Wittgenstein's *Philosophical Investigations*

Wittgenstein's *Philosophical Investigations*

Text and Context

Edited by
Robert L. Arrington and
Hans-Johann Glock

London and New York

First published 1991
by Routledge
11 New Fetter Lane, London EC4P 4EE

Simultaneously published in the USA and Canada
by Routledge
a division of Routledge, Chapman and Hall, Inc.
29 West 35th Street, New York, NY 10001

Reprinted 2001

Transferred to Digital Printing 2004

Routledge is an imprint of the Taylor & Francis Group

Set in 10/12pt Baskerville by Witwell Ltd, Southport, Merseyside

Printed and bound in Great Britain by
T J I Digital, Padstow, Cornwall

British Library Cataloguing in Publication Data

Wittgenstein's philosophical investigations: text and context.
  1. England. Philosophy. Wittgenstein, Ludwig 1889-1951
  I. Arrington, Robert L.   II. Glock, Hans-Johann

Library of Congress Cataloging in Publication Data

Wittgenstein's Philosophical Investigations: text and context/
  edited by Robert L. Arrington and Hans-Johann Glock.
      p.   cm.
  Includes bibliographical references and index.
      1. Wittgenstein, Ludwig, 1889-1951.   Philosophische
  Untersuchungen.   2. Philosophy   3. Language and languages—
Philosophy.
  I. Arrington, Robert L.   II. Glock, Hans-Johann.
  B3376.W563P638   1991
  192—dc20   91-17442

ISBN 0-415-07035-X

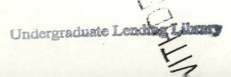

Contents

Notes on contributors

Robert L. Arrington is the author of *Rationalism, Realism, and Relativism* (Ithaca, Cornell University Press, 1989) and has published a number of articles on the philosophy of Wittgenstein. He is Professor of Philosophy at Georgia State University in Atlanta.

Gordon Baker, Fellow of St John's College, Oxford, is the author of *Wittgenstein, Frege and the Vienna Circle* (Oxford, Blackwell, 1988) and co-author, with P.M.S. Hacker, of *Wittgenstein: Understanding and Meaning; Wittgenstein: Rules, Grammar and Necessity; Frege: Logical Excavations; Language, Sense and Nonsense*; and *Scepticism, Rules, and Language*.

Stewart Candlish teaches at the University of Western Australia and is the author of several articles on, among other things, Wittgenstein, Bradley, and the theory of action.

John V. Canfield, who teaches at the University of Toronto, is the author of *Wittgenstein: Language and World* (Massachusetts University Press, 1981) and *The Looking-Glass Self* (Praeger, 1990). He is the editor of the fifteen-volume collection of major essays on Wittgenstein. *The Philosophy of Wittgenstein* (New York, Garland, 1986).

Hans-Johann Glock is a Junior Research Fellow of St John's College, Oxford and a Lecturer at St Catherine's College, Oxford. He has written, among other things, on Wittgenstein, Quine and scepticism and is currently writing a Wittgenstein dictionary for Blackwell.

S. Stephen Hilmy, currently associated with the University of Texas, Austin, is the author of *The Later Wittgenstein* (Oxford, Blackwell, 1987) and a number of articles on Wittgenstein.

John F.M. Hunter is the author of *Essays after Wittgenstein* (Toronto, University of Toronto Press, 1973), *Understanding Wittgenstein* (Edinburgh, Edinburgh University Press, 1985) and *Wittgenstein on Words as Instruments* (Edinburgh, Edinburgh University Press, 1990). He is a member of the faculty of the University of Toronto.

Andreas Kemmerling is Professor of Philosophy at the University of Munich and the author of numerous articles on the philosophy of language and the philosophy of mind.

Merrill Ring, who is Professor of Philosophy at California State University, Fullerton, is the author of several well-known articles on the philosophy of Wittgenstein and is currently at work on a commentary on the *Philosophical Investigations*.

Joachim Schulte is the author of *Erlebnis und Ausdruck* (Munich, Philosophia, 1987, English translation forthcoming, Oxford University Press), *Wittgenstein* (Reclam, 1989) and *Chor und Gesetz* (Suhrkamp, 1990). He has co-edited, with Brian McGuinness, a critical edition of the *Tractatus Logico-Philosophicus*.

Eike von Savigny teaches philosophy at the University of Bielefeld, Germany. Besides numerous articles he has published eleven books, among them a thorough study of ordinary language philosophy (Suhrkamp, 1969), *The Social Foundations of Meaning* (Springer, 1988) and a two-volume commentary on the *Philosophical Investigations* (Klostermann, 1988–9).

Abbreviations

BB   *The Blue and Brown Books*, Oxford, Blackwell, 1958.

CV   *Culture and Value*, ed. G.H. von Wright in collaboration with H. Nyman, trans. P. Winch, Oxford, Blackwell, 1980.

GB   'Remarks on Frazer's *Golden Bough*', trans. J. Beversluis, reprinted in *Wittgenstein: Sources and Perspectives*, ed. C.G. Luckhardt, Ithaca, Cornell University Press, 1979.

L30   *Wittgenstein's Lectures, Cambridge 1930–2, from the notes of John King and Desmond Lee*, ed. Desmond Lee, Oxford, Blackwell, 1980.

L32   *Wittgenstein's Lectures, Cambridge 1932–5, from the notes of Alice Ambrose and Margaret MacDonald*, ed. Alice Ambrose, Oxford, Blackwell, 1979.

LFM   *Wittgenstein's Lectures on the Foundations of Mathematics, Cambridge 1939*, from the notes of R.G. Bosanquet, Norman Malcolm, Rush Rhees, and Yorick Smithies, ed. Cora Diamond, Brighton, Harvester Press, 1976.

LPP   *Wittgenstein's Lectures on Philosophy and Psychology 1946–7*, notes by P.T. Ganch, K.J. Shah, and A.C. Jackson, ed. P.T. Ganch, Hemel Hempstead, Harvester Wheatsheaf, 1988.

LSD   'The Language of Sense Data and Private Experience', notes taken by R. Rhees of Wittgenstein's lectures, 1936, *Philosophical Investigations*, 1984, vol. 7, pp. 1–45, 101–40.

LW   *Last Writings on the Philosophy of Psychology*, vol. I, ed. G.H. von Wright and H. Nyman, trans. C.G. Luckhardt and M.A.E. Aue. Oxford, Blackwell, 1982.

LWL	*Letters from Ludwig Wittgenstein: With a Memoir by Paul Engelman*, ed. B.F. McGuinness, trans. L. Furtmüller, Oxford, Blackwell, 1967.
M	'Wittgenstein Lectures in 1930–33', in G.E. Moore, *Philosophical Papers*, London, Allen & Unwin, 1959.
MS	Manuscript from the *Nachlass*.
NB	*Notebooks 1914–16*, ed. G.H. von Wright and G.E.M. Anscombe, trans. G.E.M. Anscombe, Oxford, Blackwell, 1961.
NFL	'Wittgenstein's Notes for Lectures on "Private Experience" and "Sense Data" ', ed. R. Rhees, *Philosophical Review*, 1968, vol. LXXVII.
OC	*On Certainty*, ed. G.E.M. Anscombe and G.H. von Wright, trans. D. Paul and G.E.M. Anscombe, Oxford, Blackwell, 1969.
PG	*Philosophical Grammar*, ed. R. Rhees, trans. A.J.P. Kenny, Oxford, Blackwell, 1974.
PI	*Philosophical Investigations*, ed. G.E.M. Anscombe, R. Rhees, trans. G.E.M. Anscombe, Oxford, Blackwell, 1953; 2nd edn, Oxford, Blackwell, 1958.
PR	*Philosophical Remarks*, ed. R. Rhees, trans. R. Hargreaves and R. White, Oxford, Blackwell, 1975.
RFM	*Remarks on the Foundations of Mathematics*, ed. G.H. von Wright, R. Rhees, G.E.M. Anscombe, trans. G.E.M. Anscombe, 3rd edn, Oxford, Blackwell, 1978.
RPP I	*Remarks on the Philosophy of Psychology*, vol. I, G.E.M. Anscombe and G.H. von Wright, trans. G.E.M. Anscombe, Oxford, Blackwell, 1980.
RPP II	*Remarks on the Philosophy of Psychology*, vol. II, ed. G.H. von Wright and H. Nyman, trans. C.G. Luckhardt and M.A.E. Aue, Oxford, Blackwell, 1980.
TLP	*Tractatus Logico-Philosophicus*, trans. D.F. Pears and B.F. McGuinness, London, Routledge & Kegan Paul, 1961.
TS	Typescript from the *Nachlass*.
UW	'Ursache und Wirkung: Intuitives Erfassen', ed. R. Rhees, trans. P. Winch, *Philosophia*, 1976, vol. 6, pp. 391–445.

WWK   *Ludwig Wittgenstein and the Vienna Circle: Conversations recorded by Friedrich Waismann*, ed. B.F. McGuinness, trans. B. F. McGuinness and F. Schulte, Oxford, Blackwell, 1967.

Z   *Zettel*, ed. G.E.M. Anscombe and G.H. von Wright, trans. G.E.M. Anscombe, Oxford, Blackwell, 1967.

References to the *Nachlass* are to the Cornell version, 'The Wittgenstein Papers', Ithaca, Cornell University Microfilms. They follow the catalogue by Professor G.H. von Wright, 'The Wittgenstein Papers' in *Wittgenstein*, Oxford, Basil Blackwell, 1982 and are to MS (manuscript) or TS (typescript) number followed by page number, unless otherwise stated. Within quoted material, double obliques mark off terms or phrases that Wittgenstein entered as possible alternatives. Broken or wavy underlines (reproduced here as broken underlines) were used by Wittgenstein to indicate that he was not sure about the appropriateness of a word or phrase. Letters that follow *PI* section numbers refer to paragraphs in that section.

Introduction

Robert L. Arrington and Hans-Johann Glock

The words 'text' and 'context' in the subtitle of this volume indicate themes that serve to unite the essays found here. The authors of the essays are of one mind with respect to the proper approach to interpreting the masterpiece of Wittgenstein's later philosophy: prior to pronouncements on the tenability or philosophical relevance of remarks in the *Philosophical Investigations*, one must always carefully consider Wittgenstein's text itself, and one must locate puzzling passages in their (immediate or original) contexts in order to understand and appreciate them.

These may appear to be self-evident principles of philosophical interpretation, so obvious that there is no point in enunciating them or discussing them. Perhaps so, but one would never realize it if one examined much of what passes for Wittgenstein scholarship today. The number of articles and books that actually adduce exegetical arguments in favour of a certain reading of specific passages is astonishingly small in comparison to the vast amount of secondary literature. There has been a tendency to plunge immediately into debates about the tenability of what were, often prematurely, taken to be Wittgenstein's positions. Moreover, the apparently disjointed structure of the *Investigations* has been taken as a licence for interpreting it on the basis of isolated passages taken out of context. As a result, numerous articles and books have appeared which pay little attention to the actual text and which engage in wild speculations relating Wittgenstein to philosophical conjectures from which he surely would have wished to dissociate himself. Perhaps the most notorious example of this is Saul Kripke's interpretation of Wittgenstein's thoughts on rules and rule-following.[1] By failing to place selected remarks of Wittgenstein in their immediate context within the *Investigations*, Kripke propounds a thesis that Wittgenstein himself goes on in adjacent passages to repudiate. An examination of the original manuscript contexts from which the key remarks concerning rules are taken reveals even more clearly that Kripke has misunderstood Wittgenstein.

Kripke's misadventure is perhaps the best known, but hardly the most egregious, example of interpretive approaches to Wittgenstein that violate the principles identified above. Another commentator has suggested, for instance, that Wittgenstein develops a new approach to ontology, one that contains a novel, linguistic theory of the constitution of objects;[2] and still another writer claims that his thought is a profound reinforcement of the Kierkegaardian emphasis on 'the individual in his subjectivity'.[3] These proposals jar. The first is totally out of accord with Wittgenstein's deep suspicions about metaphysics, and the second would appear to have missed altogether Wittgenstein's critical investigations of 'the inner'. And where are we to find in the texts themselves any repeated use of, or approach to, the themes of individuality and constitution? William Alston speaks of the dangers of 'bogging down in the mire of Wittgensteinian exegesis'.[4] Difficult as it may be, such exegesis seems to be the only way to avoid a good bit of philosophical quicksand. Not only is it, trivially, a precondition for a proper assessment of the *Investigations*, it often reveals that the text provides powerful arguments against the very views it allegedly advances, as in the case of the rule-scepticism extracted from *PI* §202 or of the distinction between 'semantic mood' and 'sentence-radical' read into *PI* §22.[5]

Wittgenstein's work is popular these days – in theology, literary criticism, geography(!), and elsewhere – but is it really available to us, even today, many years after Stanley Cavell first raised the question?[6] Much of it *is* available, in highly technical, scholarly works that provide detailed exegesis of the *Philosophical Investigations* and other printed texts and frequently also involve meticulous use of the unpublished manuscripts. (We have in mind here, for example, the work of Baker and Hacker, Garth Hallett, Stephen Hilmy, Anthony Kenny, and Eike von Savigny.)[7] One may quarrel with particular interpretations found in these recent exegetical and archeological efforts, but one must admit that they take us closer to Wittgenstein himself than we were before their publication.

But much work remains to be done. There are many passages in the *Philosophical Investigations* that still defy clear understanding: some of these have been dealt with in the scholarly literature but with unconvincing results; others have been skimmed over with insufficient attention; and still others, especially those occurring after the so-called private language argument (*PI* §§316ff), have so far received little concentrated treatment. We might call these the 'knots' in the *Philosophical Investigations*. Many of these tangled lines are not only baffling but also clearly important: understanding what Wittgenstein is up to in the *Investigations* is going to require a better understanding of them. The assumption behind this volume of essays is that the knots will yield themselves to unravelling and hence understanding only if they are approached with close adherence to the exegetical principles identified above. One must look *very* carefully at what Wittgenstein himself has to say about the issues raised in these knots. As Ring puts it in his essay, we must be cartographers of territory already generally known, whose job is to provide a detailed map of districts within the country of the *Investigations*. Furthermore, one must pay close attention to the contexts in which the knots occur within the *Investigations*. Many of the authors in this volume would also insist that we attend to the original contextual homes of the problematic remarks in the manuscripts.

Consider a few of the knots in the *Philosophical Investigations*. What is Wittgenstein getting at when he talks in *PI* §206 of the common behaviour of mankind? Is he articulating a thesis of a common human nature, as revealed in common behaviour? Is this what we expect from a philosopher who seems constantly to emphasize plurality – in our use of words, in our language-games, in our forms of life? Again: what are we to make of the charming story – taken from one of Goethe's plays – of Adelheid and the Bishop playing a game of chess – *PI* §365? Wittgenstein claims that although it is a game in a play it is nevertheless a real game, and his reply to the objection that it can't be real because it doesn't have a beginning (in the play) is that it must have a beginning because otherwise it wouldn't be a real game! What kind of reasoning is *that*? As Joachim Schulte remarks in his essay, it is like saying 'It must have a beginning, because otherwise I would be wrong'. Finally, what does Wittgenstein mean when he tells us in *PI* §445 that an expectation and its fulfillment make contact in language? How could anything 'make contact' in language? In what sense is a fulfillment of an expectation dependent on *language*? And how does this puzzling remark relate to others in the textual vicinity that are equally puzzling but obviously pivotal for understanding Wittgenstein's talk about the queerness of thought and the harmony of thought and reality?

The essays in this collection are devoted to such knots in the order of their occurrence in the *Investigations*. The authors hope to show that close attention and adherence to our exegetical principles will yield clarity where before there was only obscurity. And any success that is achieved in understanding these puzzles in this way will serve as substantiation of the exegetical principles themselves.

It should not be concluded from the above that the authors represented here agree how to interpret the exegetical principles or how to apply them. Just the contrary is the case. There are a number of disagreements which are quickly apparent. As a result, this collection does not just supplement the comparatively scarce exegetical literature but also fulfills a task that no article or commentary could. As the first collection of strictly exegetical papers on the *Investigations*, it exhibits different interpretive strategies in their application to paradigmatic exegetical trouble-spots. Some of the authors, and particularly von Savigny, adhere to the conviction that the *Investigations* can be read as a coherent and independent text, and that it is unnecessary to appeal to the manuscripts to unravel the meaning of its contents. Von Savigny's approach, which he here demonstrates *vis-à-vis* the notion of 'the common behaviour of mankind' in *PI* §206, is to construct carefully the lines of argument that organize the book into its various parts and to place a particular passage in the context of one of these lines of argument. Most of the other authors would claim that while this is a necessary step in an adequate interpretation, it is not a sufficient one.[8] They find it not only illuminating but also essential to look at the context of a particular remark, or of variations on it, in the other Wittgenstein texts, either the unpublished manuscripts or those selections that have been published in book form. They do not look upon Wittgenstein as having succeeded in writing a book that is independent of what he thought and said elsewhere: in published writings, the *Nachlass*, or lectures and conversations. As he himself notes in the Preface, his lines of thought criss-cross.[9] Some of these intersections are to be found outside the *Investigations* itself, and they serve to illuminate what is only metaphorical and aphoristic – and hence often enigmatic – in the *Investigations*. Such an approach to the *Investigations* is exemplified in Stewart Candlish's 'Das Wollen ist auch nur eine Erfahrung', which deals with the discussion of 'willing' in §§611–32. Candlish rejects a 'linear' or 'sequential' reading of this passage and its surroundings, suggesting that we must think of the paragraphs as arranged like those of the *Tractatus* if we are to have any hope of understanding Wittgenstein's discussion. Sometimes we must identify the context supplied by remarks several sections removed from a paragraph in question. And sometimes it is helpful to look to earlier, 'rougher and more discursive texts'. By doing these things, we are able to identify a coherent, if largely critical and negative, set of reflections on the subject of the will. Candlish ends by claiming to discern in *Zettel* a 'positive pattern of thought' on the subject, of a very radical kind, which, unlike Wittgenstein's ideas on, say, thinking, has yet to be investigated and exploited.

Arrington's essay occupies middle ground between the view that the *Investigations* can be read as an independent work having discernible patterns of thought and argument, on the one hand, and the view that a sequential, linear representation is impossible, on the other. Arrington tries to show that a series of remarks, *PI* §§428–65, that do not have any obvious connection to one another can in fact be grouped together and construed as a commentary on a series of interrelated topics, topics such as expectation, the hardness of the logical must, the queerness of thought, and the harmony between thought and reality. Seeing the interrelationships, however, frequently requires going to other texts where Wittgenstein expands upon ideas succinctly (and cryptically) expressed in the *Investigations*. Arrington also rejects a straightforwardly linear representation of Wittgenstein's remarks. Using the metaphor of travelling up a peak, he claims that §§428–65 can be seen as an effort first to ascend the peak – and thereby attain a clear view of the surrounding environment – after which we descend and pass quickly and easily over some terrain that would otherwise be dark, mysterious, and foreboding. This is an instance, he claims, of Wittgenstein's 'circling around' a set of issues.

Still another approach to the *Investigations* is to accept the 'independence thesis' but to claim that it is not from the text alone that one can grasp Wittgenstein's meaning. This approach takes very seriously Wittgenstein's claim in the Preface that he does not wish to prevent others from thinking for themselves. What Wittgenstein does, it is therefore assumed, is to provide us primarily with a philosophical method – the dissolution of philosophical problems through the description of linguistic use. As regards *specific* philosophical problems, he only offers us a few hints about possible ways of dissolving the particular conceptual confusions that underlie them. What we then have to do is to think *our own way* through to a solution. Hence in approaching some of the knots in the book, one does not just cite Wittgenstein; one tries to generate a philosophical line of thought that achieves what he would wish us to achieve. The essay by John Hunter on Part II chapter 10 of the *Investigations* is a good example of this. Rather than pursuing the implications of Wittgenstein's reference to Moore's paradox, a line taken elsewhere by Schulte,[10] Hunter tries to illuminate the text by extracting from it a general treatment of belief which stands on its own. He does this by reflecting on hints found in the text and developing these hints philosophically. His somewhat startling conclusion is that Wittgenstein denies that in ascribing belief to a person we are ever describing a phenomenon or experience.

Still another way of being faithful to the text is found in the essay by John Canfield, namely, maintaining consistency with what Wittgenstein himself says about his investigations. Canfield can be read as applying to the private language argument Wittgenstein's insistence that he advances no disputable philosophical theses. While many philosophers have taken Wittgenstein's remarks on the impossibility of a private language to be an instance of his commitment to a verifiability theory of meaning – and have attacked Wittgenstein's remarks because of what they consider to be the demonstrable errors of this theory – Canfield shows that the project of developing a private language fails because of the demands the private linguist herself brings to the project. Wittgenstein is not defending the thesis of verifiability and urging that the private language cannot meet its demands; the private linguist, for reasons internal to her project, requires verifiability. When Wittgenstein shows her she cannot have what she asks for, the project of developing a private language collapses in on itself.

In a similar spirit, Schulte tries to dissolve the appearance that Wittgenstein's argument in *PI* §365 about the chess-game in the play having a beginning simply begs the question. However, given the fact that much less secondary literature has been devoted to this passage, Schulte's task is not one of arguing against previous interpretations. Instead, he achieves a charitable reading by structuring the initial dialogue and explaining it with the help of other passages devoted to fiction and make-believe (*PI* §§297 and 398).

Just as a reader should not assume unanimity on the part of the authors with respect to the application of our exegetical principles, this volume of essays should also not be approached with the view that the authors are slavishly dedicated to the proposition that Wittgenstein is always successful in his philosophical investigations. At least two authors, Ring and Kemmerling, reach the opposite conclusion. By looking very closely at the ways the text proceeds, or an argument unfolds, they conclude that Wittgenstein sometimes fails to achieve a totally satisfactory response to the issue he addresses. In his essay on those sections in which Wittgenstein discusses the relationship between 'Slab' and 'Bring me a slab', Ring argues that these passages are merely interpolated into the *Investigations*, that their real point is far from clear, requiring for their understanding the identification of a suppressed premise, and that organizational problems result in an inadequate discussion of the issues involved.

Kemmerling's essay is also of interest because it indicates still another way in which one can be faithful to Wittgenstein's text. One can do this by attempting to identify the philosophers and the philosophical positions to which Wittgenstein is responding. Often it is Russell or some thesis defended by him. Kemmerling shows how one can understand the remarks in §398 about the 'visual room' as mounting an attack on Frege's conception of ideas. By juxtaposing an explicit description of Frege's views and Wittgenstein's text, Kemmerling is able to illuminate the twists and turns in Wittgenstein's argument. But he concludes, as we have noted, that the argument does not succeed.

The majority of the essays in the volume are not methodological in nature but rather discuss passages devoted to substantive problems. However, in order to understand what Wittgenstein says about these problems, it is often crucial to understand how he conceived of his own philosophizing. For this reason, even those contributors who are concerned with substantive passages sometimes refer to Wittgenstein's conception of philosophy or make assumptions concerning the proper Wittgensteinian method. Given the importance of Wittgenstein's method to the exegesis of the *Philosophical Investigations* in general, it is not surprising that three of the essays are directly devoted to some of the famous – and perhaps notorious – remarks on the nature of philosophy. Baker's essay tackles a topic that Wittgenstein himself presents as being of 'fundamental importance,' the notion of a 'perspicuous representation' (*PI* §122). It points out several puzzling features of the notion of an 'Übersicht', for example, the fact that in spite of its alleged importance there is only one clear and indisputable example of a perspicuous representation in the whole of Wittgenstein's work. In order to solve these puzzles, Baker turns from the published text to its immediate sources. The result of this excavation challenges important aspects of received interpretations of *PI* §122, including the one suggested by Baker and Hacker in their commentary. Baker's suggestion is that the allegedly positive task of constructing perspicuous representations is not to be contrasted with the negative task of conceptual therapy, and that the ultimate methodological significance of the notion of a perspicuous representation lies in its connection with the idea of aspect-seeing.

A view of Wittgenstein's method that contrasts with the one suggested by Baker emerges from Glock's essay. Glock discusses Wittgenstein's claim that if one tried to offer theses in philosophy, it would be impossible to debate them because everyone would agree to them – *PI* §128. Unfortunately, Wittgenstein himself certainly appears to offer theses, and highly debatable ones at that, although some philosophers have understood him to take no philosophical positions on any topic and merely to engage in philosophical therapy. Glock rejects the latter view and seeks to explain what the indisputable, 'trivial' theses in the *Investigations* really are. Like Schulte and Hunter, Glock is concerned to show that *prima facie* untenable passages actually contain valuable insights, in this case of a methodological kind.

Methodological considerations are also to be found in Hilmy's essay, where the notion of proper and improper philosophical questions is investigated. Hilmy assembles evidence from the *Nachlass* in order to show that there are alternatives to a prominent interpretation of *PI* §133. He argues that the 'real discovery' that brings peace to philosophy need not concern the nature of philosophical problems in general, but might refer to the dissolution of specific philosophical puzzles.

Something should be said about the origination of the essays in this volume. All but two were initially presented at a conference on the *Philosophical Investigations* held in Bielefeld and Berlin, West Germany in the spring of 1989.[11] The conference, organized by Eike von Savigny, was held in celebration of the centennial year of Wittgenstein's birth, and it actually encompassed his centennial birthday. The papers were first read and discussed before a public audience at the Zentrum für Interdisziplinäre Forschung, connected to the University of Bielefeld. The participants then travelled to Berlin, where they conducted a workshop on the papers, talking at length to one another and subjecting the papers to intense debate. The workshop was held at the Institute for Advanced Studies. We are very grateful to these institutions for their generous hospitality, as well as to the Deutsche Forschungsgemeinschaft and the Stifterverband für die Deutsche Wissenschaft for their financial support of the conference.

In addition to providing ample time and numerous opportunities for discussion of a limited number of papers, the conference, being international in nature, was able to highlight the importance of language itself in Wittgenstein studies. The proceedings were conducted for the most part in English, and the German-speaking participants frequently were able to identify troublesome points of translation which in their opinion could seriously mislead an interpreter. Wittgenstein is universally acknowledged as a master of the German language, and while his way with words often leads to unsurpassed philosophical prose, it can also provoke agonizing problems of interpretation. Reflecting on the original German, pondering the uses of a word or phrase in that language, can become an invaluable tool in the effort to grasp the thought itself. Most international conferences seem to be affairs at which different nationalities and philosophical traditions merely talk at one another. The Bielefeld/Berlin conference on the *Philosophical Investigations* was, on the contrary, an instance of true international cooperation. The editors wish to to express their gratitude to Ms Anita Williams for her diligent work in preparing the manuscript for publication, and to Professor Stewart Candlish for his offer to assist those authors who had originally written in German with translating their essays into English. We are also grateful to the Wittgenstein executors for their kind permission to quote from the unpublished *Nachlass*. Our greatest debt is to Eike von Savigny. Not only did he conceive and organize the excellent conference from which these papers are derived, but he also has been a source of continuing inspiration and assistance in compiling the papers in book form.

NOTES

1 Saul Kripke, *Wittgenstein on Rules and Private Language*, Oxford, Blackwell, 1982.
2 E.K. Specht, *The Foundations of Wittgenstein's Late Philosophy*, trans. E.D. Walford, New York, Manchester University Press, 1969.
3 Charles L. Creegan, *Wittgenstein and Kierkegaard*, London and New York, Routledge, 1989, p. 71.
4 William P. Alston, 'The Christian Language-Game', in Frederick J. Crosson, ed., *The Autonomy of Religious Belief*, Notre Dame and London, University of Notre Dame Press, 1981, p. 129.
5 E. Stenius, *Wittgenstein's Tractatus*, Oxford, Blackwell, 1960, ch. 9.
6 Stanley Cavell, 'The Availability of Wittgenstein's Later Philosophy', *Philosophical Review*, 1962, vol. 62, pp. 67–93.
7 See G.P. Baker and P.M S. Hacker, *Wittgenstein: Understanding and Meaning*, Oxford, Blackwell, 1980; and *Wittgenstein: Rules, Grammar and Necessity*, Oxford, Blackwell, 1985; Garth Hallett, *A Companion to Wittgenstein's 'Philosophical Investigations'*, Ithaca, Cornell University Press, 1977; S. Stephen Hilmy, *The Later Wittgenstein*, Oxford, Blackwell, 1987; A.J.P. Kenny, *The Legacy of Wittgenstein*, Oxford, Blackwell, 1984; and Eike von Savigny, *Wittgenstein's 'Philosophische Untersuchungen': Ein Kommentar für Leser*, 2 vols, Frankfurt, Klostermann, 1988–9.
8 On the contrast between von Savigny's 'immanent approach' to the *Philosophical Investigations* and a 'source-orientated approach' that takes recourse to the *Nachlass*, see also H-J. Glock, '*Philosophical Investigations*: Principles of Interpretation' *v.* E. von Savigny, 'The Self-Sufficiency of the *Philosophical Investigations*', both in W. Brandl and R. Haller, eds, *Wittgenstein – A Reevaluation*, 1991, Vienna, Hölder-Pichler-Tempsky.
9 *PI*, p. vi.
10 J. Schulte, *Erlebnis und Ausdruck*, Munich, Philosophia, 1987.

11 Von Savigny's conference paper was unavailable for this volume. He submitted 'Common behaviour of many a kind: *Philosophical Investigations* section 206' as a substitute. Gordon Baker had been invited to present a paper at the conference, but he was unable to attend.

Chapter 1

'Bring me a slab!': meaning, speakers, and practices

Merrill Ring

My text will be those three paragraphs – §19(b), §20(a) and §20(b) – of the *Philosophical Investigations*[1] in which Wittgenstein investigates the relationship between the expressions 'Slab!' and 'Bring me a slab!'

The material in those paragraphs seems to be interpolated into that location in the *Investigations*. Where in his texts to place the discussion of that topic was a continuing problem for Wittgenstein. He first inserted it in the *Brown Book* as a very long parenthetical note immediately following §1. In his attempt to revise that dictated work for publication, the discussion remained in its original place, as a very early disruption of the central flow of thought.[2] When a few months later, he gave the revision up as a bad job and began writing the first version of the *Investigations*, these paragraphs (with changes of detail) became §§17, 18, and 19 of the new work[3] and then evolved into their final location as *Investigations* §19(b) and §20(a and b). Despite the relocation, the material still seems to me interpolated into the main text. I have not found any way of making a significant connection between it and the preceding §19(a) or the following §21. All in all, Wittgenstein seems to have been struck with the importance of the topic and largely pleased with his handling of it, and so worked to include it in what he hoped to make public of his investigations. None the less, it seems, he could never find a natural home for it in his texts.

I shall attempt to provide for this material a thorough philosophical commentary, although, as it will work out, §20(a) will elude my grasp. Since the paragraphs in question constitute the longest unit of thought in Part I of the *Investigations*, the resulting commentary will be lengthy. My aim is that of a cartographer of territory already generally known: to produce a detailed map, to give philosophers looking into Wittgenstein a useful, detailed account of one district of the country of the *Investigations*. It will turn out that the sections to be described do contain an investigation important both philosophically and to the understanding of Wittgenstein. Still, my aim here will not be to use Wittgenstein to attack a philosophical issue, but to try to understand what he is up to.[4]

It is appropriate to mention at the outset what one of my findings will be. I will argue that while there are some highly important lessons Wittgenstein wants to get across in these paragraphs, confusions, often organizational but at least once intellectual, prevent him from achieving a perspicuous presentation.

I

> But what about this: is the call 'Slab!' in example (2) a sentence or a word? – If a word, surely it has not the same meaning as the like-sounding word of our ordinary language, for in §2 it is a call. But if a sentence, it is surely not the elliptical sentence: 'Slab!' of our language.——As far as the first question goes you can call 'Slab!' a word and also a sentence; perhaps it could be appropriately called a 'degenerate sentence' (as one speaks of a degenerate hyperbola); in fact it *is* our 'elliptical' sentence.
>
> (*PI* §196)

Wittgenstein begins with a question about example (2), the language-game of §2 of the *Investigations*. It is a question as to the status of its elements: are they words or sentences? However, anyone who attempts to use that question and the notions of word and sentence as guides to the subject matter of §19(b) and §20 will become thoroughly lost.

There are two very good reasons why it would have been appropriate for Wittgenstein to investigate the status in example (2) of 'Slab!', etc. First, such a problem is suggested by a part of the Augustinian picture of language which Wittgenstein has, to this point in the text, ignored. That picture was fully specified in §1 of the *Philosophical Investigations* as the idea that words are names of objects *and that sentences are combinations of words*. In inventing a language in which the sentences are not combinations of words, Wittgenstein undermined that second conjunct of the picture. Here he calls attention to that undermining. One must also see the question in a second context. The topic will have been raised not just in criticism of the Augustinian picture generally but also in criticism of its specific deployment in the *Tractatus*. There he had held that propositions are combinations of words: 'An elementary proposition consists of names. It is a nexus, a concatenation of names' (*TLP* 4.22).

Although both those concerns are pertinent, we must not think that they provide the key to §19(b) and §20. To see that, consider his answer to the question 'Is "Slab!" in example (2) a sentence or a word?' He gives an 'Either or both' answer, although expressing a preference for calling it a limiting case of a sentence. Contrast what he does here with the tactics employed in the *Brown Book*:

> Let us now look at the different kinds of signs which we have introduced. First let us distinguish between sentences and words. A sentence I will call every complete sign in a language-game, its constituent signs are words. (This is a merely rough and general remark about the way I will use the words 'proposition' and 'word'.)
>
> (*BB* p. 82)

In that rough definition, *completeness* is the key notion. A consequence is that a sentence may consist of a single word when that word functions as a complete sign. In answer to his question about the status of 'Slab!', Wittgenstein does not explicitly offer that definition. But it surely is behind his answer that 'Slab!' in example (2) is not only a word but also a sentence, that is, a complete sign.

If we assume that Wittgenstein's fundamental concern in §19(b)–20 is in criticizing an aspect of the Augustinian picture which he had himself earlier accepted, we shall be disappointed. His response to the question about the status of 'Slab!' in example (2) runs neither long nor deep. The answer is given quickly and the machinery used in the *Brown Book* is not even presented. Nor is what he produces a deep analysis or a deep criticism: what he says merely shows the view to be mistaken.

The suspicion must be that the real issue in §19(b) is something different from what he implies it to be. That suspicion is borne out by the fact that he begins his answer by saying 'As far as the first question goes . . .'. There is, then, some second question which he had in mind. Unhappily, he does not explicitly ask that other. It is not, however, difficult to infer. The interlocutor's second and third sentences imply a question. Generally formulated, the implied question is: 'Does "Slab!" in example (2) mean the same as the corresponding expression in our language?'

Wittgenstein's interlocutor gives a 'No' answer to that implicit question. That is, it is denied that there is sameness of meaning no matter which reply is given to the explicit question. If 'Slab!' in example (2) is a word, then it does not mean the same as our word 'slab'; but if it is a sentence, that sentence does not mean the same as our sentence 'Slab!'

Consider first the claim that the word 'slab' in example (2) does not have the same meaning as our word 'slab'. In the *Brown Book* this is *the* explicit and primary issue: 'Note: Objection: The word "Brick" in language 1) has not the meaning which it has in our language' (*BB* p. 77). That *assumes* that 'Slab!' in example (2) is a word. In adapting this material for the *Investigations*, it looks as if Wittgenstein noticed the assumption and responded by tacking on an opening discussion of whether 'Slab!' is a word or a sentence. A better response, of course, would have been a more complete restructuring.

Wittgenstein also added to the original *Brown Book* material the reason for denying that, if 'Slab' in example (2) is a word, it means the same as our word: 'for in (2) it is a call.'

In the *Brown Book* Wittgenstein responded to that 'No' answer concerning the sameness of meaning of the word 'slab' in the two languages. 'This is true if it means that in our language there are usages of the word "brick" different from our usages of this word in 1). But don't we sometimes use the word "brick" in just this way?' (*BB* pp. 77–8). That is, he agrees that the word has not the same meaning in the two languages, but his agreement is conditional. They do not mean the same if the point of saying this is to note that *we* use the word 'slab' in ways other than they do. For them it is only a call. We can use it as a call and also in other ways. Hence, it would be misleading to say, as the imagined answer does, that the two expressions do not have the same meaning; but it would be equally misleading to claim that they just do mean the same.

While that reply is given in the *Brown Book*, it is not to be found in the *Investigations*. In fact Wittgenstein says *nothing* in the later work about the interlocutor's explicitly made argument that the two words do not have the same meaning. One might explain this by saying that he came to agree with the claim that the two expressions do not mean the same. While that would certainly explain his silence, such a move is not plausible. The reply given in the *Brown Book* is so characteristic of Wittgenstein. It is much more plausible to explain the omission of a reply by saying that Wittgenstein, in the *Investigations*, came to be uninterested in the issue that he had used in the *Brown Book* to structure the discussion. Perhaps that is because he has already said that the best answer to the question about the status of 'Slab!' in example (2) is that it is a degenerate sentence. That may deflect him from the issue as to whether the two expressions mean the same *if* 'Slab!' in example (2) is a *word*. This, however, is only a guess. The central point is that we have not yet identified a topic which Wittgenstein pursues in §19(b).

Turn now to the second of the interlocutor's claims: that if 'Slab!' in example (2) is a sentence, then it does not mean the same as the sentence 'Slab!' in our language. First, my account of the claim needs some defence, since I put it as a claim about *meaning*, although that is not the terminology in the text. But what would it mean to say, as does Wittgenstein speaking as critic, that their 'Slab!' and our 'Slab!' *are the same*? The issue must be whether the two *mean the same*. That reading is supported by the fact that when Wittgenstein introduced the parallel issue about the *words* 'slab', he explicitly put it in terms of whether they meant the same. The interlocutor clearly seems to be raising the same concern about the calls or sentences in the two languages.

Hence the implicit question, the one Wittgenstein had in mind but did not make explicit, is 'Does the call "Slab!" in example (2) mean the same as our call "Slab"?' Wittgenstein, again, imagines a 'No' answer. He does not immediately cite, as he did in the concern about the words 'slab', a reason for that denial, although the word 'elliptical' does, of course, provide some indication of such a reason.

Unlike his procedure with respect to the claim that the *words* 'slab' do not mean the same, Wittgenstein *does* reply to the parallel claim about the sentences or calls. And he objects to the interlocutor's denial of sameness of meaning: 'in fact it *is* our "elliptical" sentence.' That is, his claim is that the interlocutor is wrong; the two calls or sentences do mean the same.

All that Wittgenstein does, however, is to assert the contradictory of the interlocutor's answer. No argument is given for or against either answer. The upshot is that his response is left in an unsatisfactory state. I take the absence of any substantial discussion as a sign that we have not yet reached a topic which can be represented as the subject matter of §19(b). This issue of sameness of meaning will not entirely vanish, however, but the role it plays is not that of the chief subject-matter of §19(b) and its sequels.

> But that is surely only a shortened form of the sentence 'Bring me a slab', and there is no such sentence in example (2).

With the above lines, we have reached the point at which the central issue of §19(b) begins to emerge. Here Wittgenstein has the interlocutor state the reasons for his claim that 'Slab!' does not mean the same in the two languages. The reasoning can be set out as follows.

P1   Our (call/sentence) 'Slab!' is a shortened form of our (call/ sentence) 'Bring me a slab!'

P2   In example (2) there is no such sentence as 'Bring me a slab!'

C1   Hence their 'Slab!' cannot be a shortened form of 'Bring me a slab!'

C2   Hence their call cannot mean the same as ours.

Wittgenstein has already rejected the ultimate conclusion: he said their call means the same as ours. However, P2 is true given the description of example (2), and C1 follows from P2. Moreover, Wittgenstein will not deny P1: he will readily allow that our 'Slab!' is short for 'Bring me a slab!' What, then, is wrong with the argument?

There is a suppressed premise which is necessary for the conclusion to follow. P1, P2, and C1 talk about whether expressions are elliptical or not. They do not mention *meaning* at all. Yet the final conclusion says something about meaning. There must be an assumption which connects up what an expression means and whether or not it is elliptical. What must be assumed to make the argument work is something on the order of:

P3   An elliptical form of words cannot mean precisely the same as its non-elliptical counterpart.

With that premise the interlocutor's claim does follow: 'Slab!' in example (2), which is not elliptical, cannot mean the same as our 'Slab!', which is elliptical.

Perhaps surprisingly, it is the thesis expressed by that missing premise which is the long-awaited key to interpreting §19(b) and what follows. Before going on to consider the substance of the matter, it is necessary to consider a feature of the thesis which has a bearing upon our attempts to understand how the discussion proceeds.

The assumption 'An unshortened expression and a shorthand version of it cannot mean the same' is perfectly *general*. It can have application to expressions which lie wholly within *our* language as well as to expressions in *two* languages (as was the case in the above argument). It is that generality, that possibility of applying the assumption to the relation between two expressions within *our* language, which guides the remainder of Wittgenstein's discussion in the rest of §19 and until the very last words of §20.

For the fact of the matter is that after this point nothing more is said about the relation between our language and example (2). Example (2) drops out of the discussion entirely. Wittgenstein does not even attempt to show why the two calls 'Slab!' mean the same, although he has asserted that they do. His reasons for that assertion can be constructed out of what he goes on to say, but he is not at all concerned to do that himself. His interest shifts fully to the relation between *our* expression 'Slab!' and *our* 'Bring me a slab!'.

Looking back, it might be said that Wittgenstein could have saved himself and his readers a great deal of trouble had he begun §19(b) straightforwardly by having the interlocutor say, 'Our call "Bring me a slab!" cannot mean the same as our "Slab!" because the second is elliptical for the other.' For such is the real starting point of his investigation in these connected sections. Yet that brisk way of dealing with the textual difficulties has its shortcomings. It simply does not take into account the structure of the *Investigations* as Wittgenstein conceived it. The Augustinian picture and example (2) were organizationally in the saddle. To accommodate an issue that has nothing significant to do with example (2) to the main structure of the text, he prefaced the discussion with some connecting tissue which is misleading as to the nature of the problem at hand. The *Brown Book* strategy for getting the material into the text – its insertion as a purely interpolated comment – is less misleading than the solution adopted in the *Investigations*.

II

Section 19(b) is not importantly concerned with the contrast between words and sentences or with a contrast between example (2) and our language. To put it baldly, if we ignore the context and take substance only into account, §19(b) should have begun with the interlocutor saying, ' "Bring me a slab!" cannot mean the same as "Slab!" '. Wittgenstein would then have asked, 'Why do you say that?' Behind the response, 'Because "Slab!" is elliptical', would be lurking the assumption about the relationship in meaning of elliptical and non-elliptical expressions. And those claims, despite all the misguided stage-setting, do constitute the problem that Wittgenstein investigates in §19(b) and §20.

If the discussion had so begun, it would be immediately apparent that the real problem in these sections has to do with *meaning*, with what it is for two expressions to mean the same and thus with what meaning is. Understood in that way, these sections are not wholly interpolations, but rather a continuation of the investigation of meaning that has been underway since the opening paragraph of the *Investigations*. On the other hand, the view of meaning to be explored in §19(b) and §20 is not the same as that which derives from the Augustinian picture.

The interlocutor's argument here is that since 'Slab!' is elliptical for 'Bring me a slab!', the two must differ in meaning. To so argue requires, as we have seen, a general assumption about the relation in meaning of elliptical and non-elliptical expressions. But what is it that leads the interlocutor to take it that words that are shorthand and those for which they are shorthand cannot mean the same? That is not, after all, an obvious view. In fact, the more natural assumption would be that *of course* an elliptical expression and that for which it is elliptical do mean exactly the same.

Wittgenstein does not explicitly develop the answer to that, nor does he try to make the interlocutor's assumption plausible. Yet a satisfactory account of how and why he goes on as he does requires grasping something of what strikes the interlocutor about the relation of elliptical and non-elliptical expressions.

For us to say, as we all will, that 'Slab!' is elliptical for 'Bring me a slab!' commits us to treating 'Slab!' as a *dependent* form of words. What the interlocutor takes that to amount to is that 'Slab!' is parasitic upon 'Bring me a slab!' *for having the meaning it does*. On the other hand, no one would want to say that 'Bring me a slab!' has the meaning it does only in consequence of its relation to 'Slab!'.

Another way of stating the interlocutor's view, one which I shall frequently adopt because of its compactness, is to represent his claim as the thesis that 'Slab!' *really means* 'Bring me a slab!'. It is not enough for him to say that 'Slab!' means 'Bring me a slab!' – for although that is true, it is misleading in that it does not bring out the dependency and the asymmetry in meaning. To exhibit properly the relationship between the two expressions requires saying that 'Slab!' *really means* 'Bring me a slab!'.

Wittgenstein will not deny the ellipticality, even the dependency, of 'Slab!'. Instead he pursues two other issues. One, the minor one for most of the relevant text, which is not picked up again until §20(b), is whether we should follow the interlocutor in concluding, from that dependency, that the two expressions do not mean the same. The second and major issue for him concerns how to best account for the ellipticality of 'Slab!'. It is that topic which arises next in the text of §19(b).

But why should I not on the contrary have called the sentence 'Bring me a slab!', a *lengthening* of the sentence 'Slab!'.

Though these words may make it look otherwise, Wittgenstein is not intending by them to deny that 'Slab!' is elliptical or dependent in some way upon 'Bring me a slab!' Rather the question here is designed to commence an examination of the nature of that dependency by forcing the interlocutor to explain why we call it a shortened form of words. What does it mean to say that 'Slab!' is elliptical, or dependent? How should we fill in the blank in the explanation frame, ' "Slab!" is shorthand for "Bring me a slab!" because —— ' ? The true core of §19(b) concerns that issue.

Because if you shout 'Slab!' you really mean: 'Bring me a slab!'

I have argued that the central problem to be investigated is 'What is the proper explanation of the fact that the expression "Slab!" is elliptical for, and really means, "Bring me a slab!"?' Here we have the interlocutor's answer. In its most general form, that proposal claims that one linguistic form really means another linguistic form *because of some fact about the speaker*.

But what 'fact'? I shall maintain that Wittgenstein never clearly sorted out two different specifications of the relevant 'fact' and that consequently his criticism of the most significant of the two is quite poorly developed in these sections.

> The sentence is 'elliptical', not because it leaves out something that we think when we utter it, but because. . . .

The above fragment occurs not next in the text, but opens §20(b). In it, Wittgenstein prefaces his own explanation of why 'Slab!' is elliptical by contrasting it with an explanation he has been criticizing, an explanation which makes reference to a purported fact about someone who says 'Slab!' Specifically, the idea is that 'Slab!' is elliptical for 'Bring me a slab!' because the short call does not make explicit something a speaker *thinks*. The interlocutor takes it that the relevant fact about the speaker to be cited in explanation of why 'Slab!' really means 'Bring me a slab!', is a 'fact' about *the inner life* of the speaker, specifically about his thoughts.

In the sections of the *Investigations* preceding §19(b) Wittgenstein had been responding to the Augustinian picture of language and to an account of meaning derived from it. But in §19(b) a different view makes the first of many appearances in the book. Wittgenstein here exhibits for critical inspection the view that has been the chief historical competitor of Augustinian-style ideas about language and meaning. It is the idea that the meaning of an expression is to be explained in terms of what is going on in the mind of a language-user.

It is easy to see how the interlocutor gets from that general view of meaning to his explanation of the status of 'Slab!'. Suppose that someone were inclined to think that the meaning of an expression is what goes on in our minds when we utter it, and that linguistic meaning is the idea or thought we have when we speak. Because 'Slab!' really means 'Bring me a slab!' it would follow, on such a general view of meaning, that when we say 'Slab!' *we must be thinking* 'Bring me a slab!'. Hence, 'Slab!' is elliptical because it omits part of what we are thinking when we say it, namely the phrase 'Bring me a . . .'.

Wittgenstein's criticism of this account of the ellipticality of
Slab!', and with that his criticism of the general idea of meaning
which supports the account, is scattered over §19(b) and §20(a),
although never, as we shall see, clearly set in a context of its own.

> Do you say the unshortened sentence to yourself? . . . does
> (that) consist in thinking in some form or other a different
> sentence from the one you utter? . . . No. Even if such an
> explanation rather tempts us, we need only think for a
> moment of what actually happens in order to see that we are
> going astray here.

The rejection of this overly simple explanation of the elliptical
nature of 'Slab!' takes the form of reminders. Does one in fact
always think the long form while saying the other? Does
everyone? What reason have we to say that this is what other
people are thinking? We surely have only an a priori reason for
what is an empirical matter. Those responses are quite decisive
against the explanation that 'Slab!' is elliptical because it omits
something we think when we say it.

The criticism here is the first round in a long battle in the
Investigations against solving philosophical problems, including problems about the nature of meaning, by appealing to inner
states.

If that were Wittgenstein's only target in §19(b), we might (if we
ignored all the mis-steps at the beginning) treat the section and its
criticism as a success. I have already claimed, however, that he also
has a second target in mind, one which he never clearly sorts out
from the first. The consequence of that confusion is that his
criticism of that second target is far from successful.

What is this additional object of criticism? Recall how
Wittgenstein introduced the explanation to be examined:
'Because if you shout "Slab!" you really mean: "Bring me a
slab!".' That answer appeals to some (purported) fact about the
speaker in explanation of why one expression stands in a certain
kind of meaning relationship to another. I noted that Wittgenstein can and does, for example when he is summing up his
criticism prior to launching into his own account, think of that
'fact' as a fact about what a speaker is thinking, about what a
speaker has in mind. But the interlocutor's words can also be read
in a second way: namely as the thesis that one expression (really)

means another because *the speaker really means* the second expression when he or she says the first. This interpretation of the interlocutor's thesis is quite different from the other. The 'fact' about the speaker appealed to does not, at least not explicitly and directly, concern what is going on in the speaker's mind at the time of uttering the words.

Such an interpretation of the interlocutor's explanation of the ellipticality of 'Slab!' is given initial legitimacy by Wittgenstein's own formulation of the view. The scheme of the explanation is, 'Because by that you really mean this'. What is translated 'mean' there is *meinen* – to mean, to intend. Hence, it seems perfectly straightforward to understand the interlocutor to be holding that 'Slab!' really means 'Bring me a slab!' because a speaker *really intends* 'Bring me a slab!' when he or she says 'Slab!'. In fact, if Wittgenstein had not himself directed us to the alternative interpretation of the interlocutor's proposal, the most natural reading of what the text actually says would be the current one which relies upon the notion of a speaker's intentions in saying 'Slab!'.

Further, this second specification of what it is about a speaker that makes one expression mean another gains legitimacy as a interpretation of the text when it is noticed that it, as was also true of the first, is associated with a general idea of the nature of linguistic meaning. That related philosophical view is the idea that the meaning of an expression is determined by, or is a function of, a speaker's meaning. One who held such a view might well be tempted to deploy it to account for the fact that 'Slab!' is dependent in meaning on 'Bring me a slab!'. If that is the philosophical position represented here by the interlocutor, then the investigation is certainly worth undertaking.

I think that in §19(b) and §20(a) Wittgenstein was attempting to criticize the view that linguistic meaning must be accounted for in terms of a speaker's intentions. For surely there can be no dispute that, in general, Wittgenstein, in his discussions of meaning, does not subordinate the meaning of an expression to what a user means by it. There are places in the *Investigations* where he specifically rejects a speaker's intentions as providing a guide to what an expression means. See, for instance, the third paragraph of the note attached to §38: 'Can I say "bububu" and mean [meinen] "If it doesn't rain I shall go for a walk" ? – It is only in a language that I can mean [meinen] something by something.' That is, a speaker could mean (intend) 'Bring me a slab!' by 'Slab!' only where the language is such that 'Slab!' means, independently and antecedently, 'Bring me a slab!'.

The only question can be whether Wittgenstein aimed at such criticism in the sections at hand. I think that he did. In the first place, his own account of why 'Slab!' is elliptical (see §20b) stands opposed to both possible readings of the interlocutor's thesis. Second, some of the textual material in both §19(b) and §20(a), material which remains to be discussed, seems relevant only when thought of as offered in objection to making a speaker's intentions basic to the explanation of an expression's meaning.

Despite the explicit phrasing of the interlocutor's position ('Because if you shout "Slab!" you really mean [meint] "Bring me a slab!" ') and despite the fact that the verb *meinen* is used over and over in the discussion, there is something which makes it difficult to see that Wittgenstein is attempting such a criticism here. The trouble is that the objections he levels seem irrelevant to the thesis, seem to miss the mark completely. It is not that they are ineffective arguments; rather it is very hard to see them as objections to *that* supposed target.

That lack of argumentative power in these sections can be understood (in part) by noticing what happens in the text as he develops his arguments. After stating the thesis that A means B because a speaker means/intends B by A, Wittgenstein immediately launches into his criticism.

> But how do you do this: how do you *mean that* while you *say* 'Slab!'? Do you say the unshortened sentence to yourself? And why should I translate the call 'Slab!' into a different expression in order to say what someone means by it? And if they mean the same thing – why should I not say: 'When he says "Slab!" he means "Slab!" '? – Again, if you can mean 'Bring me the slab!' why should you not be able to mean 'Slab!'?

Observe how this criticism begins: he asks *what it is to mean something*. That is, he initiates an inquiry into the nature of an intention in speaking. And he supplies a potential answer: does meaning that by this amount to thinking that while saying this? He is thereby drawn back into the interlocutor's inclination to explain philosophically troubling concepts by appeal to an inner state, specifically to what someone is thinking.

Wittgenstein is tempted throughout these sections to run two projects together. He both intends to, and does, criticize the idea that the proper explanation of the ellipticality of 'Slab!' is that the linguistic form omits something a speaker thinks when he says it. He also intends to criticize a different thesis, that the proper account of why 'Slab!' is elliptical is that a speaker means the longer form in saying the shorter. Yet every time he turns to *that* thesis in §19(b) he is very tempted to give it a certain *interpretation*, namely that having an intention is to be understood as a matter of having certain thoughts. And hence the two different explanations come to look as if they are the same, as if they both have to do with a speaker's thoughts, as if the same line of criticism will deal with both. It is that lack of clarity on Wittgenstein's part which frustrates his attempt to produce an incisive criticism, in these paragraphs at least, of the notion that the meaning of an expression is to be understood as what a speaker means by it. The intended criticism of the idea that a philosophical account of *bedeuten* [meaning] is to be couched in terms of *meinen* is badly handled in these passages.

That is not wholly fair to Wittgenstein. The final three questions in the above quotation do not have any special relation to the interpretation of *meinen* as being in a certain inward condition, of thinking a certain something. They have a direct bearing on whether the meaning of 'Slab!' must be explained by what a speaker means. But though they aim at that target, they are not clear and impressive lines of criticism.

Consider the first of the three questions. 'And why should I translate the call "Slab!" into a different expression in order to say what someone means by it?' It is a consequence of the interlocutor's thesis, understood as appealing to a speaker's intentions, that one who says 'Slab!' cannot (really) intend what he or she says. This, however, is no more than an embarrassment to the interlocutor, for he or she has a clear answer to Wittgenstein's question, namely that one must so translate 'Slab!' to say what a speaker means by it in order to explain the ellipticality of 'Slab!'. It is somewhat embarrassing to be committed to holding that in the case of 'Slab!' speakers are systematically debarred from meaning what they say, but the defender of the thesis would surely think that the explanatory power of an appeal to a speaker's meaning outweighs the modest discomfort of that consequence. In short, Wittgenstein's criticism is relevant but it has only slight argumentative strength.

Wittgenstein's second question involves a criticism that is simply astray. 'And if they mean [*bedeuten*] the same thing – why should I not say: "When he says 'Slab!' he means [*meint*] 'Slab!'"?' The objection here relies upon the substitutability of expressions that mean the same. If 'Slab!' and 'Bring me a slab!' mean the same, then in the thesis in question – 'One who says "Slab!" really means "Bring me a slab!"' – we should be able to substitute 'Slab!' for 'Bring me a slab!' to obtain 'One who says "Slab!" really means "Slab!".' And that shows, Wittgenstein is thinking, that one who says 'Slab!' can really mean it.

The interlocutor, however, has an easy time escaping. At best he or she needs to deny partially the if-clause of the question. For the interlocutor's position is that although 'Slab!' does mean 'Bring me a slab!', the converse is not true. That is, the interlocutor's view is that 'Bring me a slab!' cannot mean 'Slab!'. Wittgenstein is thus not, in the interlocutor's eyes, entitled to the substitution his criticism requires, and so the objection does not work. In general, Wittgenstein here seems to forget the structure of the interlocutor's position: he fails to remember that the view under investigation differs from his own in denying that 'Bring me a slab!' and 'Slab!' do mean the same.

The third challenge is more obscure than the others, but, rightly understood, much more potent. 'Again, if you can mean "Bring me a slab!", why should you not be able to mean "Slab!"?' I take it that Wittgenstein is here asking, 'If, as you hold, it is a speaker's intentions that constitute the ultimate explanation of his or her linguistic behaviour, then why *can't* such a speaker say "Slab!" and really mean it?' On the interlocutor's view in which a speaker's meaning is explanatorily primitive, what could possibly restrict a speaker's intentions? If the last resort in explaining language is what a speaker means/ intends by what he or she says, then surely one can say 'Slab!' *and really mean it*. Consequently, the explanation 'because one who says "Slab!" really means "Bring me a slab!"' runs foul of its own insistence on the fundamental role of a speaker's intentions in explaining language and meaning.

These three questions do show that Wittgenstein did have as an object of criticism in this section an account of meaning that appeals to what a speaker intends. But the three lines of criticism vary widely in effectiveness and even the best of them is not sufficiently developed.

But when I call 'Slab!', then what I want is, *that he should bring me a slab!*

Having heard Wittgenstein's objections out, the interlocutor makes a final and powerful appeal in defence of his or her thesis that one who says 'Slab!' really means 'Bring me a slab!'. He or she appeals to what a speaker *wants* when she so speaks. And he or she has it absolutely right: one who says 'Slab!' wants to be brought a slab. Presumably, the idea is that to describe what such a speaker wants we must use the long phrase, the words 'Bring me a slab!'. We cannot describe the want in terms of the short phrase alone; we cannot say 'What he or she wants is slab' or 'What he or she wants is that he or she should be slab'. Consequently, the interlocutor would continue, the only words that strictly express what that speaker wants are 'Bring me a slab!'. That is what really must be intended and so 'Slab!' cannot really be what is meant.

Certainly, but does 'wanting this' consist in thinking in some form or other a different sentence from the one you utter?

Wittgenstein's response is not at all adequate to the power of the appeal to wants in explaining the ellipticality of 'Slab!' It strikes me that the proper reply, and one which is of a type found frequently in Wittgenstein, would be to deny that it is the want that one should be brought a slab which makes the phrase 'Bring me a slab!' basic, but rather that it is the primacy of the phrase 'Bring me a slab!' which enables us to describe the want in only the longer form rather than the shorter.

However that may be, the fact of the matter is that Wittgenstein here does not so as much hint at that line of criticism. Rather, his reply accepts that one who says 'Slab' wants to be brought a slab and then denies only a certain *interpretation* of what wanting something is. That is, he once again slides back into his aim of attacking the idea that intending is a matter of having certain thoughts. The important way of construing the issue is once more obscured by a less central version and §19(b) comes to an end on this disappointing note.

III

I have proposed that the only significant discussion in §19(b) concerns how to answer correctly the question 'What is the proper explanation of the fact that "Slab!" is shorthand for

"Bring me a slab!" ?' There are two connected issues. First, there is an issue of *meaning*: what is the relationship in meaning between 'Slab!' and 'Bring me a slab!'? The interlocutor's view is that the dependency of 'Slab!' is in its meaning, that while 'Slab!' does mean 'Bring me a slab!', the converse is not true. Second, the interlocutor attempts to offer an explanation of the ellipticality of 'Slab!', an explanation which satisfies his thesis that 'Slab!' is dependent in meaning upon the long form. He thus takes the second question to be 'Why does "Slab!" really mean "Bring me a slab!" ?'

Wittgenstein, I have argued, considers and rejects, though without adequately sorting out, two different answers to that second question. One is that 'Slab!' really means the other because we think the long form when we say the short. The second is that the one is elliptical because when we say it we intend, mean, the other. To the first and more naïve view his criticism is decisive – to the second, the criticism is not effective because he does not keep the proper target in view.

It is time to examine his own solutions to the two central problems. We have already seen part of his answer to the first topic: the point of his saying 'in fact it *is* our elliptical sentence' is to claim that the long and short forms mean just the same. But he did not then argue for that sameness of meaning. For the justification of that answer and for his own explanation of the ellipticality of 'Slab!' one must look to §20(b). While pursuing this exegetical strategy means passing over the very long paragraph that constitutes §20(a), we shall, nonetheless, be better off in so reversing the order of Wittgenstein's discussion.

> The sentence is 'elliptical', not because it leaves out something that we think when we utter it, but because it is shortened – in comparison with a particular paradigm of our grammar.

Wittgenstein thus claims that the proper way to fill in the blank in the explanatory frame ' "Slab!" is elliptical for "Bring me a slab!" because ——' is with words to the effect that our practice is to treat 'Bring me a slab!' as an ideal form, a paradigm; 'Slab!' in our practice is treated as deviant. The interlocutor's view that the dependency of 'Slab!' must relate to some fact or the other about individual speakers is replaced by an explanation that makes reference to a social practice.

The general importance of that *type* of answer can easily be overlooked. Very frequently in the *Investigations* Wittgenstein rejects *mentalistic* answers to philosophical questions, answers which claim that reference to a mental object or an inner state is the solution to the philosophical problem. Because of that manoeuvre, he has been thought to be a behaviourist. Think of what has been said of him in connection with his discussion of pain (which he took to be exemplary with respect to other significant mental concepts). When he denies that 'pain' is the name of an inner something, he has been taken to mean that giving an account of what pain is must consist of making reference only to (patterns of) behaviour.

Wittgenstein saw this interpretation of his views in the offing and antecedently denied it: see specifically *Investigations* §307 and §308. More importantly, he *exhibited* that he was not a behaviourist. Those who so interpret Wittgenstein fail to attend to what he says in §19(b) and §20(b). For there he is rejecting mentalistic answers to a philosophical problem: he denies that one expression is linguistically dependent upon another because of what a speaker who uses those expressions thinks or intends. Yet when giving his own answer, there is not the slightest reference to the individual speaker's behaviour.

Rather, what he does in answering is call attention to a feature of our *practice*: that we treat one form of words as a paradigmatic grammatical construction. The contrast found in Wittgenstein with talking about what goes on in a person's mind is not with talking about what happens in his or her behaviour. The proper contrast to the mentalistic response is not with anything inner or outer, nor anything about a person, nor something occurring at a given time, or a disposition for such a thing to happen. What Wittgenstein cites by way of answer has to do with a linguistic practice.

His answer here should be understood – and I think was *intended* by Wittgenstein to be understood – as a *model* for the type of answer that he will give when investigating psychological concepts such as pain, understanding, or belief. For in those cases he is no more a behaviourist than he is here: Wittgenstein's answer to the question 'What is pain?' or 'What is belief?' does not consist in remarks about either minds or bodies; it involves references to features of the language of pain or belief, that is, to what he calls the grammar of the concepts. (See most importantly §371 and §373.)

Of course one might object here: 'You grant that the shortened
and the unshortened sentence have the same sense. – What is
this sense, then? Isn't there a verbal expression for this sense?'
– But doesn't the fact that sentences have the same sense
consist in their having the same *use*?

Recall that the interlocutor originally claimed that since 'Slab!'
is parasitic on 'Bring me a slab!', the two cannot mean the same.
His or her explanations of the ellipticality of 'Slab!' are couched
in terms of the assumption of the subordination in meaning of
'Slab!' to 'Bring me a slab!' It is the topic of meaning which is here
resurrected by the interlocutor. Conceding Wittgenstein's account
of the elliptical status of 'Slab!', he or she now insists that
Wittgenstein's earlier claim that 'Slab!' and 'Bring me a slab!'
'have the same sense' must be wrong.[5] The demand that Wittgenstein state in words this common meaning is an attempt to secure
an admission that only the long form is a proper specification of
what they mean. And if Wittgenstein allows that, then 'Bring me a
slab!' must be primitive in meaning.

Having given his own account of in what the ellipticality of
'Slab!' consists, Wittgenstein is now prepared to reaffirm his
denial of the interlocutor's other claim. That is, he asserts once
more that the favoured status of 'Bring me a slab!' does not
require that we deny that it and 'Slab!' have the same sense.

In defence of this he makes the most explicit identification, up
to this point in the *Investigations*, of meaning and use. 'Bring me
a slab!' and 'Slab!' mean the same because they have precisely the
same use. He refuses to use words to specify the meaning which
the two expressions have in common, and instead characterizes
their sameness in meaning in terms of sameness of use.

One might demur at this move and think that there is more to
the interlocutor's view than Wittgenstein allows. To see that, ask
what it means to think that 'Slab!' is a dependent form of words
(given that you have agreed that the dependency is not a
consequence of some fact about an individual user of the words).
To put the same question differently, ask what Wittgenstein can
mean by his claim that 'Bring me a slab!' is a paradigm of our
grammar, a model construction, while 'Slab!' is treated in our
practice as deviant.

It seems to me that such an account must reside in terms of
how we explain the two expressions. Surely we are willing to

explain what 'Slab!' means by saying that it means 'Bring me a slab!'. However, we would *not*, in the normal course of our linguistic practice, be willing to explain what 'Bring me a slab!' means by saying that it means 'Slab!'. (Similarly, we would explain what 'provided that' means by saying it means 'if'; yet we would not explain 'if' by saying that it means 'provided that'.) When Wittgenstein says that 'Bring me a slab!' is a paradigm of our grammar, he cannot (and be consonant with his views elsewhere) mean 'It is an ideal form, *therefore* we do not explain it by "Slab!" '. Rather, his typical view would be that such practices of explanation *constitute* what it is to be a paradigm. That is our practice, that is what we do, and as such it is the end point of the (philosophical) explanation.

If 'paradigm' must be (and typically would be by Wittgenstein) treated in terms of explanatory practices, then the interlocutor's idea of an asymmetry of meaning has a point. Wittgenstein's answer drives a wedge between use and explanatory practices and comes down sharply on the side of use in specifying what meaning amounts to. But isn't there *something* to the idea that if the meaning of 'Bring me a slab!' cannot be explained as 'Slab!', then we rightly hesitate in saying that they mean the same? Nothing contrary to the central argument of these sections, that about the proper explanation of the ellipticality of 'Slab!', hinges upon how this matter is settled, so Wittgenstein need not have insisted so strenuously and hastily that use only, and not explanatory patterns, counts in deciding whether two expressions mean the same.

(In Russian one says 'stone red' instead of 'the stone is red'; do they feel the copula to be missing in the sense, or attach it in *thought*?)

Here at the end, in a lovely parenthetical remark, Wittgenstein reverts to the idea that it is what we think that completes the sense of an (ostensibly) incomplete form of words. (Incidentally, this also reverts to the comparison of expressions in two different languages which Wittgenstein has dropped since early in §19(b).) It would be absurd to hold that speakers of Russian think the copula (or the article) though they don't utter it. Their form of expression is shortened, but only in comparison with paradigms of *our* grammar, not of theirs. (One should not take Wittgenstein's words 'In Russian one says "stone red" . . .' literally.

Speakers of Russian normally say 'The stone is red' and not the primitive sounding 'stone red'. We cannot translate their words in that fashion. Wittgenstein's claim must be that Russian does not have a separate device for the copula and we must not be so misguided as to think that they therefore *think* something in addition to what they say.)

IV

It is disheartening to realize that despite the length of the paper, I have not yet said anything about the longest part of the material to be commented upon, namely §20(a). At least some of the pain can be alleviated by my thesis here: paragraph §20(a) could have been omitted from the *Investigations* with at most modest intellectual loss. In consequence, my commentary on it will be relatively brief.

The topic that he carries over from §19(b) is that of intending, meaning, *meinen*. The questions he poses here are three: What is it to mean 'Bring me a slab!' as four words? As one word? How do we normally mean it? He asks that third question but does not otherwise address it. That is unfortunate because the issue of how many words we mean when we speak, or of meaning what we say as some number of words, is probably bogus. Someone may know that what he or she says consists of four words or thinks it to be one word and in either case speaks accordingly, but I doubt that there is any sense to speaking of how many words we *mean* when we speak. But even if there is such a notion, it is so esoteric that Wittgenstein can make little headway by employing it as the context in which to develop an account of a speaker's meaning.

The objects of his criticism are answers to the first two questions, answers which interpret having an intention as having something going on in one, thinking something while one speaks. Thus, this additional investigation may well assist in misleading an unwary reader into believing that Wittgenstein has no objection to saying that the meaning of an expression is to be accounted for in terms of a language user's intentions.

His own answer is analogous to that given for the problem in §19(b). He holds that how many words are intended (supposing that we can talk this way) must be explained by reference to contrasts found in the language or, for the aberrant case, in the speaker's conception of that language. What he realizes is that in the normal case where a speaker intends four words as four words there *is* a relevant fact about the speaker which must be taken into account in explaining his or her patterns of speech, namely his or her *mastery* of the language. Thus, the notion of being a master speaker is introduced into the text for the first time.

In this brief description of §20(a) I have passed over some small pieces of mishandling of the material by Wittgenstein (e.g. to talk about using 'Bring me a slab!' as *four* words requires not contrasts with other *four* word expressions, as some of his examples are, but with expressions with other than four words).

I would of course welcome an account of §20(a) that shows how the discussion there makes a significant contribution to the issues discussed in the preceding and following paragraphs. I have tried several hypotheses and found them all to fail in making §20(a) a step forward in understanding the issues. Hence, I have concluded that there is nothing of substance gained by Wittgenstein and perhaps some losses incurred by the insertion of the weak inquiry in §20(a) into the *Investigations*. Given what I have argued to be the difficulties of reading §19(b) and §20(b) properly, this unnecessary material further obscures the importance of the topics taken up in these sections by Wittgenstein.

NOTES

1 All translations of the *Investigations* are by G.E.M. Anscombe.
2 Wittgenstein's attempted revision of the *Brown Book* is the second part of MS 115 (pp. 118–292).
3 MS 220 is a typescript made from the missing MS 142 and constitutes the remains of the first version of the present *Investigations*. See §§17, 18, and 19. Rush Rhees's translation, with corrections by Wittgenstein, is MS 226. See §§23(a), 23(b), and 25 (through misnumbering there is no §24).
4 Discussions of the sections I shall be considering are found in the standard commentaries on the *Investigations*, namely: G.P. Baker and P.M.S. Hacker, *Wittgenstein: Understanding and Meaning*, Chicago, University of Chicago Press, 1980; and G.A. Hallett, *A Companion to Wittgenstein's 'Philosophical Investigations'*, Ithaca, Cornell University Press, 1977. For the most extensive use of §§19(b) and 20 in the current literature, see Warren G. Goldfarb, 'I want you to bring me a slab: Remarks on the Opening Sections of the *Philosophical Investigations'*, *Synthese*, 1988, vol. 56, pp. 265–82.
5 It should be pointed out that Wittgenstein has the interlocutor say '*Du gibst zu*' ('You grant') that the two mean the same. The verb *zugeben* is properly translated by Anscombe as 'grant' – 'admit' or

'allow' will work. But on my reading of the passage the interlocutor should not be granting or allowing that – since he is denying it. I obviously prefer to take it that Wittgenstein used the wrong verb rather than to reject my interpretation on that slender evidence.

Chapter 2

Philosophical Investigations section 122: neglected aspects

Gordon Baker

A main source of our failure to understand is that we do not
command a clear view of [*übersehen*] the use of our words. –
Our grammar is lacking in this sort of perspicuity
[Übersichtlichkeit]. – A perspicuous representation [eine
übersichtliche Darstellung] produces just that understanding
which consists in 'seeing connexions'. Hence the importance
of finding and inventing *intermediate cases.* The concept of a
perspicuous representation is of fundamental significance for
us. It earmarks the form of account we give [unsere Dar-
stellungsform], the way we look at things. (Is this a
'Weltanschauung'?)

(*PI* §122)

FIRST IMPRESSIONS

This text is well known and often quoted. It seems to condense
into one short remark much of Wittgenstein's distinctive conception of philosophy. It lodges a complaint about 'the grammar of
our language' (a lack of perspicuity), and it suggests that he took
as a primary goal remedying this defect in our understanding by
providing 'representations' of grammar that would make things
perspicuous. The search for perspicuity (*Durchsichtigkeit* or
Übersichtlichkeit) is a *leitmotif* of his later philosophy, clearly
audible from the opening of *Philosophical Remarks* to the close
of *Last Writings*. It must be an integral part of the philosopher's
business of describing the actual use of language (§124). Indeed,
perspicuity might be taken to be the single ultimate end of all of
the activities of the philosopher (cf. §127), the goal to which the

dissolution of all particular philosophical problems is subordinate (cf. §§132-3).

Though clearly important, Wittgenstein's concept of a perspicuous representation is not itself perspicuous. This is hardly surprising since it is here introduced with minimal clarification and without a single example. Originally he cited the colour-octahedron as a paradigm (*PR* pp. 51-2; cf. *WWK* p. 42, *PR* p. 278). He regarded this three-dimensional model (or the corresponding two-dimensional diagram) as a 'representation' of the grammar of colours. From it we can 'read off', for example, the possibility of a spectrum of shades between red and yellow (hence also the intelligibility of the phrases 'reddish yellow' and 'yellowish red') and the polar opposition of red and green (i.e. the nonsensicality of the phrase 'greenish red'). The entire grammar of the network of colour-words seems to be condensed into a diagram that can be taken in at a glance (i.e. a diagram that has the attribute of being surveyable (*übersichtlich* or *übersehbar*)). Conversely it seems as if this whole assemblage of rules can be reconstructed by close inspection of the diagram. Here a sizable domain of grammar seems to be laid up or contained in a single sign (cf. *PG* pp. 55-6). The power to condense something complex into a simple and manageable symbol seems to be the defining characteristic of what Wittgenstein called 'a perspicuous representation'. Like the perspicuity which is said to be essential to a proof in mathematics (*RFM* pp. 95, 143-53, 174), the perspicuity of a representation is apparently to be explained by reference to its memorability and to the possibility of copying or reproducing it. Having inspected the diagram of the colour-octahedron once, most people can draw it again for themselves and make use of it to work out further relations among colours (e.g. that 'bluish red' makes sense, but 'bluish yellow' does not).

The colour-octahedron is in fact the *sole* labelled instance of a perspicuous representation (of grammatical rules) in all of Wittgenstein's published writings. This generates two major quandaries. First, how is the absence of anything closely comparable to the colour-octahedron from the text of the *Investigations* compatible with the claim 'The concept of a perspicuous representation is of fundamental importance for us'? The reader might expect explicit applications of this concept to characterize Wittgenstein's philosophizing in the same way that Ryle's criticism of the myth of the ghost in the machine is punctuated by the pinpointing of 'category-mistakes'. Does the lack of diagrammatic representations of conceptual connections from the text prove that the remark on perspicuous representations is a fossil remnant of an extinct conception of philosophy? Should we argue that the term 'perspicuous representation' covers a family of 'representations' of the uses of symbols and then go on to identify numerous *unlabelled* instances in the text? There is a *prima facie* tension in the *Investigations* which any satisfactory interpretation of §122 must seek to resolve.

The second quandary is the evident underdetermination of the grammar of the phrase 'a perspicuous representation' by the general explanation given in §122, even when this is supplemented by the example of the colour-octahedron (as in *PR* p. 52). In fact there are two different directions in which these embryonic explanations of 'perspicuous representation' could be expanded.

The first conception lays stress on the concept of a *representation (Darstellung)*. It is 'our grammar' or 'the use of our words'[1] which is said to lack perspicuity. Hence, presumably, it is 'a perspicuous representation of our grammar' which is sought to remedy 'our failure to understand'. This phraseology may be taken to indicate a contrast between 'our grammar' and '*representations of* our grammar'. The expectation of finding a contrast is fulfilled in Wittgenstein's characterization of the colour-octahedron as 'a *perspicuous* representation of the grammatical rules (for the use of colour-words)' (*PR* p. 52). Here the purpose of the diagram seems to be producing an order within the motley collection of explanations of what 'red', 'green', 'yellow', and so on mean. Wittgenstein did not avow the intention of *substituting* the colour-octahedron for explanations of the combinatorial possibilities of colour-words, but rather the intention of using the diagram to make perspicuous (to introduce system into) this set of grammatical rules. We could even state the principle for projecting the diagram onto these grammatical rules, that is, a method of representation (e.g. that the vertices marked 'red' and 'yellow' are connected by a single edge implies that shades of red can be ordered on the scale 'more or less yellow' and shades of yellow on the scale 'more or less red'[2]). Consequently there is a straightforward and important sense in which the colour-octahedron is a *representation* (or even 'picture') of grammatical rules. If we follow up this line of thought, we will conclude that what Wittgenstein called 'a perspicuous representation of grammatical rules' *must* have the characteristic that the representation is distinct from what is represented. (Neither identity nor permutation count as what we call 'a method of representation'.) In consequence, no verbal formulations of grammatical rules (and no asssemblage of grammatical rules) can properly be called 'a perspicuous representation of grammatical rules', and conversely the colour-octahedron cannot properly be viewed as a mere compendium of the combinatorial rules for colour-words. An advocate of this interpretation might summarize his conception in the claim that what Wittgenstein called a perspicuous *representation (Darstellung)* of grammatical rules is essentially different from a perspicuous *arrangement (Zusammenstellung)* of grammatical rules.

The second conception of a perspicuous representation is the polar opposite of the first. It seems to be the dominant interpretation offered by commentators who follow Wittgenstein in assigning a fundamental importance to the concept of a perspicuous representation in his practice of philosophizing. This second interpretation might be developed from the description of the colour-octahedron as 'a *rough* representation of colour-space . . . a grammatical representation, not a psychological one' (*PR* p. 51). Apparently he meant to contrast the a priori relations among colours with relations that might be established by empirical investigation (e.g. that a red after-image may be produced by looking at a white wall after staring hard at a green circle (cf. *PR* pp. 51–2)). This suggests that the role of the colour-octahedron is to describe *colour-space* by *presenting the grammar* of colour-words. But an enumeration of combinatorial rules for colour-words (e.g. 'There is no such thing as a reddish green', 'A shade of red may be more or less yellow') has exactly the same role. Consequently, the diagram and the assemblage of combinatorial rules may each be called 'a grammatical representation of colour-space' or 'a description of the use of colour-words'; the diagram simply differs in virtue of being more comprehensive than any one rule (or any succinct list of rules). The hallmark of what Wittgenstein called 'a perspicuous representation' is that it is a presentation or arrangement of grammatical rules which can be taken in as a whole. An exponent of this second interpretation might epitomize his conception by claiming that a perspicuous 'representation' is nothing more than a particular kind of *arrangement* (*Zusammenstellung*) of descriptions of 'the use of our words'.

This second interpretation might be reinforced by noting that somebody who knows how to make use of the colour-octahedron can 'read off from it' *all* of the combinatorial rules for chromatic colours. At the same time, this same thought seems to highlight the crucial difference between a diagrammatic representation of colour-space and a piecemeal description by the enumeration of many rules. In the first case, this whole domain of grammar is depicted in a single surveyable symbol, whereas in the second the full description will be impossible to take in at a glance. It would perhaps be less misleading to claim that Wittgenstein intended the colour-octahedron to *be* a formulation of the grammar of our language than to claim that he meant it to *represent* or *describe* this grammar. Moreover, since he often called grammar itself 'a form of representation', this point perhaps explains why he called a perspicuous representation 'a form of representation' (cf. §122).[3] It must be seen as an element of grammar or as a member of the set of 'descriptions of our language' (just as an architect's blueprint is to be regarded as a description of a building). Within this genus, perspicuous representations are differentiated by being *surveyable* sets of rules which constitute *complete* explanations[4] of how to use 'the words of our language'.

For the moment we shall drop the first interpretation and explore the second one. By following up and elaborating its account of the role of the colour-octahedron, we do arrive at a conception of perspicuous representations which has the merit of giving them a central place in Wittgenstein's account of the nature of philosophy.[5] On this view, the general aim of the philosopher must be to produce surveyable descriptions of the uses of words which have a high degree of comprehensiveness and which can therefore be employed to clarify sizeable domains of grammar and to dissolve many different philosophical problems all at once. What is required is the careful selection and arrangement of grammatical trivialities ('quiet weighing of linguistic facts' (*Z* §447)) to bring out features of the uses of symbols of which we have lost sight in the welter of everyday explanations of what symbols mean. The philosopher reminds us of familiar facts which have slipped out of our field of attention, and he directs our thinking into less convoluted paths by plotting a grammatical nexus embracing a wide range of related concepts (primarily by producing schemata that avoid confusing detail).[6] The production of perspicuous representations is the most general characterization of the proper goal of philosophy once we have come to acknowledge that philosophy can only describe the grammar of our language (§§109, 124). The philosopher strives to command a clear view of 'the grammar of our language'. His success is comparable to someone's looking down on a city from a height, thereby commanding a clear view of the layout of its streets and squares. The philosopher has the additional task of giving a clear description of what he surveys. Here his success is comparable to a cartographer producing an aerial map. The analogy embedded in Wittgenstein's discourse about perspicuous representations is a bird's-eye view of a city. In describing 'the grammar of our language', he is allegedly engaged in 'logical geography' à la Ryle, but he aimed to present his findings in a distinctive *style* of conceptual map.

This second conception of the nature of perspicuous representations (which I will refer to as the Bird's-eye View Model) has several important corollaries. First, it suggests that Wittgenstein left room for a positive role for philosophy which *stands in contrast* and supplements its predominantly negative or therapeutic task.[7] Though he treated particular problems as illnesses (§255) and applied various particular therapies to make them disappear completely (§133), his ideal of constructing perspicuous representations seems to indicate a striving towards a more systematic philosophy.[8] Did he not envisage descriptions of some domains of grammar which would provide accurate maps and thereby constitute a permanent prophylaxis against whole sets of philosophical problems? For example, he *seems* to have aimed at a general classification of 'psychological concepts' in which the correct treatment of each would throw light on *all* and thereby secure an understanding of conceptual connections that would dissolve many of the problems of philosophy of mind (cf. *Z* §§464–5).[9]

Second, a perspicuous representation of grammar is evidently to be contrasted with the various 'mythologies of symbolism' that philosophers are inclined to elaborate (*PG* p. 56). This contrast might suggest that the aim is simply a correct description of the uses of words ('the account books of language' (*PG* p. 85)) which will explode various mistaken philosophical theories, ranging from Platonism and intuitionism in philosophy of mathematics through Cartesian dualism and behaviourism in philosophy of mind to logical atomism and the picture-theory of the proposition in philosophy of logic. Wittgenstein often suggested that these theories can be traced to a more fundamental set of 'grammatical illusions' (§110), which are linked by 'Augustine's conception of language' (§4, cf. §1). His intention was not to replace one mythology of symbolism by another parallel theory (e.g. to replace Platonism by 'strict finitism' or Cartesian dualism by behaviourism); not even to replace 'Augustine's picture' by some alternative generalizations about the nature of language (e.g. 'anti-realism' or 'semantic idealism'). Instead he aimed at a surveyable description of 'our grammar' which neutralizes the appeal of all standard philosophical theories. On his view perspicuous representations are to stand on a different level. They make no pretensions to *explain* 'the uses of our words'. Hence they abstain from metaphysical fantasies and stick to describing the down-to-earth, ordinary [*hausbacken, gewöhnlich*] uses of 'our words' (TS 213, 412). Their function is to destroy idols or to clear the ground of derelict structures and rubble. Whereas Platonism or Cartesian dualism might be described as 'ways of seeing things' (indeed, as poor ways of seeing things which generate philosophical puzzles), a perspicuous representation does not *ex officio* embody any point of view.[10] (In this respect it resembles a report of a visual perception rather than a description of a visual aspect of things.)

Third, according to this interpretation, it is a pleonasm to say that the subject-matter of a perspicuous representation is 'the grammar of our language' or 'the use of our words'. Nothing other than descriptions of grammar are even candidates for being called 'perspicuous representations'. Consequently, there is no possibility of identifying any form of scientific theory, any hypothesis about historical development, or any observation about a religious ritual or a work of art as 'a perspicuous representation'. In particular, it would be a mistake to call Goethe's scheme of plant morphology ('All the organs of plants are leaves transformed') or Darwin's evolutionary scheme for the classification of species ('Taxonomy recapitulates phylogeny') 'perspicuous representations', at least in the context of clarifying the employment of this expression in Wittgenstein's method of philosophizing.[11]

From this sketch of the Bird's-eye View Model, we can milk out an account of the use of 'perspicuous representation' in Wittgenstein's writings.

(i) A perspicuous representation is an ordering or arrangement of grammatical rules or of descriptions of 'the use of our words'. It is tautologous to add 'of grammar' to the phrase 'a perspicuous representation' (just as it would be to add 'of a person' to the phrase 'a portrait').

(ii) What it represents is exactly what its components severally *describe,* namely the employment of symbols of 'our language'.

(iii) The adjective 'perspicuous' in the phrase 'a perspicuous representation' is used attributively. It ascribes a property to a particular arrangment of grammatical rules, namely that they can be taken in at a glance, remembered with comparative ease, and reproduced with a minimum of errors.

(iv) The adjective 'perspicuous' lacks any comparative form in the phrase 'a perspicuous representation'. A description of grammar that does not meet the appropriate criteria is simply *not* a perspicuous representation just as a sequence of mathematical propositions that does not exhibit perspicuity is simply *not* a proof. One representation of grammar cannot be 'more (or less) perspicuous' than another any more than one axiom of geometry can be more (or less) self-evident than another.

(v) There is no such thing as a mode of representation or a way of looking at rules of 'our grammar'. If there are different perspicuous representations of a single domain of grammar, they differ merely in the selection and arrangement of grammatical rules; they would be different *orderings* 'in our knowledge of the use of language'.

(vi) Perspicuous representations are roughly additive. By pasting together a map of Buda and a map of Pest we obtain a map of the conglomeration called 'Budapest'. Descriptions of grammar are similar in this respect; two of them can always be amalgamated into a more comprehensive whole. For perspicuous representations we must add a caveat since the combination of two individually surveyable descriptions may overstep the threshold of what can be taken in at a glance; perspicuity could then be restored only by some further simplification or schematization.

(vii) The criteria of identity for perspicuous representations have an indeterminacy which parallels that for such concepts as explanations of what signs mean or descriptions of character. A fragment of a description of 'our grammar' may or may not qualify as such a description on its own; certainly a fragment of a perspicuous representation may drop below the threshold of completeness necessary for a perspicuous representation. Conversely, any description of 'the use of our words' (or any arrangement of grammatical rules) may be swallowed up in a more embracing one. There is no clear answer to the question 'How many perspicuous representations are there in the *Investigations*?', just as there is none to 'How many descriptions of character are there in *Emma*?'.

(viii) There are equally no clear criteria for the success or adequacy of a perspicuous representation. Presumably each component, i.e. each individual grammatical rule, must be *correct*,[12] but in addition the whole set must have a certain degree of comprehensiveness or completeness. This crucial vagueness might give 'perspicuous representation' many of the features of an essentially contested concept.

(ix) Although to somebody at some time 'the uses of our words' may not be perspicuous, whether globally or locally, it seems that it *must* be *possible* for anybody to command a clear view of the use of any word or family of words (e.g. the use of 'psychological concepts'). This seems to be a corollary of the insight that there are no discoveries to be made in grammar given that it consists of an array of rules which competent speakers follow in speaking a language. Since nothing is hidden from us, each of us can in principle construct a map of any domain of 'our language', however extensive it may be. 'It is not a *contingent* feature of language that its grammar is surveyable.'[13]

The question to be addressed here is whether this description of its grammar squares with the actual use of 'perspicuous representation' in Wittgenstein's language. Close examination of the immediate progenitor of §122 gives some grounds for serious doubts. Careful exploration of the context of this remark leads us back to the first antithetical interpretation of his conception of a perspicuous representation. This in turn opens the way to realizing that his writings are rife with examples of what *he* called 'perspicuous representations'. This point is not merely scholastic. Acknowledging it calls for a radical redescription of what he called 'our method'.

PARENTAGE: TS 220, §100

The immediate precursor of §122 is a remark in the 'early version' of *Philosophical Investigations* (TS 220, §100). It is immediately preceded by two remarks that trace philosophical problems to analogies that have been absorbed into the forms of our language (TS 220, §98(b) = *PI* §112). The source of the difficulty is that 'the form of representation of our language' (*die Darstellungsform unserer Sprache*) has assumed 'a disquieting aspect' (*einen uns beunruhigender Aspekt*) (TS 220, §98(a)). Some examples are listed. The noun 'time' may suggest some mysterious medium. '("But here there *is* surely nothing!" – But here there is surely not *nothing*!)' ('*Aber hier* ist *doch nichts! – Aber hier ist doch nicht nichts!*') (TS 220, §98(c)). It seems problematic that we can measure the duration of an event because it is never present in its entirety. And the use of 'is' both as copula and identity-sign generates an apparent paradox. 'The rose is red and also it is surely not red' ('*Die Rose ist rot, und ist doch wieder nicht rot*'). Wittgenstein then proposed a strategy for dissolving these problems.

> We then change the aspect by placing side-by-side with *one* system of expression other systems of expression. – The bondage in which one analogy holds us can be broken by placing another [analogy] alongside which we acknowledge to be equally well justified.[14]

(TS 220, §99)

For example, the 'problem of identity in difference' can be made to disappear by adopting a notation in which 'is' is replaced in some contexts by '=' and in others by '∈' (which symbolizes set-membership). Exhibiting this *possibility* side-by-side with our use of the word 'is' suffices to break the spell of the form of representation of our language. 'It was the system of expression which held me in bondage.' (*Es war das System des Ausdrucks, welches mich in Bann hielt*) (TS 220, §99(b)). Juxtaposing one notation with another is intended to effect a change of aspect; success would consist in our seeing the use of 'is' differently, that is in our looking at the use of this word as decomposing into two distinct uses. The 'problem of identity in difference' will simply vanish for anybody who adopts this point of view since the apparent contradiction depends on seeing the two occurences of 'is' as having the same use.

Since the remark on the importance of perspicuous representations immediately follows this discussion, there is a prima facie case for linking its content to the idea of exposing new aspects of systems of expression in order to break our bondage to analogies absorbed into the forms of our language. How can this suggestion be filled out? The obvious thought is that Wittgenstein moved from illustrating some particular therapies for some particular philosophical problems to giving a more general description of the method that he has just exemplified. He suggested that the paradoxes or antinomies are themselves manifestations of the lack of perspicuity in 'our grammar'. If every particular philosophical problem is rooted in our failure to command a clear view of the uses of the words which are employed to frame it, then in making the 'problem of identity in difference' disappear by juxtaposing with it a new notation, Wittgenstein must have thought himself to be remedying this defect in a particular case by making (one aspect of) the grammar of the word 'is' perspicuous to us. We might further conjecture that he thought of this object of comparison itself[15] as a perspicuous representation of the use of the word 'is', at least if it is successful in making perspicuous an important aspect of the use of 'is'. (Its success would not entail either that 'is' has two different uses exactly matching those of '=' and '∈' in the notation of set theory or even that 'is' as a matter of fact has two distinct uses, but merely that it *can be seen as* having two uses.) The maximum of continuity in the sequence of remarks in TS 220 is secured if the observation about perspicuous representations in §100 is taken to be a generalization occasioned by an exhibition of specific instances in §§98-9.

This reading rests on two assumptions. The first is that Wittgenstein called 'a perspicuous representation of our grammar' anything that has the function of introducing 'perspicuity' into some aspects of the use of some of 'our words' (i.e. anything which manifestly helps somebody to know his way about by dissolving some philosophical problems which bother him). There is no general restriction on what form a perspicuous representation may take. In particular, it need not be either a diagram (like the colour-octahedron) or an assemblage of grammatical rules for the use of 'our words'. The set-theoretic system of notation differs from both although it is clearly introduced in order to clarify an aspect of the use of the word 'is' whose neglect generates the 'problem of identity in difference'. In this case (and in others too (TS 220, §6 = *PI* §5)), it is describing a *different* language-game (a clear and simple language-game or a calculus which proceeds according to definite rules (cf. *PG* p. 63)) and comparing this other system of notation with the complicated use of 'is' which enables us to command a clear view of 'the use of our words'. If the object of comparison itself is to be called 'a perspicuous representation', then there need be no conflict between calling something 'the *description* of a language-game *different* from our own' and calling it 'a *perspicuous represen-tation* of the grammar of *our* language'!

The second assumption is that the term 'representation' can be applied to an object of comparison which is employed to exhibit aspects of 'the use of our words'. This seems to lead to two related difficulties: the first is to make sense of the idea that the object of comparison is itself a symbol, and the second is to make sense of the idea of a method of projection which relates the symbolic representation to what is represented. The first hurdle can be surmounted by realizing that whether something counts as a symbol or not depends on how it is used. If we make use of a landscape painting to say something about a proposition or of the notation of set theory to say something about 'The rose is red', then in this particular context the painting is a symbol for a proposition and the set-theoretic notation a symbol for contrasting aspects of the use of 'is'. Anything can be used as a symbol, even if it is concrete, and something commonly used as a symbol may fail to be so used, as in using the colour-octahedron or arithmetical calculations as elements in a wall-paper design.

The problem about specifying a method of projection itself requires refinement. On the one hand, there are objects employed in comparisons or similes, for example, a landscape painting is taken as a model for part of the use of 'proposition'. Here a non-trivial method of projection can easily be supplied, for example, a correlation of picture-elements with the words comprising a proposition. On the other hand, there are simple or 'primitive' language-games which Wittgenstein used to promote a clear view of our complicated patterns of speech. Here the notion of a method of projection seems to lose its grip at least in so far as the simple language-game is taken to be a *fragment* of 'our language'. In what sense can a part of our language-game with numerals or colour-words (e.g. the use of natural numbers in counting or of colour-words without any 'is'/'looks' contrast) be said to *represent* the whole? Or is it supposed to represent only itself? This difficulty can be alleviated by considering projections in geometry. Three-dimensional surfaces may be projected onto a plane, and the resulting figures will count as 'representations' (in two dimensions) of configurations of three-dimensional surfaces. A simple language-game has a parallel role and hence has equal right to be called 'a representation' of the use of 'our words'. The converse movement of thought, from the simplified object of comparison to the full complexity of 'our language', is best conceived as adding a new *dimension* to the grammar of the symbols of the simple language-game (cf. *PI* pp. 200–1). Wittgenstein often advised that it would be best not to view the simple game itself as a *fragment* of the more complicated one; rather we should look on the simple one as a *complete* language-game which can be projected onto an *isomorphic subsystem* within the complex one (on the model of correlating the natural numbers with the non-negative whole numbers within the system of the rationals).[16] On this understanding, there seems no problem about describing a simple language-game as 'a grammatical *model*'[17] or 'a perspicuous *representation*' of the use of 'our words'.

Integrating TS 220, §100 into its context gives a highly unified account of the *method* which Wittgenstein tried to demonstrate by examples (TS 220, §116 = *PI* §133). Although there is not one single method which can be mechanically applied to dissolve every philosophical problem, there is a general strategy exhibited in all the various therapies, and the possibility of mastering it and transferring it to new problems gives substance to the conviction that the correct treatment of each problem casts light on the correct treatment of *all* (*Z* §465).

The unity of the method turns on the application to grammar and language of the concept of an *aspect* (and of the related concepts of seeing an aspect and being blind to an aspect). This concept is prominent in the text of TS 220. Philosophical problems arise 'because the forms of representation of our language have taken on a disquieting *aspect*' (TS 220, §98; emphasis added). The tyranny of a system of expression is to be broken and the problems dissolved by our effecting a change of *aspect* through juxtaposing with our language other systems of expression (TS 220, §99). We are often blind to 'the philosophically most important *aspects* of things' because of their simplicity and familiarity (TS 220, §105; cf. *PI* §129: emphasis added). And we must free ourselves from the thrall of the ideal by acknowledging it as a picture and finding its source; unless we find the concrete image that gave rise to it (*Urbild*), we cannot free ourselves from its misleading *aspect*. We can avoid ineptness or emptiness in our assertions only by presenting the model (*Vorbild*) as what it is, as an object of comparison (TS 220, §107).

Not only is the concept of an aspect highlighted, but also the method of dissolving philosophical problems by effecting changes of aspect is demonstrated. The treatment of the 'problem of identity in difference' is offered as an illustrative example (TS 220, §99). Wittgenstein then put this method to work in the text of TS 220, addressing himself to the nature of the proposition (*Satz*) as envisaged in the *Tractatus*. He had characterized a proposition as a concatenation of names, each of which corresponds to an object (TS 220, §108; cf. *TLP* 3.22, 4.22); looking back on this thesis, he now observed that 'A *picture* held us captive' (TS 220, §109 = *PI* §115). He had mistaken the possibility of a comparison (the possibility of rephrasing 'Socrates was older than Plato' as 'Socrates *stood in the relation of* being older than *to* Plato') for a state of affairs of the highest generality (namely, that all words with *material* meanings are distributed in networks of purely logical relations (TS 220, §110)). We are inclined to predicate of the thing represented what lies in the method of representing it; through a kind of optical illusion, we seem to see in the inmost nature of the thing what is etched onto our spectacles (TS 220, §110). The expression of this illusion is the metaphysical use of our words (TS 220, §110). The cure is to encourage surrender of the dogmatic claims 'Things *must/cannot* be thus and so' by exhibiting other intelligible ways of seeing things (other *possibilities*), that is by showing that we can take off the pair of spectacles through which we now see whatever we look at (TS 220, §92 = PI §103). To the extent that philosophical problems take the form of the conflict between 'But this isn't how it is!' and 'Yet this is how it *must* be!' (TS 220, §98(b) = *PI* §112), they will obviously be dissolved away once the inclination to say 'must' has been neutralized by seeing another possibility.

Wittgenstein tried to liberate our thinking from enslavement to particular analogies by bringing to light *other analogies* which are equally well supported as the ones of which we unconsciously make use (TS 220, §99).

> A simile belongs to *our* structure; but we cannot draw any conclusions from it; it does not lead us beyond itself, but it must always remain as a simile. – We can draw no conclusions from it. This is so if we compare a proposition with a picture . . . or the application of propositions, operating with propositions, with the application of a calculus, e.g. the calculus of multiplication.[18]
>
> (TS 220, §102; emphasis added)

Wittgenstein did not either recommend or practice a method of eschewing analogies in the clarification of grammar. On the contrary, he constantly introduced fresh ones. But he employed them deliberately for specific purposes, emphasizing that he was dealing with objects of comparison and hence avoiding falling into metaphysical assertions by drawing conclusions about how things must or cannot be (TS 220, §107; cf. *PI* §131). Analogical descriptions of grammar stand *on the same level* as the unexamined analogies which they are intended to displace in dissolving particular philosophical problems. Wittgenstein's therapy is, as it were, a kind of homeopathy. Conscious analogies and comparisons are useful tools for curing diseases of the intellect, whereas unconscious ones generate insoluble problems by exercising an imperceptible tyranny over our thinking.[19]

When we are held captive by a picture or analogy 'embedded in our language', we are unable to see something in more than one way. We think, for instance, that a proposition *must* consist in a set of names scattered in a nexus of purely logical relations (TS 220, §109), and we express this conception in the form of the report of a perception of a (metaphysical) fact, that is of an insight into the nature of a proposition. Our position is comparable to that of someone who *continuously* sees a single aspect in the duck–rabbit diagram (*PI* p. 194). He is aware of no other possibility, he is unable to see the figure other than as a picture-rabbit, and he reports his seeing this aspect of the figure in the form of a perceptual report (*PI* pp. 194–5). In both cases there is a kind of blindness to aspects. The remedy in both cases must be to bring hitherto unnoticed aspects of things to a person's awareness, that is to get him to *see* things differently. The aim is to effect not merely a change of opinion, but a kind of conversion (*die Umstellung der Auffassung* (TS 220, §116)). Wittgenstein suggested that *one* method is to place other objects side-by-side with the thing to be reconsidered. We change the aspect of 'the use of our words' by juxtaposing with it another system of expression, real or imagined (TS 220, §99). Indeed, 'our method is not merely to enumerate actual uses of words, but rather deliberately to invent new ones, some of them because of their absurd appearance' (*BB* p. 28). Surrounding our practice with new possibilities (language-games) may have the consequence that we *see* matters differently; it brings it about that we compare it with *this* rather than with *that*, and thereby it changes our *way of looking at things* (TS 220, §126; cf. *PI* §144). Indeed, juxtaposing 'our language' with a simple language-game may bring about our *commanding a clear view of* the use of our words! (TS 220, §6 = *PI* §5). This procedure parallels bringing someone to notice a new aspect of the duck–rabbit diagram by surrounding the figure with other picture-rabbits (cf. *LW* §165). In both cases there is an inclination to exclaim: 'Nothing has changed, yet everything looks different!'

Provided that we are prepared to call 'perspicuous representations of our grammatical rules', *inter alia*, whatever objects of comparison serve to make perspicuous to us (to bring us to command a clear view of) 'the grammar of our language', there seems to be a cast-iron case for calling some language-games 'perspicuous representations of *our* grammar'. The very same argument would apply to some diagrams (e.g. the diagram of a graduated ruler in the clarification of the mutual exclusion of parallel determinates under a single determinable[20] (*WWK* p. 64; *PR* §84)) and to certain things introduced as *analogues* in the clarification of 'the use of our words' (e.g. representational paintings in the philosophical investigation of propositions, or everyday rules of grammar in the clarification of mathematics). The range of perspicuous representations of 'our grammar' is extremely catholic. Neither divergence between the object of comparison and 'the use of our words' (e.g. its being a 'clear and simple language-game') nor lack of pretensions to *describe* 'the grammar of *our* language' debars something from qualifying as a perspicuous representation. On the contrary, simple language-games mesh with *one* preferred paradigm that Wittgenstein employed to explain what he understood by 'a perspicuous representation', namely Goethe's conception of the primal plant (*Urpflanze*). Goethe's enterprise was to describe all of the parts of plants in terms of the degree to which their forms deviated from an archetypal leaf-form; he used the primal plant as a centre of variation for plotting plant morphology.[21] Wittgenstein frequently used simple or 'primitive' language-games for exactly this purpose (cf. *LPP* 25, 142). We may come to command a clear view of the complicated and interwoven uses of 'our words' (to *see* 'our language' in a particular way) by *comparing* them with language-games in which symbols have clearly defined uses and *noting similarities and differences* between 'our language' and these prototypes (TS 220, §115; cf. *PI* §130).[22] Provided that we acknowledge the point of calling objects of comparison (when used in this manner) 'perspicuous representations', there is no obstacle to seeing that perspicuous representations have as important a role in 'our method' as Wittgenstein claimed.

At the same time, the sequence of remarks in the 'early version' of the *Investigations* points towards a very different interpretation of 'a perspicuous representation' from the one encapsulated in the Bird's-eye View Model. Many points of discrepancy are noteworthy.

First, if the paradoxes of §98 are instances of problems arising from our failure to command a clear view of 'the use of our words', and if comparing 'our notation' with a different one exemplifies the strategy of making perspicuous a particular use of one of 'our words' (§99), then the method of constructing perspicuous representations (or specifying objects of comparison) is *inseparable* from the task of dissolving particular philosophical problems. The notation which distinguishes '=' from '∈' makes perspicuous an aspect of the use of the word 'is' inattention to which generates the 'problem of identity in difference'; using this as an object of comparison makes the problem completely disappear by exhibiting a new possibility and thereby altering our way of looking at the grammar of 'is'. Here giving a perspicuous representation is essential to a conceptual therapy, not something to be contrasted with particular therapies as an independent project manifesting Wittgenstein's hankering for a more global, positive, or systematic role for philosophy.

Second, comparison with an alternative notation is clearly one method for introducing an order into 'the use of our words', but in every case it is also relative to a specific purpose, namely, the dissolution of a particular problem. If each philosophical problem arises from a particular simile 'which is taken up into the forms of our language' (TS 220, §98), if each problem manifests 'the bondage in which an analogy holds us fast' (TS 220, §99), then Wittgenstein's goal, in each case, must be to 'break the bondage in which certain forms of language hold us fast' (TS 220, §113). Consequently, in respect of each philosophical problem he wished 'to establish an order in our knowledge of the use of language' (TS 220, §113); '*an* order *for a particular purpose*, one out of many possible orders' (TS 220, §113 (emphases added); cf. *PI* §132). Both the claim that the order is purpose-specific and the acknowledgement of the possibility of different orders indicate that his aim was to produce for each problem an order which would make *it* completely disappear,[23] not to establish a single order which would make every problem disappear (or even every problem within some range of problems). It exemplifies a basic quantifier-shift fallacy to draw the conclusion that, on Wittgenstein's view, 'it is the task of philosophy to achieve an order, an order which gives complete clarity . . . an order which makes *everything* surveyable'.[24]

Third, provided that giving a perspicuous representation is the method for making a philosophical problem disappear, and provided that an effective therapy may be problem-specific, there is clearly no commitment whatever to the idea that perspicuous representations must be (even roughly) additive. The attempt to amalgamate two perspicuous representations (e.g. the colour octahedron and the graduating marks on a yardstick which exhibit two aspects of the use of colour-words) may produce nothing intelligible, or it might happen that one exacerbates the problem that the other is designed to eliminate (e.g. taking the durations of intervals on the model of the graduating marks on a yardstick may aggravate the difficulty expressed by the question 'How is it possible to measure time?'). There is no more reason to suppose that perspicuous representations are additive than to claim that the successive seeing of two different visual aspects in the duck–rabbit diagram can be combined into a single visual experience of seeing both aspects at once.

MATURE REFLECTIONS

Aside from TS 220 there is more textual evidence for a conception of perspicuous representations which differs radically from the Bird's-eye View Model. I cannot present and discuss all of the relevant material here.[25] Instead, I shall suggest how sensitive attention to the texts of both the 'early version' and the 'final version' of the *Philosophical Investigations* leads us in the direction of elaborating the first (and hitherto neglected) strand of his thinking about 'perspicuous representations'.

Perhaps the most direct route to attaining an overview of 'his method' is to address the question of what he meant by the remark 'The concept of a perspicuous representation . . . earmarks *our form of representation, the way we look at things*' (§122; emphasis added). At the very least, this concept must apply to what he considered to be his own method of philosophizing (whether or not he held that it had some claim on the attention of other philosophers or that it lay in the nature of philosophy). Consequently, it must play a role in his way of looking at and representing what he took to be the subject-matter of his investigations, namely 'the use of our words' or 'our grammar'. Does it make sense to speak of 'a form of representation *of the grammar of our language*'? This phrase may seem problematic because he sometimes referred to 'our grammar' itself as 'a form of representation'.[26] Yet Wittgenstein saw no objection whatever to this locution. On the contrary, it might be said that he regarded this idea as of fundamental importance for philosophy, and that he focused his attention not so much on accummulating data on 'the use of our words' as on confronting more general prejudices or preconceptions which stand in the way of our making effective use of these data. His therapies for particular philosophical problems involve tracing the roots of our thinking back to certain underlying 'grammatical illusions' (cf. §110), unacknowledged or unconscious ways of looking at symbolism (or 'our grammar'). This 'second-order' concern with different forms of representation *of grammar* (i.e. different forms of representations *of* forms of representation) is distinctive of what he called 'our method', and it clarifies why he held out the hope of demonstrating a *method* by means of examples (§133).

To make sense of the phrases 'our form of representation' and 'our way of looking at things' in this context presupposes that there are other contrasting forms of representation and other ways of looking at 'our grammar'. Are these ideas incoherent? Some philosophers may show extreme resistence to accepting them, but Wittgenstein identified and explored *many examples* of alternative conceptions (or 'pictures') of 'the grammar of our language'.[27] One which is prominent in many texts is what he called 'Augustine's conception of language' (§4, cf. §1). According to this schema, a difference in the meanings of two words *must* always be explained by reference to a difference between the two objects which they severally stand for, and a difference between the uses of two sentences *must* be accounted for by reference to a difference between the two facts which they severally describe. In adopting 'this general notion of the meaning of a word' (§5),

> we are asking for the expression 'This word signifies *this*' to be made part of the description [of the use of any word]. In other words the description ought to take the *form*: 'The word . . . . signifies . . . .' Of course, one can reduce the description of the use [of any word] to the statement that this word signifies this object.'
>
> (§10; second emphasis added)

Nonetheless 'this general notion of the meaning of a word surrounds the working of language with a haze which makes clear vision [*das klare Sehen*] impossible' (§5). This conception of language is manifestly a norm (or form) of representation of the 'uses of our words' to which *any* use whatever may be fitted (§13). It is not a theory which excludes anything or which could be held to misdescribe (or describe!) anything. Nothing defies being cast into this pattern, though there may be much more difficulty with some words than with others. Augustine's picture of language can be seen as a dogma that controls the *expression* of all descriptions of the uses of words and sentences. In this way it exerts an absolute, palpable tyranny over philosophers who cannot complain, however, that they are not free. It is not a *wall* setting limits to what can be noted and described in 'our grammar', but rather a *brake* which serves the same purpose (cf. *CV* p. 28). At the same time it appears to have no possible influence. It seems to be a *mere* form of representation which alters nothing in what is represented, but simply our ways of representing things. Viewed in this way it seems completely anodyne. 'When we say: "Every word in language signifies something" we have so far said *nothing whatever*' (§13). (We might even say that a philosopher who repudiated Augustine's picture would merely be objecting to a convention. What he wants is only a new notation, and by a new notation no facts of logical geography are changed! (cf. *BB* p. 57).) The pervasive, subtle, and pernicious influence of forms of representation is the very aspect of the description of 'the grammar of our language' which Wittgenstein laboured to bring sharply into focus, and his treatment of Augustine's picture of language is the prime exhibit. On this view of his intentions, it betokens grave mis-understanding of the spirit of the *Investigations* to treat Augus-tine's picture as a theory which is the least common denominator of a wide range of *theories* of meaning and to interpret his critical exploration of it as a wholesale *reductio ad absurdum* of these theories (Frege's 'philosophy of language', the logical atomism of Russell and the *Tractatus,* and so on).[28]

Wittgenstein tried to show that the roots of many more local philosophical views (both superstitions and insights!) lie in general pictures of the nature of symbolism. These explorations ranged over the conception of logical constants in the *Tractatus,* Platonism in philosophy of mathematics, and behaviourism in philosophy of mind. In every case he brought sharply into focus *general* conceptions about the essential nature of *symbolism.* All of them present particular *forms of representation* of 'our grammar', and a critic might call each and every one of them 'a mythology of *symbolism*' (*PG* p. 56), 'a *grammatical* fiction' (§307), or 'a false *grammatical* attitude' (*PG* p. 85; emphases all added).

The influence of these 'second-order' forms of representation (or ways of seeing things) on philosophers' descriptions of 'our grammar' is clearly visible not only in generating many of the celebrated 'isms' which dominate philosophical debates, but also in shaping the description of the most basic 'data' supporting their 'metaphysical uses' of the words of 'our language'. One instance is the debate about the status of ostensive definitions. It is clear enough that we do in fact teach the word 'red' by pointing to a ripe tomato and saying '*That* → is red'; moreover, it is also clear that this procedure is one paradigm of what we call 'explaining what "red" means' or 'explaining what red is'. Yet one philosopher insists that this practice *cannot* be called '*defining* or *explaining* what "red" means', since it really consists in correctly *applying* the word 'red' to a perceptible object. Another philosopher argues, on the contrary, that it is the fundamental case of assigning meaning to a word, since it actually connects a word with what it stands for (unlike the usual 'verbal' or 'dictionary' definitions). A third claims that it is indeed an explanation, but only in virtue of its endowing the recipient with the capacity to recognize the colour red when he sees it. Wittgenstein himself suggested that the ostensive definition might be viewed as a substitution-rule for symbols (which should be seen as including both a sample and the gesture of pointing), and so on. In all these cases, philosophers' descriptions of the data of 'the grammar of our language' are shaped by the adoption of particular and identifiable *forms* (or norms) of description. There is just as compelling a case for claiming that descriptions of 'our grammar' must conform to particular forms of description (employing, as it were, particular systems of coordinates) as that scientific descriptions of the world must do so (in virtue of being framed in a symbolism which has a particular 'grammar'). There seems no good reason to think (or even to think that Wittgenstein thought) that the subservience of descriptions to forms of description, and hence the 'relativism' of acknowledging the possibility of different forms of description, comes to an end at the frontiers of empirical discourse!

From close inspection of his method in conducting his own philosophical investigations, we can see clearly that Wittgenstein was committed to the intelligibility of there being *different* forms of representation of 'our grammar' or *different* ways of looking at 'the use of our words'. He thought that philosophical problems could be exacerbated or alleviated, generated or annihilated by shifting from one of these 'second-order' forms of representation to another. For example, he thought that the sterile debates of philosophy of mind could be dropped altogether if we could free our thinking from the grammatical illusion that every sentence must *describe* something. He constantly tried to sketch new possibilities (e.g. §244), to make visible hidden *aspects* of 'the use of our words' (§129), and to encourage us to look at things like *this*, not like *that* (*LPP* p. 168).

What makes a remark a perspicuous representation of 'the use of our words' are not its intrinsic features. but its function in making 'our grammar' perspicuous, by providing, for example, landmarks, patterns, analogies, or pictures, which enable us to find our way about in the motley of 'our language' (cf. §123). Such a remark *need not* have *one* form; in particular, it need not consist of a mere selection and arrangement of grammatical rules. In fact, perspicuous representations in Wittgenstein's writings have several radically different forms. Their diversity matches the diversity of procedures for bringing somebody to notice a new aspect in a drawing. This may take the form of tracing certain lines in a particular sequence, surrounding parts of the drawing with other figures, comparing the drawn figure to various three-dimensional models or other perceptible objects, or showing how the drawn figure might result from a sequence of modifications to another drawing. All of these procedures have analogues in making visible unnoticed aspects or patterns in 'the use of our words'. We may arrange various cases of following instructions for using symbols by reference to samples in order to lead someone to see a connection between the obviously normative role of the standard metre in the language of metric linear measurement and the function of everyday ostensive definitions of the word 'red' by reference to ripe tomatoes or pillar boxes (cf. §§50–4; BB pp. 85–90). We may imagine a familiar use of symbols to be embedded in very unfamiliar or abnormal contexts (§§142; *BB* pp. 9, 28, 49, 61–2). We may compare 'our grammar' with various 'clear and simple' language-games, noting respects of similarity or difference (§§5, 130–1; TS 220, §99). We may demonstrate how 'our complicated uses of words' might have grown out of 'primitive language-games' by the gradual accretion of new expressions and the adding of new joints to language (*BB* pp. 77–125; *NFL* pp. 293, 295–6; *LPP* pp. 23–5, 96; *Z* §§418–25). Provided that we acknowledge the diversity in the *forms* of what he called 'perspicuous representations (of our grammar)', we should have not the slightest difficulty in seeing that the concept of a perspicuous representation does indeed have a fundamental importance in *his* form of representation.

Failure to comprehend this aspect of his method reflects a misunderstanding of his use of the phrase 'a perspicuous representation'. The Bird's-eye View Model misrepresents almost every aspect of this use; indeed, it interposes a veil which makes clear vision impossible. I shall redraw each of its lines to exhibit a different aspect of the grammar of 'perspicuous representation' (see pp. 42-3).

(i) A perspicuous representation is a representation of some-thing which makes what is represented perspicuous (or orderly) to someone to whom it is given. It need not be a representation of 'our grammar'; its subject-matter may be the morphology of plants, the classification of animals, religious ceremonies, or magical rites. It need not consist of 'rules of grammar' (arranged in an ordering). It is not a pleonasm to speak of 'a perspicuous representation *of grammar*'.

(ii) The components even of a perspicuous representation of 'the grammar of our language' need not be *descriptions* of the employment of the symbols of '*our* language'. They may be 'centres of variation' for giving descriptions of the use of 'our words' (*LPP* p. 25); or they may be descriptions of different language-games (even of ones which have an absurd appear-ance (*BB* p. 28)) which may serve as objects of comparison in order to induce us to see things differently (or to change our way of looking at things (§144)).

(iii) The adjective 'perspicuous' in the phrase 'a perspicuous rep-resentation' is *not* used attributively. Whether a representation is perspicuous is not an intrinsic feature of it (e.g. whether it can be taken in at a glance or easily reproduced accurately from memory), but rather a characterization of its role or function. It is a representation which *makes perspicuous* what is represented. In this respect, the adjective 'perspicuous' in the phrase 'a perspicuous representation' has a use similar to the adjective 'clear' in the phrase 'a clear description'.

(iv) Wittgenstein never called one representation 'more perspicuous' than another. On the other hand, there seems no reason why one representation of 'the use of our words' should not be more comprehensive than another; it might illuminate more aspects of the use of certain words. Certainly there seem to be degrees of 'knowing one's way about a city', and corresponding differences in the knowledge conferred by maps. Wittgenstein seems to have invited some analogy with maps in drawing a comparison with 'knowing one's way about the use of our words'.

(v) It makes sense to speak of modes of representation or ways of seeing 'our language', 'our grammar', or language-games (whether actual or imaginary). Indeed, both 'Augustine's conception of language' and Wittgenstein's proposal to *view* the meaning of a word *as* its use in the language are specific forms of representing 'our grammar' or particular ways of looking at it. What seems doubtful, on the contrary, is whether it makes any sense to speak of 'descriptions of our grammar' which do *not* exemplify particular modes of representation or ways of seeing things. In particular, it seems doubtful whether we can legitimately contrast Wittgenstein's investigation of 'psychological concepts' (or his treatment of mathematics) with standard philosophical positions (such as behaviourism, Cartesian dualism, Platonism, or intuitionism, etc.) by claiming that he *merely* described 'the uses of our words' whereas other philosophers looked at the facts of grammar through the distorting spectacles of particular conceptual schemes or metaphysical prejudices. In claiming the importance of perspicuous representations for 'our form of representation', Wittgenstein seems to have been explicitly subscribing to a form of relativism which most of his would-be followers reject.[29]

(vi) Perspicuous representations need not be (even roughly) additive. If, individually, each makes visible one aspect of the use of some particular representation 'of our words', and if there are typically different aspects of the uses 'of our words', then there is no necessity that there be any single way of making simultaneously visible several different aspects 'of our grammar', still less that the combination of two perspicuous representations of the use of the same symbols make perspicuous two aspects of the use of these symbols. The mutual exclusion of different visual aspects of a diagram or drawing may be matched by the complementarity of perspicuous representations of 'the use of our words'.

(vii) There are tolerably clear criteria of identity for perspicuous representations which license the conclusions of the form that Witgenstein sometimes offered several distinct perspicuous representations of the use of a particular symbol or set of symbols. In this respect, 'perspicuous representation' is a count-noun whose use parallels the use of 'landmark' or 'point of reference'. There is no doubt that the dome of St Paul's, Nelson's Column, and Victoria Tower are distinct landmarks in the city-scape of London. Similarly, there is no doubt that the colour-octahedron and the yardstick marked off with colour coordinates are two distinct perspicuous representations of the use of words for colours.

(viii) The criteria of success in giving a perspicuous representation are strictly relative to particular situations. Adequacy must be judged with reference to the elimination of a particular person's not knowing his way about in a particular situation. In this respect a perspicuous representation 'of our grammar' is fundamentally different from the philosophical ideal of a correct conceptual analysis. In particular, it cannot be faulted on the grounds that it does not give a description that fits *every* use (or *all* aspects of the use) of the words whose use is represented. On the contrary, it is adequate provided that it makes clear *some* puzzling aspect of 'the use of our words' and that it can serve as a centre of variation or a point of reference for making clear a *large class* of cases of the use of certain symbolss.[30] For example, the slogan 'Thinking is operating with signs' (*BB* p. 6), understood as a perspicuous representation of the use of the verb 'think', should not be rejected on the grounds that a person may think without speaking or writing, or on the grounds that a parrot may utter words without cogitating or having thoughts.[31] On the contrary, its utility is to be judged primarily by whether or not it effects a certain change in the way of looking at 'our language', namely whether it dissolves the question 'What gives life to dead signs?' (*BB* p. 4) by clarifying the point that 'Thinking' is an absurd answer. To conclude, from Wittgenstein's failure to repeat this slogan in later writings about other aspects of the concept of thinking that he repudiated this earlier idea is to judge perspicuous representations by inappropriate criteria.

(ix) It is clearly not necessary that there be one perspicuous representation which simultaneously dissolves every philosophical problem into which people naturally fall in reflecting about 'the use of our words'. Moreover, it seems doubtful whether it even makes sense to delineate in advance *all* the possible *aspects* of the grammar of any word(s); there seems to be no such thing as a perspicuous representation of *all aspects* of 'the use of our words'. In respect of each particular aspect, it is a creative achievement (not a mechanical procedure) to find a means for bringing it to another's notice, and it is a task of persuasion (not a demonstrative proof) to bring it about that another *sees* things differently.

If this synopsis of the grammar of 'perspicuous representation' captures Wittgenstein's conception of the nature of a perspicuous representation (or even one facet of the employment of a family-resemblance concept), then there are important consequences for the interpretation and exploitation of his philosophical 'insights'. He constantly advocated new ways of looking at things: he urged us to examine language under the guise of a calculus, to view the meaning of a word as its use or the sense of a sentence as its employment, to regard an ostensive definition as a substitution-rule for symbols or a sample as part of 'our language', and to look at an avowal of pain as a manifestation or expression of a sensation or at an arithmetical equation as a rule of grammar. In all these cases he was manifestly trying to clarify *aspects* of 'the use of our words'. If it is correct to link up perspicuous representations of grammar with seeing aspects of the employment of symbols, then each and every one of these well-known *leitmotif*s from Wittgenstein's later philosophy appears to be a paradigm of what he understood by 'a perspicuous representation'.

The application of this concept to what he called 'descriptions of grammar' bears on what he understood by the remark that he advanced no *theses,* gave no *explanations,* and avoided dogmatism in philosophy (§§109, 126, 128, 131). If 'perspicuous representations' are connected with exhibiting *aspects* of 'the use of our words', then they do not conform to many of the features of fact-stating discourse. On the contrary, they more closely resemble descriptions of *possibilities.* If his remark that an ostensive definition of 'red' can be seen as a substitution-rule for symbols is intended to make visible an *aspect* of a form of explanation of word-meaning which dissolves the questions 'How is language connected with the world?' and 'Must any language not include indefinable or primitive concepts?', then there is no need (indeed no point) in debating whether his observation is a correct application of the everyday expression 'a substitution-rule for symbols', whether the remark encompasses *all* cases of what we call 'ostensive definitions' (e.g. explanations of proper names of the form 'That → is Mont Blanc'), or whether

it makes clear *all* of the important aspects of ostensive definitions (e.g. the differences between them and verbal or dictionary
definitions). Precisely parallel points hold for the observations
that arithmetical equations are rules of grammar, that the
meaning of a word is its use in the language, or that the
utterance 'I am in pain' is an expression of pain, etc. No fact
(even one about 'our grammar') is stated, and no thesis
advanced. There is nothing to attack, hence nothing to defend
against criticism. Wittgenstein advocated nothing more (and
nothing less!) than different possible ways of looking at things
which he offered in particular argumentative contexts for
certain specific purposes.

One might object that the conception of a perspicuous representation which I have tried to pin on Wittgenstein would rob
his writings of all interest and importance. Did his work in
philosophy of mind and philosophy of mathematics in the end
just amount to advocating mere changes in the form of representation of 'our grammar'? Did he really suggest that we can
dissolve our philosophical problems at will by deciding to see
things differently, as we can shift at will from seeing the duck–
rabbit diagram as a duck to seeing it as a rabbit? These dismissive
responses ignore the important fact that forms of representation
are deeply embedded in our thinking and even in our pattern of
activities (our forms of life). To change our form of representation (e.g. to drop the dogma of psychophysical parallellism)
may be an *enormous* thing to do (*UW* p. 434). There is every
reason to suppose that changes in forms of representation of 'our
grammar' will be equally momentous and full of far-reaching
consequences for our ways of thinking; not only momentous, but
also difficult to achieve (cf. *CV* p. 48). It is not a simple matter to
effect a total reorientation of one's style of thinking (a conversion
to a new point of view). Indeed, this may be impossible in
practice for many individuals at many times (cf. *CV* p. 61). The
point of calling aspect-seeing 'voluntary' (and in this respect
contrasting it with perception) is *not* to claim that it can be
brought about on a whim, but rather that it *makes sense* to ask
somebody to look at things differently, to say that a person has
complied with this request, or equally that he has *refused* to see
an aspect which is perfectly visible to others (*LPP* p. 334; *RPP I*
§899). We might say that changing one's way of seeing things is
difficult *because* it is voluntary, because one has to surrender

what one has always *wanted* to see (cf. CV pp. 16–17).

What I have tried to do is to bring to light a new way of looking at Wittgenstein's own conception of a perspicuous representation. This enterprise consists in making visible hitherto unnoticed *aspects* of his own philosophical methods. If the general line of my argument is correct, the most that I can accomplish is to expose a *possibility* for interpreting his later philosophy, a possibility the acceptance of which would amount to a change in our *way of looking at* his 'descriptions of the grammar of our language'. It is not possible to prove or demonstrate *contra mundum* that this interpretation captures the *nature* of *his* philosophy or that it alone fits his practice and pronouncements; it is at best possible to persuade willing readers to explore this possibility for themselves.

> Working in philosophy – like work in architecture in many respects – is really more a working on oneself. On one's own interpretation [*Auffassung*]. On one's way of seeing things [*Daran, wie man die Dinge sieht*]. (And what one expects of them.)
>
> (*CV* p. 16 = TS pp. 213, 407)

This observation is important for understanding the point or spirit of the particular perspicuous representations of 'our grammar' scattered through the *Philosophical Investigations*. It is no less important for appreciating the obstacles standing in the way of a contemporary analytic philosopher trying to grasp Wittgenstein's concept of a perspicuous representation.[32]

NOTES

1 I will usually put these expression in 'scare quotes' to remind the reader that there are many dimensions of uncertainty about how to interpret them (as well as many related expressions such as 'a simile that has been absorbed into the forms of our language' (§112) or 'a picture . . . which lay in our language' (§115)). These forms of expression in Wittgenstein's discourse need careful investigation.

2 This principle of projection applies to the simple octahedron (*WWK* p. 42), not to the more complex hexkaidekahedron (*PR* p. 278).

3 In fact, the text does not state or imply that perspicuous representations are 'our form of representation', or even that they exemplify *a* (single) form of representation. Instead it claims that *the concept of* a perspicuous representation *characterizes* 'our form of representation'.

4 The notion of completeness is fairly rough-and-ready. The criteria for distinguishing complete from incomplete explanations may be both purpose-relative and context-dependent (cf. G.P. Baker and P.M.S. Hacker, *Understanding and Meaning*, Oxford, Blackwell, 1990, pp. 78–81).

5 Cf. A.J.P. Kenny, 'Wittgenstein on the Nature of Philosophy' in Kenny, *The Legacy of Wittgenstein*, Oxford, Blackwell, 1984, pp. 42–3; Baker and Hacker, op. cit., pp. 488–91, 531–45.

6 Though comprehensiveness and schematization are logically distinct features of descriptions, they seem to be connected once the requirement of surveyability is imposed on an assemblage of rules of 'our grammar'. A perspicuous representation must focus on 'the central structure of the net of language, not the local refinements'; it would turn its back on 'the lavish detail of an Austin's descriptions of features of English grammar' because of the danger of 'getting lost in the details' (Baker and Hacker, op. cit., p. 543).

7 See A.J.P. Kenny, op. cit., pp. 38–9, 42–3; and P.M.S. Hacker, *Insight and Illusion*, 2nd edn, Oxford, Clarendon Press, 1986, p. 151.

8 Baker and Hacker, op. cit., pp. 488–91; cf. P.M.S. Hacker, op. cit., pp. 177–8.

9 Cf. Hacker, op. cit., p. 177. This reading arguably conflates two different things, the 'plan for the treatment (or classification) of psychological concepts' (*Z* §§472, 488) and 'the genealogical tree (*Stammbaum*) of psychological concepts' (*Z* §464; cf. *RPP I* §722). According to this second method of representation, certain concepts are regarded as belonging to 'primitive language-games', while others are viewed as adding new joints to these language-games (cf. *Z* §425). No logical (or psychological) priority seems to be asserted (cf. *LPP* 23–5).

10 It is, as it were, a view from nowhere. In this respect, a perspicuous representation of grammar might be said to be the heir of 'the correct logical point of view' (*TLP* 4.1213), or a part of seeing the world *sub specie aeterni* (*TLP* 6.45). (Cf. Hacker, op. cit., p. 151.)

11 Waismann did exactly this (F. Waismann, *The Principles of Linguistic Philosophy*, Macmillan, London, 1965, pp. 80–1), but one might doubt (in absence of independent evidence) whether he correctly grasped Wittgenstein's thinking about this point. There is a risk of blurring the all-important distinction between grammar and science, i.e. between description and theory-construction (Baker and Hacker, op. cit., p. 539).

12 This requirement might *seem* to be completely unproblematic. Yet some degree of simplification, schematization, or exaggeration might be tolerated (as in the qualification 'in a *large* class of cases – though not for all' which accompanies the identification of the meaning of a word with its use in the language (§43)). Likewise 'descriptions of our grammar' may include similes, analogies, and metaphors, and in these cases the true/false dichotomy has no straightforward application. What Wittgenstein called 'descriptions of grammar' have a considerable variety. The criteria for correctness of descriptions must be as variable as the language-games of giving

descriptions of grammar (or the language-games of giving 'descriptions of what is seen' (*PI* p. 200)), and therefore as indeterminate as the criteria for judging the correctness of the description of a painting (or the 'life-likeness' of a sketch of a person or even the accuracy of a *sketch* of a painting of an animated battle-scene). Indeed, the project of describing grammar, as Wittgenstein both envisaged and practised it, is not a pedestrian activity, and the skill of a philosopher is as much a matter of educated judgment as the talent of a portrait-painter. 'Die Anlage zur Philosophie beruht auf der Fähigkeit, von einer Tatsache der Grammatik einen starken und nachhaltigen Eindruck zu empfangen' (TS 220, §104).

13 ibid. p. 544. It is not clear what licenses this conclusion. Need *any* enumeration of rules for the use of 'our words' have the property of surveyability? Or even the property that *some rearrangment* must exist which would give it this property? Perhaps the idea is rather that by choosing a suitably large scale and omitting enough fine detail any map can be transformed into one which can be taken in at a glance and reproduced flawlessly from memory.

Not only are these theses dubious, but each also lacks any clear grounding. Could any of them be derived from the *grammar* of the word 'grammar'? or of the phrase 'a description of grammar'? These proposals seem to be non-starters as long as the term 'surveyable' [*übersichtlich*] is not taken to be vacuous.

14 Wir ändern nun den Aspekt, indem wir *einem* System des Ausdrucks andere an die Seite stellen. – So kann der Bann, in dem uns eine Analogie hält, gebrochen werden, wenn man ihr eine andere an die Seite stellt, die wir als gleichberechtigt anerkennen' (TS 220, §99).

15 Alternatively, he might have thought that perspicuously representing this aspect of 'is' consists in the activity or procedure of placing the notation of set theory side-by-side with the use of 'is' and noticing the similarities and differences. Here the making of the comparison would count as '*giving* a perspicuous representation', although there would be nothing that counts as 'a perspicuous representation' which is *given*. (Describing 'our grammar' in this way would be comparable to drawing a figure in the air, where no drawing is produced.)

Yet another possibility is that he thought of the listing of points of similarities and differences with an object of comparison as a distinctive form of describing 'our grammar' which he labelled 'a perspicuous representation'.

Since my aim is to expose a possibility of interpretation, not to exclude alternative ones or even the possibility that 'perspicuous representation' is a family resemblance concept, I shall not explore the merits and demerits of these two alternative conceptions of Wittgenstein's use of objects of comparison. It is clear enough what speaks in favour of treating objects of comparison themselves as perspicuous representations. The initial example of the colour-octahedron introduces a specific *diagram* which is called 'a [perspicuous] representation' (*PR* p. 52). Likewise, Wittgenstein later applied this label to the *formula* 'Thinking is operating with signs' (F. Waismann, 'Zwei Einwände', p. 3, catalogued as 'F 15' in the deposit of Waismann's papers in the Bodleian Library, Oxford). Finally he cited (or alluded to (*GB* p. 69)) Goethe's notion of the primal plant (*Urpflanze*) as a paradigm of 'a perspicuous representation'. In all these cases, something specific is isolated from a general description and singled out as a perspicuous representation.

16 For a careful exposition of this point, see F. Waismann, *Einführung in das mathematische Denken*, ch. 2.

17 This phrase is employed by Waismann, who emphasized the importance of 'the method of constructing grammatical models' for the purpose of obtaining 'a compendious scheme (*ein übersichtliches Schema*) with which we can compare language' (Waismann, op. cit., pp. 72, 74).

18 'Ein Gleichnis gehört zu *unserem* Gebäude; aber wir können auch aus ihm keine Folgen ziehen; es führt uns nicht über sich selbst hinaus, sondern muss als Gleichnis stehen bleiben. – Wir können keine Folgerungen daraus ziehen. So wenn wir den Satz mit einem Bild vergleichen . . . oder die Anwendung der Sätze, das Operieren mit Sätzen, mit der Anwendung eines Kalküls, z.B. des Multiplizierens' (TS 220, §102; emphasis added).

Here 'our construction' (*unserem Gebäude*) clearly refers to Wittgenstein's own clarification of the grammar of the term 'proposition' (*Satz*); the simile to which he called attention is the one between propositions and pictures.

19 This is one point of resemblance between Wittgenstein's method of philosophical therapy and psychoanalysis: '*Der Philosoph trachtet das erlösende Wort zu finden, das ist das Wort, das uns endlich erlaubt, das zu fassen, was bis dahin, ungreifbar, unser Bewusstsein belastet hat*' (TS 220, §106; cf. TS 213, 409). To bring something to the patient's consciousness (to bring him to acknowledge it) is the principal step in effecting a cure. Cf. Kenny, op. cit., pp. 39–41.

20 Note that there is strong, though indirect, textual evidence for calling this diagram 'a perspicuous representation': viz. it is offered as an instance of finding '*das lösende Wort* ' (*WWK*, p. 77), and Wittgenstein used this phrase (and the variant '*das erlösende Wort*') to tag what he called 'perspicuous representations' (Baker and Hacker, op. cit., pp. 552–3). This case of 'clearly articulating the rule we have been applying unawares' has certain striking features. First, it is an *example* of what it clarifies: a rod can only be assigned one length, i.e. it can coincide with only one graduating mark when held up against a yardstick (cf. *WWK* p. 77–8). Second, it provides merely an *analogy* for clarifying the grammar of other determinables, e.g. colour-words or specifications of time-durations: there is no such thing as a yardstick marked off with colours, and the closest analogue (namely a colour-chart) differs essentially in lacking a total linear ordering (cf. *WWK* p. 76). Thirdly, this perspicuous representation can come into *conflict* with other clarifications of 'the grammar of our words': in particular, the comparison of measuring

the duration of events with ascertaining the length of a rod is the root of philosophical perplexity about how it is possible to measure time and how it is possible to ascribe durations to events (*BB* p. 26; cf. TS 220, §98).

21 For a slightly fuller clarification, see Waismann, op. cit., pp. 80–1.

22 Arguably it is not sufficient for commanding a clear view of 'the use of our words' to have a discursive knowledge of points of similarity and difference with certain prototypes of language-games. In addition, it seems, we have to *see* things in a certain way.

23 Cf. 'Wie ich Philosophie betriebe, ist es ihre ganze Aufgabe, den Ausdruck so zu gestalten, dass gewisse Beunruhigungen // Probleme // verschwinden. ((Hertz.))' (TS 213, 421).

24 Kenny, op. cit., p. 43; emphasis added.

25 In particular, the immediate ancestor of TS 220, §100, viz. TS 213, 417, places the concept of a perspicuous representation in the context of a discussion which emphasizes that philosophical problems arise as much from defects of the will as from those of the intellect (i.e. from how we *want* to see things); it also connects this concept with Goethe's poem 'Die Metamorphose der Pflanzen' and with Hertz's strategy of dissolving philosophical questions. The yet more remote ancestor, viz. *GB* p. 69, applies the same concept to the description of religious rituals and magical rites (i.e. to subject-matter other than 'the grammar of our language'), and it seems to countenance various distinct forms of 'perspicuous representations' (not merely the ordering or rearrangement of descriptions of phenomena, but also comparisons with a centre of variation and fictional accounts of evolutionary development).

In addition, there is important evidence from hitherto unknown dictations recorded by Waismann in the early 1930s and partly incorporated into his book *The Principles of Linguistic Philosophy*. (Later references to them will include the catalogue number given in the deposit of Waismann's papers in the Bodleian Library, Oxford.)

26 The idea that this would be paradoxical seems to underlie a certain narrowing of the possible interpretations of *PI* §122 and the elimination of one possible interpretation of §131 (cf. Baker and Hacker, op. cit., pp. 546, 556).

27 He even referred to '*false* representations (*Darstellungen*)' of 'the every-day language-game [of describing what is seen)' (*PI* p. 200(b)).

28 *Pace* Baker and Hacker, op. cit., p. 47.

29 The final parenthesis of §122 may point towards the same conclusion. 'Is this a "Weltanschauung"?' seems meant as a genuine question, though often taken to be a rhetorical one. The case for giving a positive answer is that Wittgenstein openly adopted a particular way of carrying on philosophical investigations, viz. by looking at 'the use of our words' (e.g. focusing on the role of mathematical propositions in relation to empirical count-statements rather than on the grounds of mathematical truth or the sources of mathematical knowledge). By taking up this point of view, he cast

his descriptions of the problems of philosophy in a particular form, and his procedure therefore parallels descriptions of history, social practices, or natural history which are said to manifest the influence of particular 'Weltanschauungen'. On the other hand, there is a strong case for giving a negative answer: anything labelled 'a *Welt*anschauung' must be a way of seeing *the world*, but the subject-matter of most of Wittgenstein's own philosophical investigations is taken to be 'our language' (i.e. *not* 'the world', but rather 'our means of representation of the world'). A self-avowed relativism seems to be the only reason for his raising the question whether his own form of representation is a 'Weltanschauung'.

30 'Der Brustton der Überzeugung tut uns dieselben Dienste wie die Überzeugung, oder vielmehr bietet er uns eine einfache und übersichtliche Darstellung der Grammatik des Wortes "Überzeugung" an, die in einer grossen Zahl von Fällen dem Gebrauch des Wortes "Überzeugung" gerecht wird' (F. Waismann, 'Glaube' (F 5), p. 3).

31 This important point is not merely conjectural. Wittgenstein offered '*Das Denken . . . [ist] das blosse Kalkulieren mit der Sprache // ein Operieren mit Worten oder sonstigen Zeichen*' as one paradigm of what he called '*eine übersichtliche Darstellung*' (F. Waismann, 'Zwei Einwände' (F 15), p. 1, cf. 'Glaube' (F 5), p. 3). He canvassed various obvious objections to this description of the use of '*denken* ' (e.g. the possibility of lying or the phenomenon of trying to find the right words to express a thought). As we can infer from a parallel treatment of identifying belief or conviction with the intonation of uttering a sentence, he concluded that *none the less* he regarded this formula as the best epitome of the grammar of '*denken*'.

32 I am grateful to Dr K. Morris, Dr P.M.S. Hacker, Dr T.J. Taylor, Dr H.J. Glock, and Mr V. Politis for criticisms and improvements to earlier drafts of this paper.

Chapter 3

Philosophical Investigations section 128: 'theses in philosophy' and undogmatic procedure[1]

Hans-Johann Glock

THE DILEMMA OF WITTGENSTEIN'S NON-COGNITIVISM

In §§89–133 of the *Philosophical Investigations* Wittgenstein appears to reject the traditional view that philosophy is a cognitive discipline, that is, one that could result in knowledge expressed in true propositions.[2] No part of the *Investigations* has caused more irritation. Often Wittgenstein's attitude is understood as a rejection of science and an expression of a deep-rooted irrationalism.[3] But, I shall argue, this reaction is misguided. For whilst it is true that Wittgenstein was personally hostile towards the scientific spirit of the age (*CV* pp. 6–7), this *ideological* attitude can be separated from his *methodological* position. The latter does not condemn science but scientism, the imperialist tendencies of scientific thinking. Wittgenstein insists that philosophy cannot adopt the tasks or methods of science (cf. e.g. *CV* p. 16).[4]

There are several aspects to Wittgenstein's non-cognitivism, several entries in his index of 'unphilosophical activities'. Some of these can be explained and at least partially supported by the demarcation between philosophy and science that he was driving at.[5] Thus his prohibition of theories, hypotheses, and explanations (*PI* §§109, 126) is directed at scientific theorizing which tries to provide causal explanations of empirical phenomena. Philosophical problems, however, cannot be solved by experience (*LWL* pp. 79–80; *AWL* p. 3). They are conceptual, not factual, and arise not from ignorance about empirical reality or about a Platonist world behind appearances, but from misunderstanding the *way we talk about empirical reality*. Therefore philosophy is not concerned with explaining reality itself, but with describing our norms of representation which lay down what counts as an intelligible description of reality. Indeed, since the later Wittgenstein no longer restricts meaningful discourse to the description of reality, philosophy more generally reflects on language, the way we speak. It clarifies grammar, the set of rules by which we determine the correct uses of words (*PI* §§89–90).

The conceptual nature of its problems also explains why philosophy should be 'flat', that is to say without the inferences or proofs of deductive–nomological sciences and formal disciplines like mathematics or logic (*PI* §§126, 599). Deductive argument cannot constitute the heart of the conceptual clarification Wittgenstein seeks. Deduction establishes the consequences of a set of premisses, but it cannot clarify the meaning of these premisses or guarantee their intelligibility.

Two other aspects of Wittgenstein's non-cognitivism do not arise directly from the contrast between factual (scientific) and conceptual (philosophical) investigations, but can nevertheless be defended in a relatively straightforward manner. According to Wittgenstein, philosophy can neither justify nor revise grammar, but only describe it (*PI* §124). Both claims are based on his view that grammar is autonomous; it is not responsible to the nature or essence of reality. Our grammar cannot be correct or incorrect but only practical or impractical. This means that there are no standards by which philosophy could either justify our ways of speaking or replace them by metaphysically superior ones.

It seems, therefore, that Wittgenstein's non-cognitivism is not open to the general charge of irrationalism and that several of its aspects can be accounted for. One important aspect, however, remains puzzling and questionable. It occurs in a sub-section of the chapter on philosophy (*PI* §§126–9) and culminates in the claim that any philosophical theses would have to be platitudes to which we would all consent.

> If one tried to advance *theses* in philosophy, it would never be possible to debate them, because everyone would agree to them.
>
> (*PI* §128, cf. §599)

One reaction to this passage is to point out that it does not really condone philosophical theses of even a platitudinous kind, since this possibility is only treated as hypothetical ('If one *tried* to advance theses . . .'). But this reply is overhasty. For Wittgenstein certainly speaks in a non-hypothetical way of his own *philosophical descriptions, answers,* and *solutions* and characterizes them as closely similar to the theses of *PI* §126. The idea of platitudinous theses is therefore only the most pointed way of raising a general problem about Wittgenstein's characterization of his own philosophizing. Moreover, as we shall see below (pp. 80–3) his most promising solution of this difficulty refers to philosophical theses.

Indeed, occasionally Wittgenstein speaks of his philosophical remarks not only as uncontroversial, but even as homely (*'hausbacken'*), ordinary, trivial or as stale truisms (*'fade Selbstverst ändlichkeiten'*) (TS 213 p. 412; MS 109 p. 212; TS 220 pp. 89–90; TS 219 p. 6). In one respect such passages give a misleading picture of Wittgenstein's position. For those terms have the connotation of irrelevance or unimportance. In contrast, there is no doubt that he considered his remarks as philosophically relevant, capable, for example, of revealing traditional philosophy as 'plain nonsense' and 'houses of cards' (*PI* §118f). Strictly speaking one should therefore call such remarks *platitudes* rather than *trivialities*. But first 'platitudinous' is an awful mouthful, and second 'triviality' crystallizes the understandable suspicions of traditionally minded philosophers. I shall therefore use this term with the proviso that it is not meant to indicate insignificance but only simplicity and lack of controversy.

Unfortunately, even given these caveats, the claim made by *PI* §128 seems wildly implausible. Wittgenstein's own remarks such as 'An "inner process" stands in need of outward criteria' (*PI* §580) or 'mathematical propositions play the role of norms of description' (*RFM* p. 363) are far from uncontroversial to philosophers and laymen alike. Even worse, this claim implies that in philosophy any remarks which can be disputed must be withdrawn, a consequence Wittgenstein happily accepts.

> On all questions we discuss I have no opinion; and if I had, and it disagreed with one of your opinions, I would at once give it up for the sake of argument because it would be of no importance for our discussion.
>
> (*AWL* p. 97)

I won't say anything anyone can dispute. Or if anyone does

dispute it, I will let that point drop and pass on to say something else.

(LFM p. 22)

Such an attitude of 'philosophical pliability' leads straightforwardly into a dilemma, of which followers and critics alike have perhaps been aware, but which, to my knowledge, has not yet been stated clearly. If Wittgenstein's discussion of philosophical issues, including the nature of philosophy itself, conforms to his 'no opinion'-methodology, it cannot amount to a contribution to philosophy. For the claim to propound theses or opinions and to assess their correctness by rational argument seems essential to philosophical discourse. Consequently his work would be *incommensurable* with traditional philosophy. His remarks on philosophy in particular would amount to an antiphilosophical rejection of philosophy, not to a conception of philosophy that could be argued for.

On the other hand, if his discussions comply with the standards of philosophical discourse, that is if they put forward and defend theses of some kind, his position is *inconsistent* in several respects. For one thing, his practice would belie his stated views on the nature of philosophy. For another, he would have to base his attacks on traditional theories on philosophical positions of his own.[6] Finally, the very statement of this rejection would be self-refuting. For it would advance a philosophical thesis to the effect that there cannot or should not be nontrivial philosophical theses, a thesis which itself is anything but trivial. In either case – incommensurability and inconsistency – his attacks on traditional positions would be self-contradictory and his non-cognitivist conception of philosophy would be incoherent.

There are three ways of reacting to this very serious predicament. First, we may reject Wittgenstein's non-cognitivism as untenable. Second, we may try to develop the idea that his work is incommensurable with philosophy proper. Finally, we may try to reinterpret his remarks as consistent with participation in philosophical debate and hence as a coherent contribution to the philosophical debate about the nature of philosophy. This paper pursues the last line by linking Wittgenstein's triviality thesis to other methodological remarks in his later writings (published and unpublished). It first shows that the second option is inadequate both exegetically and absolutely. The next section starts to develop an alternative account by establishing what the trivial theses of *PI* §126 are, namely grammatical reminders which combine descriptive and normative features. Wittgenstein's willingness to abandon disputed claims can then be understood as part of his conception of an 'undogmatic procedure' arising from the *Tractatus* (below, pp. 80–3). Finally, I argue that this conception overcomes our dilemma by sketching a method of philosophizing that allows for philosophical argument while avoiding theses of the prohibited kind.

THE FAILURE OF THE 'NO POSITION'-POSITION

Wittgenstein would not have accepted the second horn of the dilemma, inconsistency. He did not hesitate to *dis*qualify contradictions. Logical contradictions, to be sure, are not nonsensical but senseless, and they have a role in assessing the validity of arguments. But this role is precisely to rule out a position which is or implies a contradiction (cf. *PG* pp. 128f; *AWL* pp. 63f, 139f; *LFM* p. 223; *RPP II* §290).[7] And as we shall see, he diagnosed conceptual inconsistency, the use of conflicting rules, as a paradigmatic form of philosophical confusion.

The triviality thesis, together with Wittgenstein's comparison of philosophy to a kind of therapy (*PI* §§133, 255, 599), has led some commentators to believe that he opted for the first horn, incommensurability.[8] According to this *'no position'-position* his work does not contain any arguments that fulfill the standards of philosophical discourse. He is not even in the business of attacking traditional positions or correcting philosophical mistakes. Rather, his remarks are therapeutic attempts to make us abandon philosophical questions for the sake of intellectual tranquillity or liberation.

Whether or not there *are* arguments in the later work cannot be decided here. (One is reminded of Lichtenberg: 'A book is a mirror: if an ass peers into it, one can't expect an apostle to peer out'.) It is clear, however, that the 'no position'-position is wrong in holding that Wittgenstein *intended* to exclude the possibility of philosophical argument. He insists in various ways on the argumentative character of philosophy. His own philosophizing he describes as the 'rejection of wrong arguments' which is open to those feeling a need for 'transparency of their own argumentation'

(TS 213, pp. 408, 421). Moreover, it is part of his philosophical pliability that disputed opinions should be abandoned *for the sake of argument* (*AWL* p. 97; quoted above). This suggests that Wittgenstein engages in a kind of argument, albeit one which undercuts matters of opinion or empirical fact.

Nevertheless one aspect of this suggestion encourages the 'no position'-position. For this approach is based on the idea that Wittgenstein did not try to provide alternative answers to traditional problems, but tried to *dissolve* them. Consequently there would be no answers to philosophical problems, no positions or views of any kind. Indeed, Wittgenstein himself occasionally suggests that we should respond to *all* philosophical questions not by giving an answer, but by asking a new question (*RFM* p. 147) and that philosophical illumination may arise from a book featuring nothing but jokes and questions.[9]

It must be conceded to the 'no position'-position that Wittgenstein typically did not take sides in traditional disputes but tried to undermine the assumptions common to the participants. He also questioned questions which lead to such misguided alternatives, including questions like 'How can one . . .?' or 'What is the foundation of . . .?' directed at commonplace practices (*BB* pp. 30f). But he certainly *did* provide answers to traditional questions of a different kind, namely Socratic questions like 'What is understanding?' (cf. *PI* §§143–84). Doing so is even a prerequisite of fulfilling the task of dissolving misguided questions. For mistaken assumptions concerning these Socratic questions are often the root of misguided constructive questions and of incoherent theorizing. What Wittgenstein rejects with respect to such Socratic questions is merely the insistence that they can only be answered by providing *Merkmal-definitions* (*BB* pp. 17ff; *PI* §§64–88).

But even where Wittgenstein rejects a traditional question as phrased, his remarks must nevertheless address an *underlying problem*. Otherwise he simply would not have anything to say on the topics at issue and his rejection would be no more than an expression of lack of interest, something those pursuing the question can ignore. Thus, when Wittgenstein rejects questions like 'What is the ground of necessary truth?' he still addresses the philosophical problem of necessity by other questions like 'What is it for a proposition to be necessary?'. Questioning a question in a philosophically relevant sense must involve taking up an underlying common problem in a more adequate way. It may be objected with reference to certain passages (e.g. *BB* p. 46) that Wittgenstein rejects the very idea that there is a genuine problem here. In that case, however, he would still be addressing the question *whether* there is a problem here, or of what kind it is. (This rejoinder sounds bloody-minded only because it has to match the obstinate silliness of seriously adopting a 'no-position'-position.)

As a matter of fact, taking up a common problem in a new way is precisely the idea behind Wittgenstein's conception of philosophy. The contrast between him and traditional philosophers is not just one between different intellectual interests, like the use of words *v.* the nature of things. Both claim to resolve the metaphysical problems which, according to Wittgenstein, constitute the subject-matter of philosophy. And he suggested his 'new method' as a new way of *dealing with* these problems, without necessarily *answering* the questions which had traditionally been thought to crystallize them. Furthermore, he claimed that this method is superior because it is based on a better understanding of the character of the problems (*LWL* p. 1; *PG* p. 193; *AWL* pp. 27f; *M* pp. 322f). He does not claim to establish true propositions or theories, but only because a grammatical investigation of philosophical problems reveals that such methods would be misguided.

Wittgenstein refuses to take sides in traditional philosophical debates and instead undermines their presuppositions. But this cannot be described as a form of agnosticism. For in doing so he is committed to the view that the question, as previously asked, evinces a confusion, or is at any rate misguided in a philosophically relevant sense. (As a conscientious objector I was asked by a committee: 'How can you be a pacifist if you are prepared to kill a person in order to prevent the destruction of mankind?' To reject this sort of question as misguided is certainly not tantamount to saying 'Gentlemen, I have no opinion on the matter!'.) One cannot completely avoid arguments or holding views without ceasing to criticize, attack or undermine certain positions or attitudes. Moreover, replacing the initial question by a new one involves the claim that the latter is more appropriate to the philosophical problem. And this claim must be capable of being backed by arguments; in other words, it must be answerable to standards of philosophical reasoning.

Therefore we cannot, as the 'no-position'-position has it, simply respond to *every* challenge by asking a new question. We must also be prepared to show that a certain question is the right one to ask with respect to a particular problem. And philosophical insights expressed in questions or jokes are at best incomplete without the support of arguments. It is unsurprising, therefore, that this is the strategy of the *Philosophical Investigations*. Wittgenstein himself allocated an important role to grammatical, as opposed to causal, explanations. And in confronting philosophical problems he searched for the 'right question', by discarding others as 'mistaken' (*'falsch'*) (cf. MS 130, p. 107; *RPP I* §600; *PI* §§189, 321). By drawing such a contrast he accepted that questioning questions has to meet certain standards and involves non-vacuous commitments of a kind discussed below. Consequently the 'no position'-position is not just untenable but incompatible with both the spirit and (by-and-large) the letter of Wittgenstein's later work.

FRAMEWORK CONDITIONS OR GRAMMATICAL REMINDERS?

If the 'no-position'-position is inadequate, can we find a more plausible interpretation of the 'triviality thesis'? That 'thesis' is obviously linked to *PI* §126, which claims that there are no philosophical discoveries, since what concerns us in philosophy is not hidden but open to view. No new information is needed and controversies are excluded since we 'constantly move in a realm where we all have the same opinions' (*AWL* p. 97). The first step is therefore to clarify the nature of this uncontroversial but nevertheless philosophically relevant realm. More specifically, what types of expressions might fit the characterization of trivial theses in §§126-9?

There are two possible answers. According to the first, trivial theses are statements about *framework conditions* of our language games. These are facts which render certain rules (im-) practical or even inapplicable, without constituting the content of these rules (*PI* §§240-2). For example, our concepts of measures are useful only in a world with relatively stable rigid objects; but this is not laid down in the rules of, for instance, metric measurement. A 'framework-reading' of §§126-9 is suggested by the fact that Wittgenstein claims, for both these 'very general facts of nature' (*PI* p. 230) and the aspects described by the trivial theses of philosophy (*PI* §129), that they go unnoticed precisely because they are so familiar and general – a 'miss the wood for the trees' effect.

Another possibility is that the pre-empirical realm of philosophy is *grammar*, the rules we use in determining the correct use of words. In this case, the triviality would not be due to the pervasive nature of certain facts but to the logical antecedence of grammar, which determines the distinction between sense and nonsense, to experience, which settles matters of truth and falsity (*PG* p. 88; *PI* §90). Grammatical rules are norms of representation. They cannot be true or false since they determine the prior question of what it makes sense to say. Familiarity with and agreement on these rules is a precondition for empirical conflicts and discoveries even to make sense. Unless we know, for example, the meaning of 'hippopotamus' we can neither dispute nor verify or falsify the biological statements in which this term occurs. And although certain terms puzzle us in philosophical reflection, we are familiar with them outside philosophy, in the sense of being able to use them and explain what we mean in using them. According to this 'grammatical' interpretation, the trivial theses of philosophy turn out to be *grammatical propositions*, or expressions of these rules.

Overall the grammatical interpretation makes sense of more aspects of Wittgenstein's methodology. It also squares better with his actual writings. Here grammatical propositions dominate. Framework conditions as such are rarely stated. Their philosophical significance lies merely in the fact *that* such conditions influence what language-games we play and that their variation makes intelligible alternative forms of representation (cf. *PI* p. 223; *Z* §§350–64).[10]

This view is further supported by the source of §128f in the *Big Typescript* (TS 213, pp. 418–19). Section 128 is here preceded by a remark in which Wittgenstein claims that 'methodology', which should be read as 'philosophy', is not interested in the relationship between framework conditions (the material of a measuring-rod) and the results of measuring, but only in the meanings of words and hence the circumstances in which we speak of, for example, having measured a length. Furthermore, an illuminating version of §127 clarifies what Wittgenstein means by 'reminders' in *PI* §127:

> Learning philosophy is *really* reminding oneself. We remind
> ourselves that we really use the words in this way.[11]
>
> (TS 213, p. 419; my translation)

At this point it is important to confront a tempting but mistaken
interpretation of this passage. For it could easily be understood
in the following way: grammatical remarks are not themselves
grammatical propositions, that is (expressions of) linguistic
rules, but statements to the effect that we actually use language in
a certain way. Such statements would not describe the framework
conditions themselves, but rather the fact *that*, partly due to
certain framework conditions, we adopt particular rules or use
signs in certain ways. Such a reading naturally leads to the view
held by some commentators that grammatical remarks differ
from scientific propositions exclusively in virtue of their thera-
peutical goal.[12] This interpretation is incompatible, however,
with the 'triviality' of philosophy and the antecedence of
grammar to experience. For such statements would constitute an
empirical description of linguistic practices, such as we find in
anthropology or linguistics. It also ignores a crucial feature of
grammatical propositions, namely their *normative* character.
Wittgenstein distinguishes statements like 'All Englishmen use
these signs in this way' from rules (*AWL* p. 154). The former are
bipolar propositions, a matter of empirical discovery, while the
latter have a normative function. Within philosophical discourse
this normative role cannot be one of explaining the meaning of a
term to someone who does not yet know the language. Rather,
grammatical propositions *remind* us of our own rules. They are
akin to explanations of meaning in that they constitute standards
for our use of words. Unlike explanations used in language
acquisition or the teaching of a foreign language, however, they
remind us of rules we have already mastered but tend to forget or
misrepresent within the context of philosophical reflection. Such
reminders point out that outside philosophy we use certain
words in such-and-such ways. That we do so could of course be
the subject of an empirical statement – made, for example, by a
foreign anthropologist recording our linguistic habits. But the
special function of grammatical reminders is to *draw attention* to
the *violation* of linguistic rules by philosophers, a violation
which results in nonsense.

The conflict in which we repeatedly find ourselves in logical reflections is like the conflict between two persons, who have entered a contract, the last phrases of which have been laid down in words which can easily be misinterpreted, while the explanatory comments to these phrases explain everything in a completely unambiguous way. Now, one of the two persons has a short memory, constantly forgets the explanations, misinterprets the rules [*Bestimmungen*] of the contract and therefore constantly gets //falls// into problems. The other one always has to remind himself afresh of the explanations in the contract, in order to remove the problems.[13]

(TS 213, pp. 424f; my translation)

Thus understood, grammatical remarks satisfy Wittgenstein's demand for triviality and his methodology proves to be compatible with theses of a certain kind – grammatical reminders. At this point it may legitimately be asked, however, why Wittgenstein's philosophy has – to put it mildly – not commanded the universal assent, which we should expect if it consisted of grammatical reminders? The first thing to remember in this context is that not all of Wittgenstein's *philosophical* remarks are *grammatical* in the sense of expressing grammatical rules. In addition, there are at least diagnostic explanations of philosophical error and statements about framework conditions. The objection is defused further by distinguishing two categories of grammatical remarks.[14] The first comprises *truisms* about the way words can be used, like 'It makes sense to say "I know that she has toothache" ' or 'A dog cannot be said to believe that its master will return in a week'. The examples mentioned above, on the other hand, such as 'An "inner process" stands in need of outward criteria', are *synoptic descriptions* in which such truisms are drawn together and related to a particular philosophical problem. Such synopses do not vitiate the rejection of theories. For the primary function of Wittgenstein's descriptions of our linguistic practices is not to disclose unity in the name of theory-construction but to emphasize diversity for the sake of philosophical clarity. Furthermore, neither kind of grammatical remark serves as either the terminus or starting point of philosophical inferences. Synoptic descriptions are not scientific generalizations from truisms but sum up truisms for the sake of dispelling conceptual confusions. They help us to find our way around in a given domain of grammar – with a view to specific philosophical problems.

GRAMMATICAL LENIENCY AND 'UNDOGMATIC PROCEDURE'

This leaves one question unanswered. How can such grammatical reminders be part of a method that is both commensurable with traditional philosophical discourse and compatible with Wittgenstein's methodology, in particular with his willingness to abandon all disputed claims? In order to solve this problem, we must find in his later work a strategy that is not so much concerned with refuting a position or confronting it with new information as with undermining a bogus question or alternative.

The solution harks back to Wittgenstein's demarcation between the conceptual and the factual. It is the idea of a *critique of sense*: there is a way of arguing which is more fundamental than contrasting opinions concerning matters of fact, since it concerns meaning or intelligibility, not truth. Accordingly philosophical theories must be shown to be not empirically false but flawed in a more fundamental way, in virtue of being meaningless, nonsensical, or incoherent. Such an approach emerges already in the early work. The *Tractatus* advocates, but does not practise, a dialectical critique of sense which refrains from making assertions of its own and confines itself to revealing the nonsensical character of the metaphysical propositions advanced by traditional philosophers (*TLP* 6.53). In the *Tractatus* this strategy is linked to the distinction between saying and showing, which excludes all philosophical propositions as nonsensical (*TLP* 6.54–7). The idea that grammatical remarks are on the index of illicit statements is given up in the later philosophy (*RFM* pp. 395f, 402f). But the dialectical method envisaged in the *Tractatus* resurfaces as what Wittgenstein later calls his 'un-dogmatic procedure' (*WWK* p. 186).

> I once wrote, 'The only correct method of doing philosophy consists in not saying anything and leaving it to the other person to make a claim.' That is the method I now adhere to. What the other person is not able to do is to arrange the rules step by step and in the right order so that all questions are solved automatically . . . The only thing we can do is to

tabulate rules. If by questioning I have found out concerning a word that the other person at one time recognizes these rules and, at another time, those rules, I will tell him. In that case you will have to distinguish exactly how you use it; and there is nothing else I wanted to say.

(*WWK* pp. 183-4)

Thus I simply draw the other person's attention to what he is really doing and refrain from any assertion. Everything is then to go on in grammar.

(*WWK* p. 186; cf. *PR* pp. 54-5)

In spite of their sketchiness, these remarks provide the means of explaining Wittgenstein's philosophical pliability. The characterization of grammatical remarks provided in the previous section already suggests that the fact that we actually have certain rules, engage in a particular linguistic practice, is in one sense philosophically irrelevant. There are two reasons for this, both of which are linked to the autonomy of grammar. First, if we had different rules we would play a different language-game. But this would not create a philosophical problem, although it may well create a practical one. Second, there is no such thing as a metaphysically correct or incorrect rule or concept, but only a more or less useful one. A philosophical position cannot be criticized merely for employing concepts that differ from our ordinary ones.[15] For our concepts are not metaphysically superior: they may be more convenient than any alternative that philosophers could dream up, but not because they are true to the facts or express the essence of reality. A philosophical position can be criticized undogmatically, however, by pointing out that there is an incompatibility between the use a philosopher makes of a word and the account (explanation) he provides of this use.

What is it that is repulsive in the idea that we study the use of a word, point to mistakes in the description of this use and so on? First and foremost one asks oneself: How could *that* be so important to us? It depends on whether what one calls a 'wrong description' is a description that does accord with established use – or one which does not accord with the practice of the person giving the description. Only in the second case does a philosophical conflict arise.

(*RPP I* §548; cf. *RPP II* §289)

These considerations indicate that statements about our actual linguistic practice can be set aside within undogmatic procedure. If our opponent openly acknowledges that he is introducing a new concept by using a familiar expression in an unfamiliar way, we shall, for the moment, disregard ordinary use and challenge him instead to explain his novel use. However, if subsequently he claims to elucidate our concept or to address a question which is couched in terms of it, we shall have to remind him of the rules governing its use. Provided they are correct, these grammatical reminders cannot simply be surrendered, not because they describe *our* rules, but because they concern rules *our opponent trades on*.

On the other hand, even such reminders are not the ultimate purpose of Wittgensteinian argument. In the *Tractatus* the propositions used within the dialectical process had to be thrown away, because of the saying/showing distinction. And although the later philosophy no longer puts grammatical remarks on the index, it retains the idea that they are not the ultimate end of philosophical reasoning but its chief instruments. As mentioned earlier (p. 75), the subject-matter of Wittgenstein's philosophizing is metaphysical problems. Its result is, in the first instance, a clear understanding of a particular segment of grammar, in the second, *clarity* with respect to a philosophical entanglement in these rules, and, in the final instance, the rectification of philosophical 'mistakes' and 'injustices' with the consequence that the original problem disappears (*PI* §133; TS 213 pp. 407, 418ff). This ultimate purpose explains why Wittgenstein's conception of philosophy is non-cognitivist not just by traditional standards. In spite of its 'quiet weighing of linguistic facts' (Z §447) his philosophizing is not a doctrine of *any* kind, but an activity in pursuit of clarity.

Against this explanation of the 'triviality thesis' and Wittgenstein's philosophical pliability via the notion of undogmatic procedure, it might be objected that it is questionable to base an interpretation of passages from the *Philosophical Investigations* on remarks from 1931 and earlier. But *Remarks on the Philosophy of Psychology*, vol. I §548 stems from TS 229, which was finished in 1947. Most importantly, it has been suggested that the term 'theses' in *PI* §128 may hark back to Waismann's *Thesen* (*WWK* pp. 223ff).[16] This is confirmed by the fact that the term 'theses' and the 'triviality' claim of *PI* §128 both make their first appearance in Wittgenstein's comments on Waismann's theses (which Waismann intended as grammatical remarks).

> With regard to your theses I once wrote: were there theses in philosophy they should occasion no debate. That is, they would have to be so stated that everyone would say: yes, yes, that is obvious.
>
> (*WWK* p. 183)

This passage shows that the key to *PI* §128 lies indeed in 'undogmatic procedure'. For it occurs in the discussion of dogmatism in which Wittgenstein presented this procedure. Consequently the idea of undogmatic procedure elucidates one of the most obscure aspects of his methodology.

UNDOGMATIC PROCEDURE AS IMMANENT CRITIQUE

This solves the exegetical problem concerning the triviality thesis. But what about the philosophical dilemma which created the need for a better interpretation in the first place? What kind of argument is compatible with an undogmatic procedure? Someone ascribing a 'no position'-position to Wittgenstein might attempt a comeback at this point by claiming that the undogmatic procedure does not allow of conclusive arguments against traditional philosophical positions. For it seems as if grammatical reminders could do no more than point out new aspects of the use of words employed in philosophical theories, without ever challenging such philosophical usages. The most that could be expected is that one of these aspects will allay our philosophical puzzlements. ('Look at it this way . . ., if that doesn't calm you down, look at it that way . . . .')

Wittgenstein's methodology indeed excludes refuting philosophical positions in the sense of showing them to be false. It is also correct that changing one's perspective on grammar plays an important role in his philosophical investigations (*PI* §§90, 130–2, 144, 593). Nevertheless it is precipitate to conclude that Wittgensteinian argument cannot be conclusive, or to reduce it to 'grammatical aspect-seeing' for the sake of intellectual acquiescence. This latter suggestion has the unpalatable consequence of obliterating the difference between persuasive rhetoric and sound dialectical argument. For the only criterion of success it provides room for is dissolving an individual 'patient's' urge to ask certain questions. It cannot distinguish between achieving this goal by completely *external* means, such as drugs or a knock on the head, and achieving it in the only way that is *internally* related to the nature of the problems at issue, namely by pinpointing conceptual mistakes.

If Wittgensteinian philosophy is to be logically distinct from mere manipulation, it must involve argumentation that reveals the illegitimacy of the position it attacks. The undogmatic method promises such a rigorous kind of argument. Moreover, whether or not it is persuasive to all persons, it at any rate aims to be conclusive. It may be granted that mere deviance from ordinary linguistic practice does not constitute a philosophical mistake. But the idea is to demonstrate a certain kind of inconsistency in the philosophical positions or questions attacked, an *inconsistency concerning the use of words*. The point is that it is constitutive of metaphysical theories and questions that their employment of terms is at odds with their explanations of these terms and that these theories use deviant rules along with the ordinary ones. As a result, traditional philosophers cannot coherently explain the meanings of their questions and theories. They are confronted with a *trilemma*: either their new, technical uses of terms remain unexplained (unintelligibility), or it is revealed that they cross language-games by using incompatible rules (inconsistency), or their consistent employment of new concepts simply passes by the original philosophical problem, which is based on our ordinary use. This means that the only way of explaining philosophical uses of terms reveals them to be based on an *ignoratio elenchi*: they purport to address problems expressed in our concepts, but in doing so tacitly introduce new concepts.[17]

Finally, contrary to the 'no-position'-position there are limits to philosophical pliability even within undogmatic procedure. Statements to the effect that ordinary people use words in specific ways can be set aside at certain stages of a philosophical critique. What cannot be surrendered, however, is the claim that non-philosophical usage excludes certain ways of using words as *nonsensical*. For only if our grammatical rules establish the bounds of sense for our concepts can philosophical questions or theories be accused of violating these rules, of employing incompatible rules, or of tacitly fluctuating between different language-games. To the notorious 'I'll concede everything' Wittgenstein therefore adds 'as long as I know what I am conceding' (TS 219, p. 224). This means: there will be no disagreement about the truth of the opponent's views, but very much about their intelligibility.

The Wittgensteinian philosopher will try to get his opponent to recognize an inconsistency or unintelligibility in his position. This does not indicate the need for a kind of conversion, but rather is a methodological requirement.[18] For an undogmatic *reductio ad absurdum* it is essential to transform a latent piece of nonsense or inconsistency into a patent one (*PI* §464).[19] The opponent should realize that the proposition or question he advances stems from a grammatical conflict, an inconsistency in his use of words.

To give up the critique of underlying inconsistencies would amount to the acceptance of philosophical nonsense. There is no reason to believe that Wittgenstein would have tolerated such an attitude, which is manifest for example in Nietzsche's 'gay science' or Rorty's 'edifying philosophy'. He even describes his confrontation with philosophical nonsense as a fight (*PI* §109). What we have to realize in order to appreciate his 'triviality thesis' and his philosophical pliability is that the grammatical nature of the confrontation excludes any reliance on statements of fact or matters of opinion in the ordinary sense.

CONCLUSION

Wittgenstein's rejection of 'non-trivial' theses does not commit him to philosophical silence and is hence consistent with his own philosophizing. It is part of a particular conception of philosophical argument which is sketched in his remarks on undogmatic procedure. This critique of sense is not just in line with Wittgenstein's methodological remarks. It is also a kind of argument traditional philosophers will have to accept. To put it crudely: no one can deny that the questions must be intelligible in order for constructive or theoretical answers to make sense. As we have seen, in some respects Wittgenstein's undogmatic procedure is closely linked to the disclosure of familiar fallacies.[20] Moreover, his undogmatic procedure expresses a venerable ideal of philosophical methodology which has come to be known under its Hegelian label of an immanent critique: in criticizing a philosophical position we should not have to rely on dogmatic assumptions of our own but only to point out its internal inconsistency. Wittgenstein provides a new rationale for this vision: due to their conceptual nature, philosophical problems must be resolved by reference to what lies open to view – once we are reminded of it (grammar).

It might finally be objected that this view of philosophy is incompatible with the immense complexity of philosophy. But whereas the results of Wittgensteinian philosophizing (insight into the way we use words and consequent resolution of philosophical puzzlement) must be trivial, its arguments cannot be. For they have to mirror the complexity of the confusions and inconsistencies they reveal. These difficulties are not inherent in the phenomena philosophers discuss, but rather arise from philosophical misconstrual (Z §452; PG pp. 154–5; PI §125). Once more Wittgenstein's methodological views turn out to be consistent. This does not mean that they have been vindicated, but it does show that they should not be rejected *ab initio*.

NOTES

1 I am grateful for comments by Gordon Baker, Peter Hacker, John Hyman, Ernst-Michael Lange, and Eike von Savigny, as well as to points made during the conference, especially by Robert Arrington and Joachim Schulte.

2 This characterization must be qualified in so far as Wittgenstein's philosophy features grammatical *descriptions*. But we shall see that first, this renders it 'cognitive' only in a low-key sense, and second, these descriptions are only a means of Wittgenstein's philosophizing, not its ultimate aim.

3 For example, M. Dummett, *Truth and Other Enigmas*, London, Duckworth, 1979, pp. 454ff. Occasionally this suspicion is reinforced by followers. Thus S. Hilmey (*The Later Wittgenstein*, Oxford, Blackwell, 1988, chs 5–6) gives the impression that Wittgenstein's main concern was not with dispelling conceptual confusions engendered by venerable linguistic forms (*PI* §109; TS 213, p. 424), but with opposing a twentieth-century belief in science and progress.

4 This demarcation of philosophy and science originated in the early philosophy (*NB* p. 106; *TLP* 4.002ff), inspired partly by the philosopher-scientists Hertz and Boltzmann. Unlike Wittgenstein's cultural attitudes, it was shared by the Vienna Circle. Their differences

concerned not so much philosophy, but other non-scientific forms of discourse, which the Vienna Circle tended to regard as inferior to science or even as meaningless.

5 Some of the points mentioned here are defended in greater detail by P.M.S. Hacker, *Insight and Illusion*, 2nd edn, Oxford, Clarendon Press, 1986, chs 5–6.

6 Cf. Dummett, op. cit., p. 434; R. Rorty, *Consequences of Pragmatism*, Brighton, Harvester Press, 1982, pp. 22ff.

7 His attitude towards contradictions in mathematical and logical systems is a complex issue that cannot be discussed here. Cf. S. Shanker, *Wittgenstein and the Turning Point in the Philosophy of Mathematics*, London, Croom Helm, 1987, ch. 6. It seems that he did not advocate the use of calculae which lead to an *actual* contradiction in which application comes to a halt but criticized the fear of *hidden* contradictions.

8 The first to adopt such a position was O.K. Bouwsma ('The Blue Book', in K.T. Fann, ed., *Wittgenstein, the Man and His Philosophy*, New York, Dell, 1967), who reads the assimilation of psychoanalysis and philosophy of the *Blue Book* into the *Philosophical Investigations*. In a less medical and more 'post-modern' vein R. Rorty (*Philosophy and the Mirror of Nature*, Oxford, Blackwell, 1979, pp. 370ff) includes Wittgenstein among his 'edifying philosophers', thinkers who have got nothing to say. Aspects of a 'no position'-position, albeit in an exegetically much more refined form, can also be found in G.P. Baker, 'Philosophy – Eidos or Simulacrum', in S. Shanker, ed., *Philosophy in Britain Today*, London, Croom Helm, 1986.

9 N. Malcolm, *Wittgenstein, A Memoir*, Oxford, Oxford University Press, 1959, p. 29.

10 Two points are noteworthy here: first, the facts of the 'natural history' Wittgenstein has in mind are predominantly socio-historical or anthropological rather than biological. (G.P. Baker and P.M.S. Hacker, *Rules, Grammar and Necessity*, Oxford, Blackwell, 1985, p. 240). Second, the nexus between framework conditions and language-games is not deterministic. The same conditions may lead to different forms of representation (Z §351).

11 'Das Lernen in der Philosophie ist wirklich ein Rückerinnern. Wir erinnern uns, dass wir die Worte wirklich auf diese Weise gebraucht haben.'

12 This has been suggested by D. Pears, *Wittgenstein*, London, Fontana, 1971, pp. 38, 108ff and K.T. Fann, *Wittgenstein's Conception of Philosophy*, Oxford, Blackwell, 1969, pp. 42f.

13 'Der Konflikt, in welchem wir uns in logischen Betrachtungen immer wieder befinden, ist wie der Konflikt zweier Personen, die miteinander einen Vertrag abgeschlossen haben, dessen letzte Formulierungen in leicht missdeutbaren Worten niedergelegt sind, wogegen die Erläuterungen zu diesen Formulierungen alles in unmissverständlicher Weise erklären. Die eine der beiden Personen nun hat ein kurzes Gedächtnis, vergisst die Erläuterungen immer

wieder, missdeutet die Bestimmungen des Vertrages und kommt //
gertät daher// fortwährend in Schwierigkeiten. Die andere muss
immer von frischem an die Erläuterungen im Vertrag erinnern und
die Schwierigkeiten wegräumen.'

14   Baker and Hacker, op. cit., pp. 23f.

15   This constitutes a major difference between Wittgenstein and Austin
(see *Philosophical Papers*, Oxford, Oxford University Press, 1970,
pp. 182–5).

16   G.P. Baker and P.M.S. Hacker, *Wittgenstein: Understanding and
Meaning*, Oxford, Blackwell, 1980, p. 552.

17   Two caveats are in place. First: it is not clear whether
unintelligibility, incoherence, and irrelevance are the only types of
philosophical error. Second: the dialectical situation is not always as
'black or white' as the distinction between sense and nonsense.
Wittgenstein conceded that philosophical errors ('Irrtümer') contained a kernel of truth (Z §460).

18   This is not to deny that the idea of aspect-seeing or of a *Gestaltswitch*
is methodologically important. But arguably its place lies in the
move from a presentation or articulation of grammar which creates a
deadlock, to one which does not. This *presupposes*, however, that
such deadlocks can be exposed by way of argument.

19   My understanding of this passage differs from that of A. Kenny (*The
Legacy of Wittgenstein*, Oxford, Blackwell, 1984, p. 40). He relates it
to the unveiling of the repressed core of philosophical puzzlement
(which is akin to psychoanalysis), whereas I link it to the *reductio ad
absurdum* involved in undogmatic procedure. There can be no doubt
that both ideas feature in Wittgenstein's discussion of philosophy.
The question is where to place this specific remark. The same
problem is posed by the claim that in philosophy we seek to find the
'redeeming word' (*NB* 6.6.15; *WWK* p. 77; TS 213, p. 409 – the
translation of '*erlösendes Wort*' as 'key word', is too weak). It sounds
like part of the psychotherapeutic model. But the fact that in TS 220,
§106 this remark follows a version of *PI* §129 suggests that it may also
be linked to undogmatic procedure.

20   H.J. Glock, 'Stroud's Defense of Cartesian Scepticism – A
"Linguistic" Response', *Philosophical Investigations*, 1990, vol. 13,
tries to apply Wittgenstein's method, as understood here, to a
paradigmatic philosophical problem.

Chapter 4

'Tormenting questions' in *Philosophical Investigations* section 133

S. Stephen Hilmy

Wittgenstein states in *Philosophical Investigations* §133 that the 'proper [*eigentliche*] discovery' in philosophy is the one that 'gives philosophy peace, so that it is no longer tormented by questions which bring *itself* into question'. This is an intriguing remark, but characteristically opaque and puzzling, especially given his declaration on the preceding page of the *Investigations* (§126) that one might call philosophy 'what is possible *before* all new discoveries and inventions'. Unfortunately, Wittgenstein gives us no obvious clues as to the nature of the 'tormenting questions' which allegedly bedevil the discipline (perhaps even to the extent that the discipline itself comes across as a suspect and dubious enterprise). Given the lack of elaboration in §133 one can only assume that the sort of 'discovery' proper to philosophy and which would bring relief to a philosophical perplexity is markedly different from the 'new discoveries' that Wittgenstein seems to shun in §126 as inessential to the philosophical enterprise. Thus the different modifiers (*neuen* and *eigentliche*) could only have been a deliberate attempt to distinguish between the sort of discoveries that are not philosophy's concern, and those that he felt are appropriate to philosophy – though Wittgenstein might have been better off not using the word 'discovery' for the latter. The expression 'new discovery' would seem to be a redundancy, and to the extent that one can discover something that is not new, it would perhaps be better to use an expression such as 'rediscovery', or 'recollection' (depending on the nature of what is recovered). Immediately following §126 this would seem to be Wittgenstein's point, when he characterizes philosophy as a matter of 'assembling reminders' (§127) – a recalling of something familiar rather than a discovering of something new.

A prominent interpretation of the third paragraph of §133 takes Wittgenstein as suggesting that philosophy 'constantly torments itself by questioning its own legitimacy' and that the 'real discovery' which will bring peace is that of 'grasping the true nature of the philosophical enterprise, viz. the resolution of philosophical problems by methods that will yield, not philosophical knowledge, but an *Übersicht*'.[1] This reading of §133 of the *Philosophical Investigations* is not without merit. However, it has at least two shortcomings. On the one hand, it fails to take advantage of Wittgenstein's rather alluring invitation to explore his notion of a 'tormenting question' – a notion which recurs under various guises as an important theme in his later philosophy. If one does exegetically probe his notion of 'tormenting questions', the passage will become more transparent; it is intimately intertwined with a host of other salient and more familiar motifs in his later writings. And second, the notion of 'the proper discovery which brings philosophy peace' ought perhaps to be interpreted also in a more problem-specific way. Given a specific philosophical conundrum or torment, certainly a modicum of peace comes by knowing what kind of discovery needs to be made (for example by grasping the general nature of the philosophical enterprise), but also more specifically peace (*Ruhe*) can be said to come by making the proper discovery that resolves (or dissolves) the specific conundrum or torment.

In his chapter on 'Philosophy' in TS 213 Wittgenstein explains:

> The way I do philosophy, the task of philosophy is to formulate the expression in such a way that certain disquietudes [*Beunruhigungen*] //Problems// vanish . . . . If I am right, then philosophical problems must really be capable of complete resolution, in contrast to all others . . . . The problems are in a real sense dissolved [*aufgelöst*] – like a lump of sugar in water.
>
> (TS 213, p. 421)

The suggestion seems to be that the *Ruhe* or peace of which Wittgenstein speaks in §133 has also a more problem-specific import; specific disquietudes will vanish by in a real sense dissolving the problems, and this is not merely a matter of grasping the nature of philosophy (though first grasping the nature of philosophy might certainly be instrumental in achieving peace at the problem-specific level).

Furthermore, the tormenting questions to which Wittgenstein alludes in *Philosophical Investigations* §133 need not themselves question the legitimacy of philosophy. Rather, the issue of the legitimacy of philosophy may arise as a by-product of the sorts of questions that philosophers tend to be tormented by (or with which they torment themselves), without those tormenting questions themselves being concerned with the legitimacy of the enterprise. If the legitimacy of the enterprise arises as an issue not *in* the questions, but rather because of the types of questions we tend to raise, and it is Wittgenstein's ambition to criticize the questions themselves, then the overall import of *Philosophical Investigations* §133 is as much a *challenge* to the status quo enterprise of philosophy as a legitimation of the discipline. My task here, however, is not to address the issue of the legitimacy of the philosophical enterprise, but rather to flesh out exegetically Wittgenstein's obscure allusion to 'tormenting questions' and expound a bit on the problem-specific dimension of his notion of a 'proper discovery which brings peace'.

It is touchy business for Wittgenstein to try to criticize the nature of philosophical questions, since any apparent attempt to put restrictions on the nature of philosophical questioning may well be viewed as antithetical to what is stereotypically taken as the sweepingly probative nature of the enterprise. But throughout his later writings one finds indications that he was indeed critical of the philosophical *questions* some of his contemporaries (and perhaps even he himself formerly) were inclined to raise, and this not because they are so profound that they are *difficult* to answer, but rather because there is something wrong or amiss in the very questions themselves. This preoccupation with a criticism of the questions themselves is echoed in his remarks that:

You ask this question again and again. – How can one make you stop doing this? By drawing your attention to something else.

You are under the misapprehension that the philosophical problem is *difficult*, whereas it's hopeless.

I want you first to realize that you're under a spell.

(MS 158, p. 64)

and

> The first mistake we make in a philosophical investigation is
> (as always) the philosophical question (itself).
>
> (MS 165, p. 55)

Thus it may be that the tormenting questions to which Wittgenstein alludes in §133 are tormenting not because they are so
profound as to be beyond our grasp or abilities, but rather
because there is something wrong with the questions themselves,
or at least the misleading way in which we formulate them.

Wittgenstein does in fact make such a suggestion in the context
of drafts of early versions of parts of *Philosophical Investigations*
§133, when he asserts that:

> To a philosophical question one can always answer: 'As it is
> now put, it is unanswerable. We must examine how the
> question ought to be put in order to allow of an answer
> (solution). Were we to put it in such and such a way, then
> answering it will pose *no* difficulty.'
>
> (MS 116, p. 186)

Or similarly in other contexts:

> The philosophical puzzle seems insoluble if we are frank with
> ourselves, and *is* insoluble. That is until we change our
> question.
>
> (MS 149, p. 56)

> In order to solve a philosophical problem one must turn away
> from the question (formulation of the question
> [*Fragestellung*]) which so forcefully imposes itself on us.
>
> (MS 130, p. 38)

These remarks clarify to some extent what might be the nature of
Wittgenstein's notion of 'tormenting questions', but the remarks
are also very misleading in at least two respects. First of all, by
'philosophical question' Wittgenstein cannot be referring to just
any question that might be classified as philosophical. Rather,
he must be referring to a specific sub-class or sort of 'philosophical questions'. Clearly, if a question can be reformulated or posed
differently so as to allow of an answer, whereas it did not allow of
an answer as initially formulated, the different formulation itself
would still be classifiable as philosophical, even though it would

be answerable. The more narrow class of 'philosophical questions' to which Wittgenstein refers, therefore, in all likelihood is constituted by the sorts of 'tormenting questions' which are the subject of *Philosophical Investigations* §133, and they 'torment' [*gepeitscht*: lash, whip] philosophy *because* as formulated they are unanswerable. It is perhaps on this point that the notion of 'tormenting questions' ties in with the broader issue of the 'legitimacy' of the philosophical enterprise. A discipline that could not answer the very questions it raises would certainly itself be brought into question, and in any event such a discipline could hardly be expected to achieve even temporary repose or peace (*Ruhe*) in its handling of the problems that are its subject matter.

There is also the suggestion in the above passages that by properly reformulating a philosophical (or so-called 'tormenting') question, or perhaps by asking a different and more appropriate question, the difficulty or conundrum can be rendered solvable or dissolvable. Thus the suggestion is that asking the right sorts of questions is necessary for the 'proper discovery' (or recollection/reminder) which allows philosophy to overcome the seemingly insuperable difficulties posed by the 'tormenting questions' alluded to in §133. What is misleading, however, is the apparent claim that, once one has asked the right sorts of questions, there should be no difficulty in answering them. It is unlikely that Wittgenstein wanted to claim that answering even the right sorts of philosophical questions (of whatever nature they may be) is by any means an easy task. Just as it is the *unanswerability*, not the degree of difficulty, that makes the alleged 'tormenting questions' tormenting, it is the *answerability* of the 'right questions', not their degree of ease, that makes possible the 'proper discovery' which would bring peace or repose with respect to a given conundrum.

In the prewar version of the *Investigations*, two pages prior to portions of what we now know as §133, one again finds Wittgenstein giving a general characterization of his philosophical task as essentially involving a criticism of the philosophical questions themselves:

We bring words back from their metaphysical to their everyday use. . . . And so it seems for the solution of all philosophical troubles. Our answers must, if they are correct, be ordinary and trivial. – Because these answers, as it were, make fun of the questions.

From where does the investigation get its importance, since it after all seems only to destroy everything interesting, that is, everything great and important? (As it were all edifices, leaving behind only bits of stone and rubble.) But it is only edifices of mist [*Luftgebäude*] that we destroy, and we are exposing the terrain of language on which they stand.

(TS 220, pp. 89–90)

Much of this passage obviously consists of what we are now familiar with as *Philosophical Investigations* §§116 and 118. Note however in this early version of the *Investigations* how intimately linked the familiar themes of §116 and §118 are to the notion of 'tormenting questions' in §133 and the underlying theme of a criticism of philosophical questions. It is the questions themselves which must be, not answered, but treated; the questions themselves which are only 'edifices of mist' (*Luftgebäude*) which must be destroyed. As Wittgenstein put it in his *Brown Book*:

The question itself keeps the mind pressing against a blank wall, thereby preventing it from ever finding the outlet. To show a man how to get out you have first of all to free him from the misleading influence of the question.

(*BB* p. 169)

In his 1937 revision of the *Brown Book* he elaborated in another passage:

Our language admits of questions for which there are no answers. And it leads us to ask these questions through the *metaphorical character* [*Bildhaftigkeit*] of the expression. An analogy captivates our thinking and irresistibly drags us on.

It has always been Wittgenstein's view that language gives rise to the questions that torment philosophy.[2] The stress one finds in the above passages is that the task of freeing oneself from the tormenting questions is to be accomplished simply by laying bare the linguistic terrain that gave rise to those very questions.

Given that language is the source of the tormenting questions, it now becomes somewhat more clear what is the nature of the 'real or proper discovery' that §133 alleges will bring philosophical peace or repose, and more importantly why the notion of discovery in §133 does not clash with the allegation in §126 that philosophy is what is possible *before* all new discoveries and inventions. The sort of 'proper discovery' mentioned in §133 is not so much a grasping or discovering of the essence of philosophy (or of the essence of language[3]) as an exposure of the particular linguistic terrain that gave rise to a specific 'tormenting question'. Thus Wittgenstein, in the context of a discussion of a specific philosophical question, can claim that:

> The philosophical problem seems unsolvable, until one sees that it is an illness [*Krankheit*] (a torment [*Leiden*]) that lies in our form of expression.[4]

Furthermore, an exposition of the linguistic terrain that gave rise to a 'tormenting question', although it might be characterized as involving a 'discovery' appropriate for the dissolution of the tormenting question, can hardly be characterized as a '*new* discovery', given that for Wittgenstein the linguistic terrain is that bedrock of ordinary use which is familiar to us as masters of the language and in terms of which the very questions that initially perplexed us were raised (cf. *PI* §120). But this is not to say that it is the linguistic terrain of everyday use itself which constitutes the perplexities; our language itself is not deficient or defective, rather the tormenting questions arise because we, misled by analogies in language, have lost our way on the contours of that terrain. Thus ordinary language is viewed not only as the source of philosophical conundrums (which was always Wittgenstein's position), but also as the *means* by which those conundrums are to be eliminated.[5] For this reason Wittgenstein has characterized philosophical problems as having the form 'I don't know my way about',[6] and for this reason the 'proper discoveries' mentioned in §133 as bringing peace to philosophy are not the repudiated 'new discoveries' of §126, but rather perhaps more appropriately characterized as the 'reminders' of §127.

Wittgenstein's prosaic, figurative allusion to 'tormenting questions' as 'edifices of mist' to which language gives rise, is much more directly, if mundanely, expressed in another of his many discussions of the relationship between philosophical problems and language, in which context he asserts that it is a characteristic feature of a philosophical problem that:

> a confusion is expressed in the form of a question that doesn't
> acknowledge the confusion, and that what *releases* [*erlöst*] the
> questioner from his problem is a particular alteration of his
> method of expression [*Ausdrucksweise*].
>
> (*PG* p. 193)

This passage more directly speaks to what Wittgenstein considered to be the linguistic origin of philosophical questions.
Apparently part of what makes such questions tormenting is that
the alleged linguistic origins of the questions are not
acknowledged or are not manifest in the questions themselves
(hence their unanswerable and apparently unassailable character).

There is also echoed in this latter passage the suggestion
Wittgenstein makes in several other passages, namely, that a way
out of the philosophical perplexity is perhaps a reformulation of
the forms of expression in terms of which the question has been
couched – this presumably in order to lay bare the linguistic
terrain that gave rise to the tormenting philosophical question.
Such reformulation, however, is not a matter of *reforming* a
language that is inadequate, but rather for Wittgenstein a matter
of reformulating our questions (or asking different ones) such
that they are directed at disclosing the terrain, the grammar, of
language itself. Thus one finds Wittgenstein making suggestions
such as:

> When a philosophical question feels cold and unpleasant,
> then remember that the *right* question has not yet been posed.
>
> (MS 130, p. 107)

and

> What I strive to do is present the matter in a new, unusual
> way; though not because the old way is not right, but rather
> because placing the new next to the old throws new light on
> the latter and eliminates philosophical questions.
>
> (MS 133, p. 138)

The centrality of this theme of a criticism, a treatment or an
elimination of philosophical questions themselves is evidenced
by the fact that one can open virtually any notebook in Wittgenstein's *Nachlass* or for that matter virtually any of the collections
of remarks posthumously published as representative of his later

philosophy, and find numerous instances of Wittgenstein, rather than answering a given question, attacking the question itself. His attacks on the questions take various forms. Most frequently his attacks involve the charge that a given question is itself 'mistaken' or involves some sort of error (cf. above). For instance, in the *Investigations* in response to the question: 'But are the steps then *not* determined by the algebraic formula?', he charges that 'The question contains a mistake [*Fehler*]' (*PI* §189). In *Remarks on the Philosophy of Psychology*, in response to the question 'What makes my image [*Vorstellung*] of him into an image of *him*?', Wittgenstein answers that 'The *question* makes a mistake' (*RPP I* §262). And similarly in one of his notebooks, in response to the question 'What is the difference between imagining and seeing?', he retorts: 'In the question already lies a mistake'.[7]

Often, however, his attacks on the questions involve the more obscure accusations that the questions themselves are nonsensical or even false (prima facie it is not at all clear that a *question* can be false – more about this presently). For instance in the section of the Big Typescript concerned with the issue of how the word 'not' negates, he wrote:

> One might say: the sign of negation is just an occasion for doing something very complicated; but what? The question does not allow of an answer, thus it is nonsensical, and so also is that initial assertion.
>
> (TS 213, p. 108)

A type of question which seems particularly to have irritated Wittgenstein was that of the form: 'What happens when . . .?' For instance, in a discussion of the notion of 'talking to oneself', in response to the question 'What happens [takes place] here?', he exclaims: 'False [*falsche*: mistaken] question!'[8] In one of his notebooks he even more broadly proclaims that in the sort of investigation he is undertaking, the question 'What happens when . . .?' is completely misleading and is an instance in which 'The philosophical question itself bars the way to clarity.'[9]

All of these examples can be taken as illustrative of the 'tormenting questions' to which Wittgenstein alludes in *Philosophical Investigations* §133. There are a countless number of such examples in his books and unpublished papers. Before exegetically examining a specific example in order to probe in more depth the nature of Wittgenstein's criticism of such so-called 'tormenting questions', there are three striking things that ought to be pointed out about such questions. First of all, quite clearly the 'tormenting questions' are indeed problem-specific, that is to say they tend to address specific philosophical problems without themselves addressing the issue of the legitimacy of philosophy, though the issue of the legitimacy of philosophy might arise by our asking but allegedly not being able to answer such questions.

Second, it would appear that the alleged 'tormenting questions' are unanswerable not in the sense that one could not in good faith come up with a reply that seems to fit what is being asked, but rather they are unanswerable in the more subtle sense that the conundrum that may have given rise to them is not resolvable by the answers we might be inclined to give to the questions. Thus the questions as it were miss their mark, they miss what is essential to the conundrum.

For example, to the allegedly irrelevant or nonsensical question 'What complicated activity is the sign "not" an occasion for our doing?', one might well in good faith reply as Russell and James did; namely, that

> 'not' must derive its meaning from experiences of rejection, and 'or' from experiences of hesitation. Thus no essential word in our vocabulary can have a meaning independent of experience.[10]

As Russell more elaborately replied to the question with respect to the sign 'or':

> We wish to know what are the occurrences that make the word 'or' useful. . . . The only occurrences that demand the word 'or' are subjective, and are in fact hesitations. In order to express hesitations in words, we need 'or' or some equivalent word.[11]

But if the issue is how a sign *functions* as a negation sign, or what is the meaning of a negation sign, then asking about the 'psychological accompaniments for which the sign is an occasion' may well be irrelevant in spite of the fact that a good faith reply to the latter question can be given by way of introspection. For Wittgenstein the issue of how a negation sign functions or what a negation sign means is an issue of which grammatical/logical conventions govern our use of the sign, not an issue of introspective psychology – just as it is a matter of grammatical convention, not a matter of psychology, that a double negation *means* we are to take what follows affirmatively, rather than that it is the occasion for a doubly intense feeling of 'rejection'.

The third point that should be noted about Wittgenstein's examples of so-called 'tormenting questions' is that they do not at all seem to be exclusively comprised of what might be called the traditional, grand, metaphysical questions of philosophy; questions about the existence of God, the soul, the ultimate nature of reality, and so on. I do not point this out in order to claim that Wittgenstein would not have considered some of the traditional, grand questions of philosophy to fall into the category of 'tormenting questions'.[12] Rather my purpose is to stress that in his notebooks, in his day-to-day philosophical struggles, the alleged 'tormenting questions' that were the subjects of his criticisms were questions much closer to home; questions which most often his own twentieth-century contemporaries or even he himself had been inclined to ask. So many of Wittgenstein's disciples have interpreted Wittgenstein as primarily engaged in an effort to debunk traditional philosophy in favour of a triumph of the modern. Indeed with great arrogance Wittgenstein has at times been wielded as a tool for dismissing great swaths of traditional philosophy, and in particular traditional metaphysics. However, given that the 'tormenting questions', which were the focal points of his criticisms in his notebooks over the last twenty years of his life, were questions that had been raised by Wittgenstein himself and his own contemporaries (most of whom considered themselves at the forefront of the assault against traditional metaphysics), it would seem that if there is any deliberate debunking going on in Wittgenstein's later philosophy, it is ironically more a debunking of aspects of the twentieth century philosophical scene as he experienced it than a direct assault on traditional metaphysics.

Let us now examine in more detail a specific instance in which Wittgenstein criticizes a 'tormenting question'. This not in order conclusively to dissolve or eliminate the specific tormenting question, but rather in order to give more concrete meaning to the points Wittgenstein has made about the nature of his concern with the criticism of so-called 'tormenting questions'. The specific question to be examined arises in the following passage in Wittgenstein's notebooks:

One is tempted to ask: how does one think the proposition p, how does one expect that such and such will happen (how does one do that)? And in this false question lies the whole difficulty . . .

(MS 109, p. 174)

Wittgenstein went on here and in his many revisions of the remark to couch this question in terms of a host of other psychological verbs such as 'understanding', 'believing', 'wishing', and so on.[13] His characterization of the above question as 'false' is a tell-tale sign that it falls into the category of the 'tormenting questions' to which he alluded in *Philosophical Investigations* §133. Note also that this question too is to a significant extent problem-specific. It seems to address the problem of the meaning of a proposition of language, but by means of a question or questions about how a given proposition is 'thought', 'understood', 'expected', and so on. In effect one has a cluster of specific 'tormenting questions' here, each casting the problem of the meaning of a proposition of language in terms of a different 'psychological verb'.

Wittgenstein claims that the question itself is false – but in what sense is this so? In the notebook he continues by explaining:

The false analogy here consists in our conceiving of the matter as like that of a mechanism whose outside we are aware of but whose inner workings are (still) hidden.

It is a principle function of philosophy to warn against false analogies. To warn against the false analogies which lie embedded in our forms of expression without our being fully conscious of them.

I believe our method here resembles psychoanalysis which also makes conscious the unconscious and thereby renders it harmless, and I believe that this resemblance is not purely superficial.

(MS 109, p. 174)

It would seem that the tormenting questions of the sort 'How do we understand (or think, expect, believe, etc.) the proposition *p*?' are false questions in the sense that they rest on a false analogy rooted in our forms of expression, but of which we are not fully aware. And it is a principle task of Wittgenstein's, perhaps resembling here to some extent the task of psychoanalysis, to bring to our awareness the false analogy that has given rise to the tormenting questions.

Wittgenstein goes on in another draft of the above tormenting question to explain in more detail what the false analogy involves when the question is specifically cast in terms of the concept of 'believing':

'How does thought work, how does it use its expression? – this is analogous to //sounds like// the question: 'How does the Jacquard loom work, how does it use the cards?'

The feeling is that with the sentence 'I believe that p is the case' the process of belief isn't described (that only the cards of the loom are given and everything else is merely hinted at). That one could replace the description 'I believe p' by the description of a mechanism wherein p, that is to say now the series of words 'p' would only occur as *one* component like the cards in the loom.

The false analogy, then, is that a sentence of the form 'I believe p' appears to be like those which describe, refer to, or report processes, except that in the case of 'believing' those processes must be hidden. Therefore it is suggested that an expression of the form 'I believe p', because of the false analogy embedded in our language, *tempts* one to think that a hidden psychological mechanism or process is being reported but not described in its inner workings, and that it is these inner workings which are constitutive of the signification of the sentence 'p'. The question 'How does one believe that p is the case, how does one do that?' is thus itself, as Wittgenstein would poetically put it, an edifice of mist to which language has given rise.

And such questions are 'tormenting' in that they are unanswerable, but in a special sense unanswerable. As Wittgenstein explained in yet another revision of his discussion of this particular tormenting question:

It seems: 'believing' describes something which occurs with the sentence – as 'digesting', something which occurs with the meal.

One could then understand the belief if one knew what really went on at the time. One would then have analysed the 'process of belief'. . .

To the question 'How does one do that?', the one who

answers perhaps through introspection will not come up with
~~anything useful~~ – an answer that one could use. It is reported
at the time: I say this, I imagine such and such, and the like.

(MS 117, pp. 128-9)

The question 'How does one believe that p is the case?' is not
unanswerable in the sense that one cannot give a good faith reply
to the question, for example, by introspecting and perhaps
describing the images that flowed past one's mind's eye as one
uttered the words. One needs only to read some of the works of,
for example, Russell, James, or Hume to see what elaborate good
faith answers can be given to such a question.[14] Rather the
suggestion is that the tormenting question is unanswerable in
the sense that the *meaning* of the proposition 'p' or indeed the
meaning of the proposition 'I believe that p' is not explained by
the types of answers for which the tormenting question asks. The
conundrum which gave rise to the tormenting question will not
be resolved by some new discovery about the inner workings of
the 'mind', such as Russell's attempt to discover a new sort of
'belief-feeling' which attaches to an 'image-proposition'
accompanying speech.[15] Not that there are no such inner workings; the point is simply that a description of those workings will
not resolve the conundrum that gave rise to the tormenting
question; it will not dispel our confusion about the meaning of
the expression 'I believe that p'.

But what then would dissolve the tormenting question, and
what would resolve the conundrum or confusion that gave rise to
it? In both of his revisions of his treatment of the specific
tormenting question, Wittgenstein explains that the dissolution
of the question, the resolution of the conundrum, is to be
accomplished by redirecting our efforts away from an
introspective description of a hidden psychological mechanism,
and to the terrain of language itself:

> here is the error: whatever this description includes, besides
> just the sentence 'p' *with its grammar,* would be worthless for
> us. That [its grammar] is as it were the real mechanism in
> which it [the sentence 'p'] lies embedded.

(TS 213, pp. 211-12)

Or as he similarly, but more figuratively, put it in a later
revision:

It is absolutely not unexplored processes of belief that interest us, ~~the mechanism which we don't understand is no mental~~ – but rather the use of our well-known processes of belief, e.g. of the expression of the sentence 'I believe . . .'. The mechanism which we don't understand is not anything in our soul, but rather that of the life in which this expression swims.

(MS 117, p. 129)

And by this Wittgenstein means:

Don't think (so much) about the images which accompany a word, a sentence, but rather about its use in the language game. Don't ask whether this sentence 'can be thought' and try to decide it through introspection . . . .

(MS 160, p. 54)

Thus for Wittgenstein it is not the inner psycho–physical goings-on that are determinative of the sense of the sentence 'p' or the sentence 'I believe that p', but rather the *grammar*, the use in the language game; and to the extent that one can speak of the sentence being linked to or embedded in a 'mechanism', the grammar or the language-game in which the sign is embedded is that mechanism. Consequently the question about the meaning of signs has been transformed from a question of introspective psychology into a question about the contours of the terrain of language itself. Although in this instance Wittgenstein has not actually gone ahead and described for us the grammar or use of these particular expressions, one can call this redirecting of our attention to the contours of language a transformation or a reformulation of the form of the question, or one might simply characterize this as asking a different and more appropriate question – a question that for Wittgenstein allows of an 'appropriate discovery' about language which would free us of the spell of the false analogy.

Such a discovery of course would not involve a *reform* of language itself; quite the contrary, it would be a matter of getting clear about or eliminating our confusion about the extant misleading terrain of our given language. The type of 'proper discovery' required to get clear about the terrain of language that gave rise to the tormenting question, the type of discovery that makes clear the grammar or use of the expression (e.g. of the form 'I believe that p') in the language-game which is its home, accordingly would not in any significant sense be a 'new discovery'. Rather the 'proper philosophical discovery' would be, as Wittgenstein was inclined to phrase it: 'really a remembering. We recall that we really use the words in this way.'[16] In the process the 'tormenting question' would dissolve, the edifice of mist would dissipate, and presumably one would achieve at least a modicum of philosophical peace from the 'tormenting questions' alluded to in *Investigations* §133.

NOTES

1. G.P. Baker and P.M.S. Hacker, *Wittgenstein: Understanding and Meaning*, Chicago, University of Chicago Press, 1980, pp. 558–9.
2 Cf. *TLP* 3.001.
3 See S. Hilmy, *The Later Wittgenstein*, Oxford, Basil Blackwell, 1987, pp. 61ff and 79ff, for an extensive discussion of Wittgenstein's own comments on the clash between his early and later philosophy on the issue of the 'nature of language' and the relation of this issue to how one characterizes the project of dissolving the conundrums to which language gives rise.
4 MS 115, p. 110; *PI* §255.
5 See Hilmy, op. cit., pp. 56ff, on the contrast between the early and later Wittgenstein on the latter point.
6 *PI* §123.
7 MS 136, p. 11.
8 *RPP I* §600. Cf. MS 133, p. 29.
9 MS 129, p. 167.
10 B. Russell, *An Inquiry into Meaning and Truth*, New York, W.W.Norton, 1940, p. 368. Cf. William James, *Principles of Psychology*, vol. 1, New York, Henry Holt, 1890, p. 245.
11 Russell, ibid., pp. 264–5 (see also p. 263).
12 On occasion one does find Wittgenstein identifying some of the traditional grand questions of philosophy as tormenting questions. See, for example, his comments on St Augustine's question 'What is time?', in *The Blue and Brown Books*, p. 26. Cf. TS 213, p. 521: 'What is time? – already in the question lies the error.'
13 See, e.g., TS 213, p. 211.
14 See my extensive discussion of this in S. Hilmy, op. cit., especially chapter 4.
15 See Bertrand Russell, 'On Propositions: what they are and how they mean', *Proceedings of the Aristotelian Society*, 1919, supp. vol. 2, pp. 1–43. Cf. B. Russell, *The Analysis of Mind*, London, George Allen & Unwin, 1921, pp. 250–2.
16 TS 213, p. 419.

Chapter 5

Common behaviour of many a kind: *Philosophical Investigations* section 206

Eike von Savigny

HUMAN BEHAVIOUR AND LANGUAGE-USING CAPACITY

There can be no doubt that there is a close connection in the *Philosophical Investigations* between being human, behaving in human ways, and mastering a language.[1] Wittgenstein suggests, in many ways throughout the *Investigations*, that there is a range of typically human behaviour which is involved both in learning and using a natural language. And one might conjecture that both the range of behaviour and the linguistic capacity are manifestations of one and the same deep-rooted human nature. Mastering some natural language may be due to a unique competence for mastering language, and behaving in human ways may depend on sharing an essential human nature.

None of this is particularly clear, but as a characterization of the general orientation of the *Investigations* it has some plausibility. Moreover, such an outlook lies behind the generally accepted reading of a passage which, so understood, might even serve as a motto for linking human nature and language:

> The common behaviour of mankind is the system of reference by means of which we interpret an unknown language.
>
> (*PI* §206(c))

On the whole, the exegetical literature on this passage (not to mention the bulk of writings where it is quoted out of context) makes short work of interpreting it.[2] The common view is that Wittgenstein here presupposes the existence of a set (or even of a structured system) of human behavioural dispositions, a capacity by which man is distinguished from creatures which by their nature cannot master language (except for simple rudiments of

pre-linguistic behaviour). This capacity permits people to interpret, learn, understand, and master languages very remote from
their own native tongue, provided only that these languages are
used by other human beings.

I shall argue that this standard interpretation is mistaken. My
argument will consist of two parts, an indirect and a direct one.
In the indirect argument, presented in the following section, I
shall first sketch what I take to be the most plausible defence of
the standard interpretation, namely the defence that starts from
the premise that all language-use is embedded in a form of life,
and then go on to argue that this line of defence fails. In directly
attacking the interpretation, I shall try to establish in the next
section that, contrary to appearance, Wittgenstein does not, in
the passage quoted above, presuppose the existence of any
common behaviour of mankind. In the final section I shall
consider a more plausible interpretation that seems to preserve
the idea of there being something general about the way
language is embedded in human behaviour. But although more
plausible than the received interpretation, it is, I shall argue, still
inadequate and would, if true, not even save the idea of a
common behaviour of mankind, or of a human nature.

LANGUAGE-USE EMBEDDED IN A FORM OF LIFE

In the *Philosophical Investigations*, being able to use a given
language depends on sharing a form of life. So much is clear, and
there does not seem to exist a more promising line for defending
the standard interpretation of §206(c). The argument would start
from the premiss that one cannot master a language without
mastering the corresponding form of life, and it would conclude
that one cannot interpret the language of foreigners unless one
shares enough of their form of life. The link between premiss and
conclusion might be provided either by the assumption that
interpreting is a reduced kind of linguistic mastery, or by the
assumption that interpreting another language involves at least
understanding its associated form of life, which in turn requires
that this form of life be sufficiently 'common' to 'them' and 'us'
even if we fall short of completely sharing it.

It should be noted that the standard interpretation is in need of
very strong support, since it is strikingly un-Wittgensteinian in
(coming close to) postulating the existence of an explanatory
human nature! However, if we turn to the passages where

Wittgenstein connects forms of life with language-use, we do not meet with such support. At §§241 and 242, Wittgenstein says only that in order to share a common language, people have to share a common form of life which (among other things) involves agreement in judgments. (These judgments, as indicated by the context, include applications of colour words and of algebraic rules.) This is of course compatible with there being one general human form of life; but no such thing is hinted at. At *Philosophical Investigations*, p. 174, mastery of a language is called a 'complicated form of life'. But this is consistent with very different forms of life embedding very different languages without there being any common range of behaviour – provided that all of the forms of life are sufficiently complicated. After all, Wittgenstein's point in *Philosophical Investigations*, p. 174 is simply that the applicability of certain psychological predicates requires a degree of complexity in behaviour which is only reached through the use of an articulated language. The reference to forms of life in *Investigations*, p. 226 stresses the *differences* among forms. For the context contains a discussion of different kinds of *being sure*, each one requiring a specific kind of 'shelter' from specific kinds of 'attack', namely, specific social guarantees (rather than all of them involving one and the same kind of 'certainty' or 'incorrigibility'). Without forms of life providing such guarantees there is no safety from attack, and the kinds of safety that exist are provided by varying forms of life.

Let us consider in this regard two other passages, §19 and §23. According to §19(a), it is easy to imagine 'innumerable' languages. The examples given are 'a language consisting only of orders and reports in battle' and 'a language consisting only of questions and expressions for answering yes and no'. Here the sentence, 'And to imagine a language means to imagine a form of life' can only mean that *different languages belong to different forms of life*. (The form of life imagined in each case cannot refer to something like the form of life of using language; given the text of §19(a), this latter notion would have had to be expressed by something like: 'Nonetheless, to imagine some language always means to imagine one and the same form of life.')

The same result is reached through a careful interpretation of §23(b), even though the English translation of this passage might favour aberrant interpretations which fail to take into account its context:

> Here the term 'language-*game*' is meant to bring into promi-
> nence the fact that the *speaking* of language is part of an
> activity, or of a form of life.

'The *speaking* of language' corresponds in the German text to
'das *Sprechen* der Sprache'. If Wittgenstein really had meant 'the
speaking of language', '*das Sprechen*' or '*das Sprachverwenden*'
would have been likelier expressions, particularly because 'das
Sprechen der Sprache' here (as opposed to §25) has the perfectly
natural reading 'das *Sprechen* der jeweiligen Sprache', that is, the
speaking of the language under consideration, of the respective
language. Furthermore, this reading is required by the context.
The word that brings into prominence the fact that a language is
spoken or used, rather than being just a symbolic system, namely
(the italicized) language-*game*', is used in §23(a) where Wittgenstein points out that there are '*countless*' types of language. In
sum, then, speaking a new language is a new language-game –
and this is precisely what is being claimed in the context.

Thus the text does not suggest the existence of some unique
human form of life[3] that would lie at the bottom of all language-
use. Just the opposite – in this context, Wittgenstein uses the
possible variations of forms of life to establish his idea that
languages can differ in boundless ways. In order to see this, it is
useful to look closely at the word 'countless', which is applied in
§23 to sentences, kinds of use of symbols, types of language, and
language-games; the word 'innumerable', as applied (in §19) to
languages, translates the same German word, namely
'*unzählige*'. Now, 'countless' does not mean 'infinitely many',
but, in its most idiomatic sense, 'indeterminably many'; here,
however, it also means 'indefinitely many'. For in §23(a) it is said
that 'new types of language . . . come into existence', and the list
of examples in §23(c) is obviously to be construed as an explanation by examples as *open* and as *capable of continuation*.
Consequently, new types of language may evolve at any time.
Why is this? Notice that Wittgenstein's examples of different
languages do not differ because they exhibit different words or
different syntactical types of sentences, but rather because they
involve different uses. Therefore it is reasonable to assume that
the indefiniteness of the number of languages is precisely due to
the indefinite number of possible variations of forms of life. This
is indeed the most plausible explanation for Wittgenstein's

otherwise surprising claim that the examples of languages which he gives in §19(a) (see above) are 'easy to imagine'. Imagining these involves imagining forms of life very different from ours: for the first language we need to imagine a form of life which involves battles but lacks a language for ordnance blacksmiths, that is, with an organization of handicraft very different from ours; for the second language we need to imagine a form of life which involves asking questions but lacks reports, and hence lacks the social recognition of the role of eyewitnesses. If we construe 'form of life' – as I think we ought in general, but at least ought in this context – as a set of social rules, then it becomes clear why the possible variations of forms of life lead to boundless possible differences among languages: we just have to add or to drop such rules, or to modify or substitute others for them. There are no orders in a society lacking specific authority relations, and there is no such thing as making gifts in a society that lacks the institution of personal property. A less exotic and more recent example: challenging somebody to a duel became extinct together with the corresponding code of honour.

If the general conception of language-embedding forms of life is to provide the support required for the standard interpretation of §206(c), then we ought to find textual evidence, either for there being elements in common to all languages (which seems unlikely in view of the examples quoted in §19(a)), or for there being elements common to all language-embedding forms of life that are presupposed by different languages. I think that for Wittgenstein rule-following and learning are indeed such elements. However, it would be rather odd to invoke them in the present context. All different systems of rules have in common, of course, that they are systems of rules, but this is trivial. And if two quite different systems are both preserved by social learning (rather than by hereditary transmission), this does not make them more like each other than they are. In any event, presupposing that a form of life is rule-governed and that it is learnt would not help us in interpreting the language – if there is any – embedded in it. In fact, there are *no* indications in the text of the *Investigations* of significant universal elements among forms of life, indications which might counter the strong impression that on those occasions when Wittgenstein is concerned with similarities between forms of life, he is really more interested in the unexpected ways in which these may differ.

Thus the standard interpretation of §206(c) is not borne out by Wittgenstein's insistence on the connection between forms of life and language use. It is difficult to detect support from other aspects of what he writes in *Philosophical Investigations*. In fact, at one point he explicitly rules out the idea that understanding a language depends on sharing a common, universal form of life, in *Philosophical Investigations*, p. 223:

> We also say of some people that they are transparent to us. It is, however, important as regards [the present consideration] that one human being can be a complete enigma to another. We learn this when we come into a [foreign] country with entirely strange traditions; and, what is more, even given a mastery of the country's language. We do not *understand* the people. (And not because of not knowing what they are saying to themselves.) We cannot find our feet with them.
>
> (Translation modified between the square brackets)

I cannot determine whether the last sentence of the passage accurately and fully conveys the point of the German *'Wir können uns nicht in sie finden.'* Therefore, let me just affirm that this does *not* mean 'we cannot get along with them' (*'wir können uns nicht mit ihnen zurechtfinden'*). It means, rather, that their behaviour is full of surprises for us, and that what was surprising about it in the past does not become the basis of new regularities that can guide our expectations for the future. We are unable to adapt to the regularities in their behaviour which, nevertheless, undoubtedly exist, given that this behaviour embodies 'traditions'. I think there is no way to avoid the conclusion that in this case the human behaviour of the foreigners, far from being shared by us, is not even understood by us. This is so even though, according to this passage, we may *master* the language of these foreigners! (Mastering, for Wittgenstein, is more than interpreting, for 'to interpret' is precisely his technical word for something which is insufficient for understanding and meaning. Recall §§28, 85, 198, 201, passages where Wittgenstein makes substantial use of his 'one interpretation after another' argument against the possibility of meaning or understanding expressions disconnected from use.) Far from sharing the form of life of some human beings, we may not understand it at all, even though, presumably, we might master their language.

I should concede that *Philosophical Investigations*, p. 223 does not provide me with a conclusive argument. One might argue that the 'common behaviour of mankind' may in fact be shared by people who cannot even understand one another's form of life. However, the actual content of such common behaviour should then be specified. Ingenious as they are, the relevant speculations on *Investigations* §206 offered, for instance, by Baker and Hacker,[4] neither find satisfactory textual support in the *Investigations* nor make intelligible why such common human features should be necessary for interpreting language: and such necessary common features are what is needed to support the standard interpretation of §206(c). (It is of no avail to claim that §206(c), taken as it stands, states a sufficient rather than a necessary condition for interpreting an unknown language; in its context (§207), it is adduced only as a necessary condition.)

The notorious lion example – 'If a lion could talk, we could not understand him' (*PI* p. 223) – has a related standard interpretation, too. The received interpretation of this line dates back at least to Pitcher[5] and is all the more attractive as it appears very Wittgensteinian, even when it quotes the passage out of context. Let a lion be a competent speaker of some natural human language, competent in the sense preferred by linguists, namely, able to utter syntactically and semantically non-deviant sentences *ad libitum*. His utterances could not possibly be embedded in situations, reactions, and responses such that we could make sense of them. We should not be able to understand why he makes the utterances he makes or why he reacts to our utterances in this or that way. 'Good morning' would not come out when it would be appropriate for a greeting; 'thank you' might come as a reaction to a lash from a whip, and so on. These sentences, though perfectly good English, would not be used in the behavioural activities of greeting and thanking, and the lion in uttering them would not greet or thank someone. Hence these sentences would not have their standard English meanings, and the same would hold for any such utterances in so far as the lion does not share a form of life in which there are places for utterances with such meanings. In short: the lion does not share our form of life, and this is why we could not interpret anything he produces as an utterance that is translatable into a natural human language. So goes the standard interpretation.

Now of course this line of argument does not provide a knock-down argument against my view. Even if Wittgenstein wanted to say, in *Investigations*, p. 223, that it is the remoteness of the lion's form of life from ours that deprives him of any chance of being understood, it might be equally remote from *all* human forms of life. There is a more interesting point to note, however, namely that this standard, and very Wittgensteinian, interpretation of the lion example unnecessarily burdens it with tacit suppositions that would be completely idle in the context and argument to which it belongs. (And the fact that careful interpretation should consider the context is surely indicated by the fact that the lion aphorism occurs just two paragraphs after Wittgenstein's claim concerning the mastery of a language whose speakers are completely strange to us.) As is always the case with the *Investigations*, everything depends on what the context of the lion example is taken to be. Here is my answer: the lion example is the concluding statement in Wittgenstein's discussion of what kind of knowledge we can claim of another person's 'inner life', a discussion that begins with 'I know what I want, wish, believe, feel, . . .' on p. 221. The discussion on p. 223 leads up to the result that another person's feelings are not hidden from us. (This discussion is motivated by considerations of privileged access to one's own inner speaking – beginning with 'silent "internal" speech' on p. 220 – which connect to the question of meaning experiences. It is followed by a consideration of the very different kinds of social guarantees that can back up claims to knowledge: 'The kind of certainty is the kind of language-game' (p. 224), a consideration which exhausts the remainder of section IIxi.) Having reached the result that the feelings of others are not hidden from us, Wittgenstein makes the remark quoted above about strange traditions. I think we can now grasp his point:

> We do not *understand* the people. (And not because of not knowing what they are saying to themselves.) We cannot find our feet with them.

> 'I cannot know what is going on in him' is above all a *picture*. It is the convincing expression of a conviction. It does not give the reasons for [what one is convinced of].[6] *They* are not readily accessible.

> If a lion could talk, we could not understand him.
> (*PI* p. 223, translation altered between the square brackets)

The '*picture*' expresses the experience of not finding one's feet with another person. The statement 'It does not give the reasons for what one is convinced of' simply repeats the parenthetical clause 'And not because of not knowing what they are saying to themselves', and what is repeated here is *argued for* in the lion example: hearing a lion talking would help us to understand what he says exactly as much as perceiving nothing but the signs used by people in speaking to themselves would help us understand them. With a lion, we should not know how to construe his utterances; by the same token we should not know how to do so in the case of a person. The argument is identical with another one which belongs to the context:

> If I were to talk to myself out loud in a language not understood by those present my thoughts would be hidden from them.
>
> (*PI* p. 222)

We could not understand the lion; this is all that matters for the argument. Further explanations for why we could not understand him are unnecessary in this context; the lion example might well be read with a supplement: 'Why – if a lion could talk, we could not understand him either.' Thus whatever Wittgenstein's own possible further justifications might be, they cannot be adduced in order to weaken the exegetical point that the context explicitly envisages mastering a language embedded in a strange form of life.

THERE IS NO 'COMMON BEHAVIOUR OF MANKIND' IN §206(c)

In translating §206(c), Professor Anscombe made a kind of mistake which is otherwise rare in her translation: she excluded a possible reading of the German text even though English provides a way of preserving it. Whereas her translation renders one possible meaning of '*Die gemeinsame menschliche Handlungsweise*', there are two further ones: 'The human behaviour common to the foreigners and ourselves' and 'The human behaviour common among the foreigners'. The second reading would only force us to weaken the standard interpretation while preserving the connection between interpreting a language and having access to the form of life embedding it. The third reading, however, would do away with the whole idea, and I shall establish that it is the correct one. ('Shared human behaviour', 'Common human behaviour' would have preserved all possibilities.) Once more, one has to respect the context of the passage in order to interpret it. Here it is:

> 206. Following a rule is analogous to obeying an order. We are trained to do so; we react to an order in a particular way. But what if one person reacts in one way and another in another to the order and the training? Which one is right?
>
> Suppose you came as an explorer into an unknown country with a language quite strange to you. In what circumstances would you say that the people there gave orders, understood them, obeyed them, rebelled against them, and so on?
>
> The common behaviour of mankind is the system of reference by means of which we interpret an unknown language. 207. Let us imagine that the people in that country carried on . . .[7] usual human activities and in the course of them employed, apparently, an articulate language. If we watch their behaviour we find it intelligible, it seems 'logical'. But when we try to learn their language we find it impossible to do so. For there is no regular connexion between what they say, the sounds they make, and their actions; but still these sounds are not superfluous, for if we gag one of the people, it has the same consequences as with us; without the sounds their actions fall into confusion – as I feel like putting it.
>
> Are we to say that these people have a language: orders, reports, and the rest?
>
> There is not enough regularity for us to call it 'language'.

The language in question in §207(c) is that of 'these people' in §207(b), namely, 'the people in that country' of §207(a). These are also 'the people there' of §206(b) who seem to use 'a language quite strange to you', which is an example of 'an unknown language' in §206(c). The resulting symmetry (§206(a)–§207(c), §206(b)–§207(b)) is remarkable and provides the most immediate, if least weighty, argument for claiming that §206(c) must correspond to §207(a). Both have as their topic the relevance of common human behaviour for interpreting a foreign language. In §207(a), this attempt must fail because, contrary to appearances there simply is no language (§207(c)), because there is nothing that could possibly be interpreted as a language. According to the standard interpretation, the attempt is to be expected to fail because the behaviour of the foreigners is too far removed from the common behaviour of mankind. Why does it actually fail?

The text of §207(a) offers just one reason: that there is no regular connection between *their* sounds and *their* actions, and this reason is repeated in §207(c). It is not the case that their behaviour lacks any regularity whatsoever. This is shown by the fact that gagging them leads to confusion. For the fact that only as long as the people are not gagged their actions do not become confused, is, of course, a regularity. (We might imagine them to be in need of constantly keeping contact through something like the contact-noises of Konrad Lorenz's greylag geese.) The same consequence – confusion of action – would arise in our case as well, if we were gagged. Thus a regular connection as unspecific as that between contact-keeping sound-making and controlled or coordinated actions is not sufficient for the sound-making to be linguistic. The regularities must be sufficiently specific to permit us to describe certain sounds as orders, other as reports, and so on (§206(b), §207(b)).

Let us be quite clear about the fact that the people envisaged by Wittgenstein lack a language because their sounds cannot be interpreted as linguistic utterances and that any interpretation of these vocalizations fails because there is no regular, sufficiently specific connection between their sounds and their actions. This is an objective fact, quite independent of whether or not we could learn their language if they had one. Wittgenstein's description of the example indicates how we would find out that they do not have a language, namely, by unsuccessful attempts at finding out which language they have. There is one very efficient method for such attempts, namely trying to learn the putative language, and the failure of this method is used here to illustrate the objective fact that there is no language to be found. On this point, the text is completely explicit: *there is no* regular connection; *there is not* enough regularity. This is the reason why it cannot be called 'language' in our sense of 'language', that is, 'language' *tout court*.

Thus the attempt at interpreting the behaviour of the people in Wittgenstein's example as linguistic, rather than failing because there is no *behaviour common to them and ourselves*, actually fails because there is no *behaviour common among them* that would be sufficient for specifying their sounds as meaningful utterances. Common behaviour is what matters, according to §206(c), for interpreting a foreign language. What is missing in order for there to be language embedded in the behaviour characterized in §207 is specific, regular behaviour common to the foreigners. There is no way around the conclusion that 'the system of reference' in §206(c), far from being 'the common behaviour of mankind', is specific regular behaviour common to the people who use the foreign language.

More than that: §207(a) explicitly states that the foreigners actually do share with us a considerable part of human behaviour. They carry out typical human activities that normally are controlled or even cooperative; we find their behaviour intelligible, it seems 'logical'. Recalling *Philosophical Investigations*, p. 223, we might say, 'We do *understand* the people. We can find our feet with them.'[8] It might be suggested that their share of human behaviour is not large enough to count as 'the common behaviour of mankind'. But then why does Wittgenstein call them 'people' ? (It is no use pointing out that since the argument of §207 is a *reductio*, its premisses need not be true. This is correct, but the purpose of §207 is to prove wrong the hypothesis that the creatures have a language; in order to prove one premiss wrong, the others must be assumed to be true.) More important, perhaps, falling back on this line of defence commits one to establish from the text what precisely this 'common behaviour of mankind' is taken to consist in.

Thus what §206 says is this: (a) if one person reacted in one way and another of *the same group* in another, none would be right; an 'order' would be without content and would thus not be an order at all in their group; (b) modes of behaviour suspected to be orders would have content if giving orders, understanding them, obeying them, rebelling against them, manifested themselves in ways *common to the people there* (I shall suggest some details in the final section); (c) these modes of behaviour must involve a regular connection between the sounds and actions of people in order for those people to have a language. Human behaviour typically, but not always, displays this kind of regularity; however, it is not the only kind of behaviour that could display it.

The text preceding and following §§206 and 207 does not point to any different interpretation. The language-specific regularities clearly are on a par with the 'way of grasping a rule' (§201), the 'regular use' (§198) which Wittgenstein frequently offers as an alternative 'source of meaning' (not his words, of course!) in place of the awareness of expressions of rules (§§28, 29; §§84–7; §§139–41; §§185–90; §§198, 201). The claim that in order for an utterance to be meaningful in the language of a given group, it is sufficient that the corresponding specific regularities should prevail in that group, fits in very well with one of his points in the discussion of rule-following up to §242: given that people have learnt to follow a rule in a certain way, there can be no further question as to whether they follow it correctly (§§211–14, §§224–7). On the whole, what one would expect from Wittgenstein is the advice not to be surprised if we encounter communities where people are completely different from ourselves.

BEHAVIOURAL REGULARITIES REQUIRED FOR LINGUISTIC MEANING

As noted above, not any regular connection between sounds and actions will do for making the sounds meaningful. Rather, the connections must be sufficiently specific to differentiate, for example, orders from reports. This idea has been elaborated in speech-act theory, and I shall conclude by sketching a speech-act theoretical interpretation of §206(c) which would save the generality of the behaviour in question – at the expense, however, of sacrificing all connections with any nature of man. Let us accept the following sentences as the kernel of rough-and-ready incomplete definitions of orders and reports:

(O) With respect to action H, speaker S is in an authority position relative to addressee A. If S orders A to do H, A is obliged to do H.

(R) Speaker S is expected to know whether or not event E has occurred; addressee A is expected to be interested in finding out whether or not E has occurred. If S reports to A that E has occurred, A may rely, at the expense of S, on the fact that E has occurred.

As an explorer in an unknown country, you would have to find out under what circumstances people there acquire authority positions relative to others and how far their competence extends; then you could test your hypothesis that a certain utterance in given circumstances is an order by finding out whether or not the addressee becomes obligated. (I am disregarding holistic qualifications on testing such theories.) Sentences (O) and (R) describe complicated behavioural regularities on a very theoretical level. The advantage of taking them as instances of common human behaviour is twofold: first, 'the system of reference' gets a pretty intelligible meaning, for if you complete the list beginning with (O) and (R) you get a definition of language. Second, (O) and (R) illustrate the kind of specificity required for regularities that are to endow sounds with meanings.

As far as Wittgenstein's aversion to rash generalization is concerned, this interpretation is, of course, as weak as the standard interpretation is, and this is why I hesitate to attribute it to him. In contrast to the latter, however, it is consistent with the text. For if §206(c) states that we have to refer to specific regularities typical of what we call human orders, reports, and so on in order to interpret a language, §207(a) describes a very appropriate example of a form of behaviour in which the regularity is not sufficiently specific. According to this interpretation, §206(c) presupposes that we have a concept of a meaningful utterance such that differences in meaning go with differences in behavioural regularities, and do so universally. In the expression 'common human behaviour', 'common' would then mean, 'common to all human language use', rather than 'common to all mankind'. The interpretation does not presuppose that any 'meaning' or pattern of linguistic behaviour is realized in all languages, or that any corresponding behavioural regularity prevails among all or only human beings.

NOTES

1 In order to convince oneself of this point, just recall some passages where it is highlighted in contexts that are significant for the present problem: §§25, 281-7, 346, 357, 390, 415, 445, 649-50; and pp. 174, 179-80. There are passages which are even more significant than some of these, but the point is not immediately clear in those cases.
2 I have met with but two exceptions where the text is analysed with some patience (the result being the customary interpretation): R. Haller, 'Die gemeinsame menschliche Handlungsweise', *Zeitschrift*

für philosophische Forschung, 1979, vol. 33, pp. 521–33, esp. 531–3; G.P. Baker and P.M.S. Hacker, *An Analytical Commentary of the 'Philosophical Investigations', Vol. II: Wittgenstein, Rules, Grammar and Necessity*, Oxford, Blackwell, 1985, pp. 186f, 189f.

3 N. Garver, 'Form of Life in Wittgenstein's Later Work', *Dialectica*, 1990, vol. 44, 175–201 was published too late to be discussed properly here. Prima facie his argument for a unique form of life does not seem to be at odds with my position. For Garver concedes the possibility of modifications of this form of life, where I speak of different forms of life (see pp. 178–90). He provides no textual evidence for the view that there is a common kernel of behaviour.

4 Op. cit. pp. 186f.

5 G. Pitcher, *The Philosophy of Wittgenstein*, Englewood Cliffs, Prentice-Hall, 1964, p. 243.

6 I suspect that Professor Anscombe's translation, 'the reasons for the conviction', does not suggest my reading of 'die Gründe der Überzeugung', but rather one's psychological motives for being so convinced.

7 Professor Anscombe supplies 'the' which is not in the original.

8 But see my qualms about this translation of *'Wir können uns in sie finden'*. The latter is well instantiated by the case of §207(a).

Chapter 6

Private language: *Philosophical Investigations* section 258 and environs*

John V. Canfield

Only one person, the 'speaker', can understand the words of a 'private language', because she will refer to items in the metaphysically exclusive domain of the immediately given. Since Norman Malcolm's ground-breaking review of the *Investigations*, the following passage from §258 of that book has been commonly supposed to voice some would-be powerful argument intended to show the impossibility of such a language:[1]

> precisely by the concentration of my attention . . . I impress on myself the connexion between the sign and the sensation. – But 'I impress it on myself' can only mean: this process brings it about that I remember the connexion *right* in the future. But in the present case I have no criterion of correctness. One would like to say: whatever is going to seem right to me is right. And that only means that here we can't talk about 'right'.

Attempts to explain this argument are myriad; the ground is so trodden as to threaten mud. Naturally I would not approach the matter yet again unless I believed I had succeeded in finding some previously overlooked elements of Wittgenstein's line of thought.

Let us put to one side the point that the search for a knockdown argument to establish some thesis central to metaphysics (or anti-metaphysics, for that matter) is antithetical to Wittgenstein's mode of procedure in the *Investigations*. For whether or not section §258 somehow encapsulates *the* private language argument, it is clear enough that it states *an* argument relevant to the issue of private language. This argument, I believe, has been consistently misunderstood by readers of the *Investigations*. (Kripke's reflections in his well known piece on Wittgenstein do not help directly in understanding the argument, although perhaps they do indirectly, by raising some relevant concerns about the nature of rule following.[2])

The misunderstanding is to interpret the passage from §258 along verificationist lines: a person attempting to create and employ a word in a private language cannot verify that it is being used correctly. This was one of the earliest readings of Wittgenstein's argument, and one of the most natural ones. One can find both implicit and explicit versions of it in the recent literature. At the same time, of course, many critics have rejected Wittgenstein's argument *because* they thought it was verificationist in nature – verificationism being out of favour as a theory of meaning.

In this paper I argue that Wittgenstein's reflections in §258 are not verificationist ones, and at the same time I explain why they appear to be so. The argument in §258 might be described as an internal deconstruction of the idea of a private language. Wittgenstein does not there construct a hypothetical proposal for a private language and then impose an external, verificationist criterion of meaning on it – a criterion that it cannot fulfil. Rather, any theorist who attempts to conceive of a private language must *himself* or *herself* demand that the uses of this language be subject to verificationist conditions. The demand is not imposed from without on the basis of some assumed criterion of meaning; rather it is generated by the very metaphysical picture that lies behind the attempt to conceive of a private language. When the would-be private uses of words or signs are seen to fail to satisfy that demand, the idea of a private language internally deconstructs.

In general two main points support my interpretation. First, if Wittgenstein's argument were a verificationist one it would be plainly inconsistent with other things he has to say about language. He would be imposing on the uses of a private language conditions that he explicitly refuses to impose on regions of public language. If we assume he is consistent, we must look elsewhere for an interpretation of the argument. Second, there is a textual justification for my reading of the text. Section 288 of the *Investigations* can be viewed as a commentary on §258, and, it will be seen, this supports my reading of the latter.

I

The misunderstanding of §258 that I have spoken of has the form of a mistaken attribution.[3] It is, at first blush, quite plausible to read Wittgenstein as arguing there that:

> The private diarist needs a criterion of correctness for establishing the truth of his private language assertion (for example, the claim 'S'). For *all uses of language require such a criterion*. Because he lacks such a criterion, he is in the untenable position of not being able to distinguish between what seems right and what is right.

Thus it is tempting to attribute to Wittgenstein some form or other of the dogmatic demand that all legitimate uses of language (of the appropriate sort) are governed by a criterion that functions to adjudicate correctness. Judith Jarvis Thompson, for instance, found an argument like the one above in Malcolm's reading of §258 (though it is not clear she interprets him correctly.[4]) She believes that Malcolm, along with others who argue in a similar way, presupposes that it is Wittgenstein's view that:

> A sign 'K' is not a kind-name in a man's language unless it is possible to find out whether or not a thing is a K.
>
> ('Private Languages' p. 29)

If the possibility of so finding out presupposes a criterion, then the argument she had in mind becomes identical with the one given above. Thompson says that arguments using the premiss about K, or a similar one, presuppose a verificationist theory of meaning, which theory has gone the way of the dodo.

More recently, Benjamin F. Armstrong Jr has offered an interpretation similar to the one just culled from Thompson, although, unlike her, he seems to accept the argument.[5] He states what he calls 'necessary conditions on the *existence* of a correct use for a sign; they are conditions that must be satisfied if a sign is to qualify as a word' ('Wittgenstein on Private Language' p. 51). These are conditions for something's belonging to language. Since the would-be private signs fail to meet the conditions, there can be no private language; or so goes the interpretation. Here are two of his three necessary conditions:

(i) There must be something that *counts* as 'thinking that one is using a sign correctly';

(iii) It must be possible for what counts as 'thinking that one is using a sign correctly' to occur when what counts as 'using a sign correctly' does not occur.

Armstrong explicitly says that to fail to satisfy his conditions is just 'to be in the situation Wittgenstein describes at the end of section §258'. As in Thompson's reading of Malcolm, the reading has Wittgenstein holding a questionable general thesis: there is no meaningful use of a sign unless there is a criterion for adjudicating its correct application in a given case – so that, as Armstrong indicates, there will be possible a distinction between thinking one is right and being right. The alleged words of a private language fail the test; therefore there can be no private language.

This familiar argument is attractive as an interpretation of our passage. But such a gloss runs up against the principle of charity. It makes Wittgenstein hold a thesis about all language that is inconsistent with his clearly stated views about how certain parts of our public language work.[6] Thus on the interpretation in question the sentence 'But in the present case I have no criterion of correctness' is read as if Wittgenstein is there implying that one ought in general to have such a criterion. He would then naturally assume that in the case of a public use of, say, pain-language, one will have such a criterion. But in fact a speaker, in the case of our public language, does not employ a criterion to recognize that he or she is in pain again. At least not according to Wittgenstein, who says:

> Of course I do not identify my sensation by means of criteria; rather I use the same expression (I had used earlier).[7]
>
> (*PI* §290)

For example, I say, again, 'I am in *pain*'.

It now looks as if Wittgenstein is both demanding that the private diarist have a criterion to employ, and saying also, in later remarks, that one who speaks of his or her pain coming back does not employ a criterion. Why should the diarist have to supply what the public speaker does not?

The point carries over to the concluding sentences of §258: 'One would like to say: whatever is going to seem right to me is right. And that only means that here we can't talk about "right" '. But again consider our common way of talking about pain. We judge a person's statement, 'I am in pain', by a criterion of truthfulness.[8] By this Wittgenstein means that if we accept that the person speaks sincerely ('truthfully') then we cannot also doubt the truth of what he says. Ruling out slips of the tongue, and assuming the person understands what he says, if I believe someone is sincere in saying he is in pain, then by the grammar of this 'language-game' I must accept it as true that he is in pain. This is unlike the case where he says, for instance, 'There is a dictionary in the drawer'; no criterion of truthfulness operates here. When a hearer employs a criterion of truthfulness, the speaker himself employs no criterion, and hence could not (logically could not) adjudicate a mistake he might have made. The speaker, in such a case, could not look within himself, see he had misapplied a criterion, and conclude that it is not really pain he is feeling. Thus Wittgenstein's well-known claim that if someone professed to be in doubt as to whether what he feels is pain or not we would not understand him. (§246: 'It makes sense to say about other people that they doubt whether I am in pain; but not to say it about myself.')

One is drawn to say, therefore, that for Wittgenstein our public talk of pain is such that for the speaker 'Whatever is going to seem right is right'. This temptation is doubtless to be resisted, because even here it is not a case of something seeming right to the speaker; it does not *seem* to me that I am in pain. But I am at least in a position *similar* to the one for whom 'Whatever is going to seem right is right'. Similar, because no criterion governs my first-person talk of pain, and because it makes no sense for me to be mistaken about whether I am in pain or not.

The last two lines of §258 look as if they fashion a *reductio* argument for the private language diarist, leaving him in the uncomfortable position of saying that what seems right is right, and hence of not being able to talk of right. But we are all in a very similar 'predicament' when we speak ordinarily about our sensations, so it cannot be such an uncomfortable place to be, and the alleged *reductio* loses its force.

If we attempt to restrict the generality of the key principle about the need for a criterion, we shall require a clear statement of the qualification, and a justification for believing that the rule applies everywhere outside the embargoed cases. Pain-talk, for example, would not be governed by the principle and hence would need no criterion, but a would-be private language word would be governed by it and would require a criterion. But Wittgenstein has stated no such restriction, let alone justified one, and if we try to do these things for him the argument begins to take on an ad hoc and unconvincing air.

If Wittgenstein is not arguing, in those last sentences in §258, in some such way as Armstrong and others have suggested, then how are we to read the text?

The missing idea here is that it is the private language advocate himself who cannot embrace or adapt to his own purpose the premise that in public pain-talk the speaker employs no criterion of correctness. If he tries to construe the private language that way, the result is one he does not want. His picture of what a private language is itself demands a criterion of correctness. The demand is not imposed from without by some dogmatic view of Wittgenstein's about what language is or how it must function.

I shall try, then, to show the following: it is the picture of a private language itself that excludes the possibility of treating the private recording of sensations after the manner of our public talk of them; and in particular bars, for the private case, the possibility of doing without a criterion of correctness. What is demanded is no general thesis of the sort quoted from Thompson or Armstrong, applying to all 'kind terms' or all uses of signs. It is a local requirement, so to speak, and could be read – where 'I' is the private diarist – as 'In this situation I need a criterion of correctness'.

II

To establish these points I shall first consider some consequences of the notion that the private language advocate ostensibly defines a *sensation*.

A key example of Wittgenstein's (§257) assumes that none of a people give natural expression to pain; consequently, they have never learnt to speak of pain. But a genius invents a private name for it. Now if it is really a sensation she has named, then her word 'S' (let us say) should be governed by the rules common to sensation words. What are those rules? I shall give some of them below, relying on various of Wittgenstein's discussions, including *Zettel* §§472, 483, and 621, and, correspondingly, the *Remarks on Philosophical Psychology II*, §§63ff. The question is, can the genius imagined by Wittgenstein take those rules, as they apply to other sensation terms like 'feeling of heat' or 'felt pressure' and the like, and apply them to her new word?

The rules as they exist govern interactions; they allow us to speak and to be understood, for instance when we say that a feeling of pressure is getting more intense. So, one might say, the genius will not have succeeded in extending those rules to the new case unless she is able to make herself understood by means of them; but then 'S' would not be a private word.

But could she not extend the rules *privately*? Or adapt them privately to this new phenomenon? In such a case, she could not tell others what S is, but would use S in accord with rules that make S a sensation; it is just that others could not know what sensation she is talking about.

One of our rules is that a criterion of truthfulness governs statements such as 'My forearm feels hot'. So the diarist might take this up and stipulate: 'If I am sincerely convinced that a certain feeling is S, then it is.' And, she might argue, by Wittgenstein's own account in other passages, that she has a perfect right to do so! For one cannot be in error about whether *this* (say) is pain (§288);[9] I do 'not . . . identify my sensation by criteria' (§290); and I cannot *justify* my saying 'I am in pain' (§289). How can we deny the diarist the right to proceed without a criterion of correctness in her private language when we do just that in parts of our public one?

The diarist notes also that S, being a sensation, must be capable of being timed, its inception and departure noted, its synchronization with other feelings established. She also tells herself things like: when S is like this I shall say it is barely perceptible; when it is like that I shall say it is intense (see *Z* §472).

So now in addition to the private word 'S' she also introduces signs that serve to measure the duration of S, mark its inception and departure times, describe its intensity, and so on.

If asked to justify saying S is a sensation, she might reply, 'Well, "S" behaves just like other sensation words. I can note S's duration, intensity, and so on'.

But still she cannot tell anyone what S is; it is a sensation, but, it seems, we could not know what sensation it is. In the situation Wittgenstein considers, where there is no natural expression of pain and consequently no public talk of pain, we could not even know, apparently, what sort of sensation S is, unless we were somehow able to correlate her 'S' with an appropriate one of our sensations.

Someone who has learned, as we all do, to speak of pain might use a special sign to keep a record of some recurring pain and note its duration, writing down, for example, 'Alpha, 11 a.m., 20 minutes'. A private diarist might do the same, only using 'S', say, in place of 'alpha'. The person who writes 'alpha' could tell us, if she wished: 'That is the sign I am using to keep track of this recurrent headache; it came on at eleven and lasted twenty minutes.' The private diarist says, in parallel: 'I can't tell you what sensation "S" names; we have no name for it. But it came on at 11 and lasted for twenty minutes.'

So now it looks as if the private diarist could take over for her own purpose the grammatical rules governing public sensation-words, including the rule that there is no first-person criterion in operation. In describing a case where this happens, it seems we can successfully hypothesize a private language, since what the diarist speaks of remains inexorably private. It also appears to be a counter-example to Wittgenstein's seeming implicit claim in §261 that there is an incompatibility between the possibility of justifying the assertion that S is a sensation, and 'S' being a word in a private language. The justification is that the private words obey the rules for public sensation-words.

Let us explore this further. If the diarist is truly to employ sensation-rules, then she must assume that her assertion that S came on at 11 a.m. and lasted twenty minutes will be accepted as true by us if we grant her sincerity.

It might then be objected to our example that the diarist herself cannot 'extend' the sensation rules to cover the case of 'S'. It is not in her power to do so. Those rules assume that others will take her words in a certain way, namely as governed by a criterion of truthfulness. And while we are already geared to apply such a criterion to the extant sensation words, we do not apply it to 'S'.

But why can this objection not be met? It certainly seems possible that a group of speakers – some 'tribe' – adopt a truthfulness criterion as regards 'S'. Then we would have a speaker whose utterances are taken as true, provided he is taken as speaking with no intent to deceive, but who speaks of a private entity S which the hearers cannot know. They must grant that S is a sensation, because, we assume, the sensation-rules indicated above apply here. The speaker will mark S's duration, speak of it becoming more intense, and so on. Her hearers will grant both that S has those properties, and that when she says 'S' it has indeed recurred. So the example only seems reinforced by these considerations.

But this example is really a *reductio* of the private language advocate's position.

To see this we must return to the metaphysical picture that lies at the beginning of these reflections. What does the one who proposes keeping the diary really want? Not merely that the diarist, and those around her, engage in some ritual, where she makes certain marks in a calendar and they sagely nod their heads, or solemnly say, and even believe, 'Ah yes, she has had S again!'[10] No, she wants the diarist really to *have* a certain sensation, to fix her attention on it when she in some way or other baptizes it 'S', and then *recognize* it when it recurs. The picture is: when S comes round again, the diarist rightly takes *it* to be another occurrence of S.

She wants, that is, to be able to name the sensation correctly. That she wants to be right follows from what the private language advocate is supposing (or picturing). The diarist wishes to name or impress upon herself some recurring sensation, and then name *it* again, or recognize it when next it occurs. That is simply built into the picture of a private language. And to say she wants to name *it* again, or recognize *it* again, implies she wants to be right or correct in taking it to be another instance of S. The assertions, 'She wants to call it by the same name, "S", when next it recurs', and, 'On its next occurrence she wants to correctly take it to be S' mutually entail one another (given that 'S' here names S).

But it is also built in that she has no means of ascertaining whether she is right. Her earlier mere concentration on the sensation while she says or writes 'S' will not in itself guarantee she will get it right in the future (but see the discussion below). She cannot bring the sample S through time with her, so in the future she can only appeal to her memory of what she had called 'S'; and there is no way to check the correctness of that memory. She cannot get a criterion by extending our normal sensation-talk; for it employs no such first-person criterion. If she looks to our talk of objects as supplying a model for the criterion she needs, she will not be able to find such a criterion operative in her imagined private instances. (This last point, however, needs extensive additional discussion.)

Without a criterion, the private language diarist herself is forced to admit what she also wishes to repudiate. She must say that, given her picture, 'Whatever is going to seem right to me is right'. This is to admit she cannot get what she wants, a recognition of S – that is, a knowing, and correct affirmation of the recurrence of S.

This inner (correct) recognition is neither required nor entailed by the events of our extended example. At the level of the underlying metaphysical picture, it could certainly happen that the diarist mistakes some other sensation for S; while her peers, duly applying a criterion of truthfulness, agree that she has correctly picked out S once again.

The way of 'extending' the sensation-rules to the case of S that I have envisioned, then, does not give the would-be private diarist what she really wants, a way of correctly marking the recurrence of S. What she gets rather is a mere parody, a ritualistic shadow of language, where the speaker writes down certain signs and the rest of the population duly nods in affirmation. And thus it is really a *reductio* of the idea that one can, in something like the way attempted, extend our public sensation-rules to cover the example of S.

III

But granted that she wants to name the same thing S as she had earlier focused on in baptizing the sensation, and granted that therefore she wants to be right in saying it is S, why does it follow that she needs a criterion of correctness? To show that she does I shall consider an objection. It is that after all one might be able to get by, in the situation in question in §258, without a criterion of correctness: 'Look, you have to admit that the following is possible: every time the diarist writes "S" in her diary, then, as a mere matter of fact, she experiences the same sensation she had earlier baptized "S". So although perhaps whatever is going to seem right to her is right, in the situation just imagined whatever seems right to her is *in fact* right. So she is correct in her judgments; and nothing seems to stand in the way of our saying she has hypothesized or conceived a private language.'

Another way of putting this objection is in response to a claim I made earlier, that 'Her earlier mere concentration on the sensation while she says or writes "S" will not in itself guarantee she will get it right in the future'. For someone could object that it is possible that her concentrating does as a mere matter of fact causally result in her getting it right in the future.

But the would-be example of the person who, as a mere matter of fact, gets it right in future, and for whom whatever seems right is in fact right, is one that rebounds on its proponent.

Given the 'assumptions' of the objection, there could well be another private diarist who associates a term, say 'S_2', with a certain sensation, but who, when she goes on in various future instances to write 'S_2' in her diary, makes numerous 'mistakes' – that is, in many cases she notes down 'S_2' when that original sensation is not present but some quite different one is. (Or, in another case, a person's concentrating on a sensation has the causal result that she uses the name in question wrongly in future.) So the only difference between this person and the original diarist is that the latter is lucky. The advocate of a private language will certainly not count the case of S_2 as giving her what she wants. But by the same token she will not accept the first case, as elaborated in the objection.

The picture of a private language demands more of the diarist than mere extensional 'success'. The diarist is supposed to come upon S again and recognize that this is the sensation she originally baptized. Not only must she line up a series of 'S's with a matching series of S's, but she must convince herself that she has done so correctly. For she must be able to distinguish herself from the anomalous diarist of S_2, and to do that she must be able to know her labellings are correct. So she needs some way of establishing that this sensation really is an occurrence of S. Thus it is part of the metaphysical picture of a private language that she have some way of telling whether a given awareness-element is S or not. And here 'way of telling' and 'criterion' are interchangeable (see below, p. 135).

Can we get a close-up of this portion of the picture? Subjective experience flows past the mind's eye. A particular awareness element draws my attention, and I focus on it especially. It has a certain striking and distinctive quality which resonates in the mind. *This*, I say, is important, memorable! I shall dub it 'S' and if it recurs, I shall note that down. The particular experience passes away. And now I am having the experience again – or am I? I recall my friend who, I am told, several times recorded 'S_2' in his diary, but in vain, for sometimes it was indeed S_2 and sometimes not. I want to be sure that *this* which now resonates in my mind is truly that experience I noted earlier. I do not want just to guess that it is the same; and I don't want just to be lucky. I want to know it is the same. But how can I? I was not able to stash the original experience away somewhere; so I cannot now consult *it*. I experience this present awareness-element vividly; and I had experienced that other equally vividly. But I need some way of finding out whether they are indeed the same. Do I *remember* that this is the same as that? But my friend thought he remembered too. What I know is that I think I remember it. Whether I do remember it is just the same question I started with: is this the same? I want a way of establishing whether it is or not. But none is to hand. What is there is a certain vivid experience, which seems to me the same as the earlier one. But *seeming* didn't help my friend, and it doesn't help me. I need something more. I need some way of telling whether this is truly S.

If she were speaking a public language, she would be counted right merely in virtue of her having sincerely used the word again, for example in virtue of sincerely saying, 'Oh, there's that pain again'.

IV

But now we must deal with a question that has been in the background of our previous discussions. Why is the public speaker counted right simply in virtue of her sincere say-so? Simply because that in fact is the way the language-game works. And there is a point to the language-game. There is a point to speaking of pains and other sensations. To tell of one's pain can bring help or sympathy on the part of others. It can call forth their natural reactions to one in pain, just as a child's cries can call forth such reactions. And in these cases we do not stop for a moment to wonder whether the person who speaks of her pain has really recognized her sensation correctly. Or in another case, if someone is having a tooth probed by a dentist who asks her to say when it hurts, then the patient's interjection, 'There is pain now', can hardly be questioned on the grounds that she may have failed to recognize the sensation correctly.

The private speaker has attempted to drop the whole complex context that gives our talk of sensations point and meaning. That is why, in the example we considered at length, the result seemed farcical. The diarist kept the outer form of our way of speaking, saying for example, 'S lasted twenty minutes' and getting from her peers the response, 'Yes, she is sincere, so S lasted twenty minutes'. But nothing happens in addition to this sort of empty exchange. There is no point to it. The complex context I spoke of in the case of pain – the context of helping, curing, comforting, and so on – is missing.

But now one might raise a further objection. Suppose we supply such a context as well. Won't we still have a private language? This is exactly the sort of case discussed in that difficult remark in §270, where a use for the sign 'S' is imagined, in terms of a correlation between S and the diarist's blood pressure rising, as measured by a manometer. The puzzle is why the development of this new use is supposed to make it 'quite indifferent whether I have recognized the sensation *right* or not'. The answer is because the use will have shifted, from private to public. I shall now impart the message 'S' to various people who are able to help or otherwise cooperatively react to the prognoses of my illness. For instance, if I inform someone that I am experiencing S then she might withhold certain bad news, in order not to excite me further, knowing I am at risk. And she will now apply a criterion of truthfulness to my statement 'S' just as she would in the case of a report about feeling pain. The supposition that I identify the sensation wrong must be made now from inside some picture of the sensation as private; for the actual use of 'S' – as spelled out in the present case in terms of the manometer, and so on – does not allow that supposition to make sense, any more than we can in our ordinary talk about pain make sense of the supposition that someone knows what pain is, only is perhaps mistaken about whether what she is now experiencing is pain. That supposition concerning S 'will not matter in the least' because it is irrelevant to the role the use of 'S' now plays in the language-game. Quite independent of that supposition, others will still react to my statement 'S' by bringing medication, trying not to overexcite me, and the like; and anyone's speculations about my possible 'mistakes' are irrelevant.

The point with respect to the objection broached just above is that adding such a context transforms the private language to a public one, where a criterion of truthfulness does properly operate, and where there is, properly, no sense to the idea of getting 'S', or whatever the once would-be private word is, wrong.

V

Another protest against my interpretation might be to wonder why Wittgenstein himself did not call attention to the disparity between our ordinary talk of sensations, which gets by without a first-person criterion of correctness, and the would-be private language of sensations, which requires one. The answer is that he did. In §288 he writes:

> That expression of doubt [over whether this, that I now have, is pain or not] has no place in the language-game; but if we cut out human behaviour, which is the expression of sensation, it looks as if I might *legitimately* begin to doubt afresh. My temptation to say that one might take a sensation for something other than what it is arises from this: if I assume the abrogation of the normal language-game with the expression of a sensation, I need a criterion of identity for the sensation; and then the possibility of error also exists.

Note that it is one who assumes 'the abrogation of the normal language-game with the expression of a sensation' – that is, one who is in the grip of the picture of a private language – who needs a criterion of identity. And again, the demand is not imposed from without, dogmatically.

In §258 there is an attempt to hypothesize a private language; an attempt, that is, to conceive of such a language. The words used in the attempt have certain pictures connected with them. For instance, the words 'I impress on myself the connexion between the sign and the sensation' have associated with them the picture of some mind-substance S, which can recur to consciousness and which can be recognized when it recurs – and recognized correctly. Wittgenstein draws this picture out and gets the metaphysician to see he is committed to saying that he can remember the supposed connection he has impressed upon himself right, and yet must admit that all he can do now is count as right whatever will seem right. Then Wittgenstein, by a grammatical remark on the word 'right', points out to him that he has now lapsed into nonsense, so that the original attempt to conceive a private language has once again failed.

That does not destroy the idea of a private language once and for all; the picture has multifarious roots, and must be 'treated' extensively.

VI

At a much simpler level of criticism, it may be objected to that sentence in §258 that it employs the notorious word 'criterion', the meaning of which has been debated in the secondary literature for decades now. So someone might reject this key passage from the 'private language argument' just on the grounds that it contains a technical term from Wittgenstein's own philosophy of language, and so is no stronger than the defence that can be given to the term. Or it might be rejected on the allied ground that no one has yet made clear what a 'criterion' is, let alone justified such claims made in terms of this notion.[11]

But I do not think Wittgenstein means his remark in §258 to presuppose some technical sense of 'criterion'. He does not intend that it be accepted only by some one who uses the term in that assumed special way, for instance in the way he defined it in the *Blue Book*. Such an interpretation would be at odds with the manner in which he approaches philosophical problems in his later work.

What then is he up to? Let us take still another look at 'But in the present case I have no criterion of correctness'.

This remark can be compared to someone who says to a child, concerning a puzzle picture, 'Look, this horse has three eyes'. That is, Wittgenstein is addressing the one who has the metaphysical picture and drawing his or her attention to a feature of the picture. But what feature exactly is he drawing attention to? We might put it: the speaker has no way of establishing or telling if this is really another instance of S. Such a 'way of telling'

Wittgenstein calls a 'criterion'. The word functions here not as a technical but an ordinary one. It could without loss have been replaced by 'way of telling' or 'way of establishing'.

When Wittgenstein says, then, 'But in the present case I have no criterion of correctness', he is not using 'criterion' in a special sense, and he is not imposing a requirement from the outside – some dogmatic claim that there must always be a 'criterion'. To repeat, the one who has the picture sees that it is a feature of her picture both that she needs and lacks a way of establishing the reoccurrence of S, that is, needs a 'criterion'.

At this point she may be driven by that unfilled need to the idea of a 'subjective justification'. And now that 'idea' must be matched against the grammar of the word 'justification'. This is the point the private language passages take up next.

The idea of a private language is enormously attractive – it was to Hume, say, and Russell, and is to virtually all who philosophize. One or several guided tours, where we are shown what's wrong with this picture will not cure us of that attraction, but only move us to defend it in some other way.

For instance, we might turn to the notion of a private rule in order to justify the claim 'S' or to allow us to tell that S has recurred. Or we might move to the case of 'red', where it seems clear that this word has, in addition to its public significance, a private meaning – *this* (pointing within) is what 'red' means to me, or really means. And so the 'treatment' of private language will proceed.

NOTES

* I am indebted to colleagues at the Bielefeld/Berlin Wittgenstein conference for criticisms of an earlier draft of this paper, and to the editors of this volume for their support and comments.

1 Norman Malcolm, 'Review: "Wittgenstein's *Philosophical Investigations*" ', *Philosophical Review*, 1954, vol. 71, pp. 67–93. Some representative papers on the private language argument are collected in J. Canfield, ed., *The Philosophy of Wittgenstein*, vol. 9 (*The Private Language Argument*), New York, Garland, 1986. See also Saul A. Kripke, 'Wittgenstein on Rules and Private Language', in Irving Block, ed., *Perspectives on the Philosophy of Wittgenstein*, Oxford, Blackwell, 1981. Some papers on this famous study can be found in vol. 10 (*Logical Necessity and Rules*) of my anthology, *The Philosophy of Wittgenstein*.

2 Kripke, op. cit.
3 There are two distinct lines of thought to be considered in reading §258. They concern possible ways of avoiding the seeming *reductio* fashioned there. One has to do with our public talk of such 'external' things as colours. The idea, suggested by Kripke's paper on private language, would be roughly this: at some point a person, in learning a criterion for a public word like red, just does make the judgment 'This is red' and does so without justification; justification must come to an end. So why therefore expect the private language speaker to provide a 'criterion of correctness'? The second point, very similar in intent, has to do with our public language for 'pain'. Here too it looks as if the demand Wittgenstein makes on the would-be private language practitioner is one he would not make on the corresponding public-language speaker, so that again the seeming *reductio* has no force. In this paper I shall confine myself to the second issue.
4 Judith Jarvis Thompson, 'Private Languages', *American Philosophical Quarterly*, 1964, vol. 1, pp. 20–31.
5 Benjamin F. Armstrong Jr, 'Wittgenstein on Private Language: It Takes Two to Talk', *Philosophical Investigations*, 1984, vol. 7, pp. 46–62.
6 Thompson discusses at some length the seeming incompatibility between the principle I quoted from her and Wittgenstein's writings on 'pain'. She tries to save the Wittgensteinian from this preliminary objection, in order, perhaps, to spare him for her own objection, as one might cure a prisoner's superficial wounds before hanging him. But I do not find her intervention successful. She notes, for instance, that the Wittgensteinian might deny that 'pain' is a 'kind term'; but that seems much too frail a premiss to support a private language argument.
7 I have altered Anscombe's translation slightly.
8 See *Philosophical Investigations*, p. 222. I believe the view stated there to be central to Wittgenstein's account of 'pain' and similar psychological or mental words; it may safely be presupposed in interpreting the private language passages.
9 Perennially, philosophers, thinking over this matter, conclude that it is possible, for example, for there to be sensations which are as it were intermediate between pain and something else – perhaps, a tickle – so that the introspecting philosopher is in doubt about whether some particular *this* is a pain. But this would-be piece of language is a fantasy dreamt up in someone's study; in fact if someone in a real situation cannot be certain whether something is pain or not, then it isn't. The man in the dentist's chair who responded, 'Wait a minute now, is that pain, or a tickle?' would be rightly considered frivolous; certainly he would not, in Berkeley's phase, be speaking with the vulgar. That is, he would not be making sense within the confines of natural language.
    One can perhaps produce initially more plausible examples where a person is mistaken about whether he is in pain, but only by imagining the circumstances in which one speaks of pain radically

altered, so that the examples are of that special kind, treasured by philosophers, where one is asked to have 'intuitions' about what to say in circumstances outside the scope of normal usage. In circumstances, that is, where language does not dictate an answer, and where we must ourselves extend the use of the term to cover the new, extraordinary case.

10 One is reminded here of Wittgenstein's remark (§269) that 'sounds which no one else understands but which I *"appear to understand"* might be called a "private language" '. Here the others too 'appear' to understand; this bizarre social ritual could also be called a 'private language' – if the quotes are scare quotes.

11 There has, of course, grown to be a standard interpretation of 'criterion'. This was put forward originally by Albritton, made prominent by Shoemaker, and later taken over, in a somewhat modified way, by Dummett, and by Baker and Hacker. Evidence of the interpretation's having become standard is that it is cited as an obvious and incontrovertible truth in a recent popular presentation of Wittgenstein (A.C. Grayling, *Wittgenstein*, Oxford, Oxford University Press, p. 88). Its present popularity is a bit paradoxical, however, since, as I understand, Albritton, Shoemaker and Baker and Hacker now themselves repudiate it. Moreover, it is wrong.

Chapter 7

Adelheid and the Bishop – what's the game?

Joachim Schulte

Section 365 of Wittgenstein's *Philosophical Investigations* consists of a short dialogue between two interlocutors, and in order to avoid confusion I shall give them names. The first interlocutor will be called Rodolfo, the second one Valentino. The dialogue runs as follows:

> RODOLFO: Do Adelheid and the Bishop play a *real* game of chess?
> VALENTINO: Of course. They are not merely pretending – which would also be possible as part of a play.
> RODOLFO: But, for example, the game has no beginning!
> VALENTINO: Of course it has; otherwise it would not be a game of chess.

Adelheid and the Bishop are figures from Goethe's drama *Götz von Berlichingen mit der eisernen Hand*; the game of chess to which Wittgenstein alludes in this passage occurs at the beginning of the second act. From the text of the play we can gather that the game is near its conclusion, for Adelheid is just putting the Bishop in check; a minute later she checkmates him. (She remarks that he has evidently not been keeping his mind on the game; thus the game may have been a brief one.)

The notion which is to be illuminated by this short dialogue is the concept 'real', emphasized in Wittgenstein's text. The fact that this is the subject-matter of that dialogue is Wittgenstein's reason for inserting it at this point of the *Investigations*. The context in which this dialogue occurs will be dealt with later.

Looking at it more closely we shall find that our dialogue has some rather puzzling features. From the very start there is a certain contrast between the subject of the discussion and the example by means of which the problem at issue is to be clarified. After all, the figures who are – allegedly or apparently or seemingly – playing chess are not real people but characters in a play. And if the stage plays any philosophical role at all, it counts as an example of mere appearance and not as a paradigm of reality.

A typical example of this philosophical attitude is the case of an actor or impresario who comes running onto the stage shouting, 'Fire! Fire!'. The audience may greet this performance with applause but does not understand it as an invitation to leave the theatre as quickly as possible and without panic.[1] It seems that the place where those words are spoken deprives them of their usual sense. They cease to deal with reality and come to be about a different, a fictitious world (if it is at all legitimate to claim that they are 'about' anything). In some senses the stage may – as in a well-known line by Schiller[2] – signify the world, but the *real* world is a place which (to the extent that it *can* be reached by words spoken on the stage) can be reached only indirectly, for instance by the author using one of his figures as a mouthpiece to get across in a more or less veiled fashion what he himself thinks about, or demands from, the world.

This way of looking at the matter is surely not a strange one and it can no doubt be justified. Thus it must come as a surprise when Valentino, in his answer to the question whether the game of chess between Adelheid and the Bishop is a real one, replies that of course it is a real game because they are really playing, not pretending to play. That is, they are not behaving like people who wish to evoke a false impression in a possible observer and make him believe that they are absorbed in their game of chess.

What is Valentino's point? In order to make it clear we shall try to picture to ourselves a scene from an imaginary film in a café on Montmartre. Cary Grant and Audrey Hepburn are trying to eavesdrop on a conversation between Edward G. Robinson and Orson Welles. Nonchalantly they will take their seats at the next table and, looking as innocent as possible, they will ask the *garçon* to supply them, not only with their usual aperitifs, but also with a chessboard and chessmen. Then they will put the chessmen on the board and start to push them hither and thither while 'in reality' they are pricking up their ears and trying not to miss a word of the terrible schemes that are being talked about at the next table. If Grant and Hepburn play in accordance with the rules of chess (start from the right position, move the pieces correctly, start a new game after mate or stale-mate) they play chess *as a pretext*. But they might just as well simply move the pieces irrespective of these rules. In that case (and in contrast with the game between Adelheid and the Bishop intended by Wittgenstein) they make it *appear* as if they were playing chess. Their gestures and their moves are pretence, they are a pretext and a feint, and in this sense our protagonists are not playing chess.

So far we must agree with Valentino's claim. It is true that even regarding a fictitious game of chess – as it may occur in a play, in a film, or in a novel – we distinguish between a real game and a sham game, between a game that involves winning and losing and a game where nothing is at stake, between being in earnest and bluffing.

But now our friend Rodolfo may reply, Of course you are right in this, we are in complete agreement. I do not wish to dispute that actors may be able to represent either a real or a sham game of chess, as the case may be, and they may also be able to convey by means of gestures, facial expression, and tone of voice whether they are playing a real game or a sham game. Similarly we make a distinction between a situation where, in a play, a bill is paid with counterfeit money and a situation where real money is used. But even if on the stage genuine money is used to represent counterfeit money and toy money to represent real money, this makes no difference as far as the fact is concerned that we are not dealing with reality but with the world of appearance or fiction. On the stage real money is a mere prop, even if an actor will afterwards use it to pay his restaurant bill. And even if an actor's tears are real tears, their function in the play may be that of crocodile tears. We must make a fundamental and clear-cut distinction between reality on the one hand and fiction on the other; and in terms of this distinction that which happens on the stage is, if it is part of the play,[3] never real.

This is what Rodolfo's answer basically amounts to, although in Wittgenstein's text he merely speaks the following line: 'But, for example, the game has no beginning.' When the curtain rises the game of chess between Adelheid and the Bishop has nearly reached its end. In the play we are not shown the beginning of the game. This game of chess is essentially part of the fictitious world of the play we are watching, just as the

money or the tears of our previous paragraph. Even if the actors
representing Adelheid and the Bishop have before the beginning
of the second act actually started playing a game of chess which
they are now, after the curtain has risen, bringing to an end in the
course of the first scene, then this is just as irrelevant to the
question of the reality of the game played in the drama as the fact
that one of the actors in the other example uses a banknote
employed as counterfeit on the stage to pay his bill at the
restaurant.

Now Rodolfo clearly appears to be the winner of this dispute.
What could his interlocutor reply to that? After all, it is quite true
that in the play this game of chess has no beginning; and that is,
just as Rodolfo asserts, a good reason for accepting the claim that
this game is not a real game. But in spite of that Valentino does
give a reply – he simply denies Rodolfo's claim, which appeared
so very plausible, that the game has no beginning. 'Of course it
has', says Valentino, and what he means is that it does have a
beginning. And then he continues with the following remarkable
piece of reasoning, 'otherwise it would not be a game of chess'.

That is the end of our dialogue. Valentino has the last word,
and one gains the impression that Wittgenstein agrees with him.
But how is that possible? Rodolfo, we have seen, has persuasively
argued that the beginning of the game is essentially *not* part of
the play. Now it seems sheer stubbornness on Valentino's part
when he denies that the game between Adelheid and the Bishop
does not have a beginning. His reason – 'otherwise it would not
be a game of chess' – does not sound any better than the simple
statement, 'otherwise I should be wrong!'.

Now the question is whether we can make any sense of the last
sentence of our dialogue. Is it possible to justify and establish as
correct that brief last line of Valentino's, or is it Wittgenstein's
intention to make it clear by means of wording and context that
the position defended by Valentino is absurd?

Apart from what we have here reproduced, §365 itself does not
contain any statements that could be used to give a direct answer
to any of these questions. But there are a few scattered remarks in
the *Philosophical Investigations* and other writings which one
may think could be used to throw some indirect light on our
questions. Two of these passages will be mentioned presently,
and we shall try to find out if they can be of any help.
Furthermore we shall have to have a close look at the immediate

context of §365 in order to see whether any answer can be derived from it. In Wittgenstein's writings, fiction, images, and make-believe play an important role, or, rather, a number of roles, which a reader of those writings must not leave out of account. But as far as the game of chess between Adelheid and the Bishop is concerned, two passages from the *Philosophical Investigations* seem particularly relevant, inasmuch as they exhibit certain parallels and might thus help us to arrive at a better understanding of §365. The first of these passages is §297:[4]

> Of course, if water boils in a pot, steam comes out of the pot and also pictured steam comes out of the pictured pot. But what if one insisted on saying that there must also be something boiling in the picture of the pot?

Even if we pay no attention to the context of this remark, this much is obvious: of course it is absurd to suppose that a picture and that which it depicts are to agree in such a way that the picture must contain things that correspond to all the hidden or visible background phenomena of the state of affairs represented by the picture. Thus a painting may be called 'Good news' and it may succeed in getting this idea across, even though in the picture itself there is no letter and no telephone or carrier-pigeon that might have served to transmit the news, but only the happy face of a girl. The example described by Wittgenstein is less subtle. A picture of a pot with boiling water may only depict a pot and steam, but we are nevertheless able to understand this picture without having to suppose that the painted pot really contains something which is boiling (and without objecting to the painter that he did not bother to show at least a little bit of bubbling water).

Applying this idea to the dialogue quoted at the beginning of this paper, it seems plausible to conclude that Valentino is wrong in insisting that the game must have a beginning. In this case the scene that is being performed would correspond to the painting, and just as it is possible to grasp that which is represented by the painting even though there is nothing in it which is bubbling up in a visible or concealed fashion, so it is possible to gather from what is happening on the stage that Adelheid and the Bishop are playing a game of chess without our having to assume that the game has a possible hidden beginning. To suppose that the game which is being enacted must have a (necessarily invisible) beginning appears just as superfluous and almost as absurd as the idea that a visibly boiling pot in a painting must contain something which is bubbling up in the same way as a pot which is *really* boiling in my kitchen.

There is another passage in the *Philosophical Investigations* which may seem to be sufficiently parallel to our dialogue about the game of chess to be possibly helpful. This is the concluding paragraph of §398.[5] Here Wittgenstein writes:

> Think of a picture of a landscape, an imaginary landscape with a house in it. – Someone asks 'Whose house is that?' – The answer, by the way, might be: 'It belongs to the farmer who is sitting on the bench in front of it.' But then he cannot, for example, enter his house.

In this case too we shall have to ignore the context of Wittgenstein's remark. If we can here see a parallel to the topic of our dialogue and apply that parallel to the game of chess, it seems that we cannot help concluding that there is no reason to suppose that the game of chess represented in the play must have a beginning. Just as the farmer fails to be able to enter 'his' house in the painting, so a game of chess which in a play is represented only in its final stages fails to have a beginning. Valentino's claim that the game does have a beginning – for 'otherwise it would not be a game of chess' – is thus equally absurd as the assumption that the pot in the painting must contain something which is bubbling up or the notion that the farmer in the painting must be able to enter the house which is represented in the same painting.

For the time being, however, these parallels which at first blush seem so plausible do not really help us in trying to understand whether the game of chess between Adelheid and the Bishop may be called a real game and whether Valentino is justified in claiming that the game does have a beginning. We should now have a closer look at the context of our §365 in order to see if it will get us any further.

Both the preceding §364 and the following §366 deal with the topic of calculating in one's head, and here the question is raised whether calculating in one's head is less *real* than calculating on a sheet of paper. Of course, this question is in turn connected with a fair number of further problems which in Wittgenstein's later philosophy are discussed again and again and in a variety of contexts. Here, however, the neighbouring paragraphs of our §365 will be taken into account only to the extent that they may help to illuminate the obscure parts of §365 itself.

In §364 it is shown that there are several possible ways of questioning the legitimacy or reality of calculating in one's head, and finally the following question is raised, which I shall put into Rodolfo's mouth:

> RODOLFO: Is calculating in the imagination in some sense less real than calculating on paper?

And Valentino's reply runs as follows:

> VALENTINO: It is *real* – calculation-in-the-head.

Up to this point the parallel between §§364 and 365 is virtually complete. In the latter the general question is raised whether the game of chess between Adelheid and the Bishop is a *real* one, and in the same way the former leads to the general question whether calculating in one's head is less real than a – public – calculation on a sheet of paper. And just as the final answer with respect to the game of chess is that the specific game between Adelheid and the Bishop (in contrast, for example, to the sham game between Cary Grant and Audrey Hepburn) is a real game, that is, no make-believe, so the final answer concerning the calculation in the head referred to in §364 says that it is a real calculation in the head (in contrast, we may add, to a sham calculation in the head as in the case of an examinee who, with a frown of concentration, mentions the correct result which he *seems* to have calculated in his head but which in reality he has read off his cuff).

Thus in this sense it is a real calculation in the head. But now Rodolfo asks a further question:

> RODOLFO: Is it like [*ähnlich*] calculation on paper? –

And Valentino's answer runs as follows:

> VALENTINO: I don't know whether to call it like [*ähnlich*]. Is a bit of white paper with black lines on it like a human body?

This is a very clever reply, but in order to appreciate it, we should elucidate the dialogue a little more fully. The first question which springs to mind is: why does Rodolfo mention the problem of likeness or similarity at all? Now, it is likely that

Rodolfo's reason for asking that question is the following. If that which is normally or in paradigmatic cases called 'calculating' is something which is done by means of a pen on a sheet of paper in such a way that every single step in the calculation can be retraced and checked, then a kind of calculation which is performed, not in this public manner on a sheet of paper, but as it were hidden – that is, in the head – must in some way be similar to the normal or paradigmatic procedure, for otherwise there would simply be no reason to regard it as a related activity and subsume it under the same concept.

Valentino's reply to Rodolfo's misgivings is an indirect one but he none the less succeeds in driving his point home. Without a twinkle in his eyes he remarks, 'I don't know whether to call it similar'. But then he turns the tables on Rodolfo and cites a paradigm example of what in normal cases we tend to call 'similar' or 'like', namely a portrait of a human being,[6] and asks how it is possible to call a thing like that – a white sheet of paper with black lines on it – similar to a human body. If you look at it from this point of view – a flourishing human face full of expression and life on the one hand and a pale scrap of paper with some black scrawls on the other – then there will of course be no similarity at all. But if you look at it in a different way and see it as a portrait of the Emperor Maximilian, for instance, then you may even want to say that it is a better likeness than a mirror image.

Applying this reply to the case of calculating in one's head, we shall see that from a certain point of view there appears to be no similarity at all between calculating on a sheet of paper and calculating in one's head, while if one looks at it from a different point of view numerous similarities become visible.

On the one hand, there is no similarity in so far as there is nothing in our heads which we may point to and which corresponds in an equally verifiable way to the individual steps of a calculation effected on a sheet of paper. On the other hand, a man who really knows how to calculate in his head will always or often be able to give the correct reply when asked what the solution of a given problem or what a certain step in his calculation is. And in this respect there is a similarity between calculating in one's head and calculating on a sheet of paper.

That which is misleading is the fact that we tend to expect or demand a similarity to occur in the same place as it were and that with regard to calculating in one's head we are tempted to say what Wittgenstein in §366 puts as follows:

> it was some mental process *corresponding* to the multiplication on paper. So it would make sense to say: '*This* process in the mind corresponds to *this* process on paper.' And it would then make sense to talk of a method of projection according to which the image of the sign was a representation of the sign itself.

You cannot deny the reality of a calculation in the head merely for the reason that it does not exhibit similarities with a (paradigmatic) calculation on paper in the same (or homologous) places. In spite of clear external differences, we should characterize calculating on paper and calculating in one's head as related activities; often we should not bother explicitly to keep them apart, and this tendency is evidently due to the fact that, owing to the sameness of results and the general agreement in technique, they prove to be closely connected. The appearance of unreality could arise only because a difference without any practical relevance was emphasized and connected with unsuitable but tempting analogies.

The public character and the checkability of a calculation effected on paper are not essentially due to the materiality of the sheet of paper. Calculating in one's head is equally public and checkable, for the person who calculates in his head must be able to answer a number of questions which will then correspond to certain steps of a calculation on paper. But that does not mean that there have to have been any corresponding events in his mind which we should be justified to call mental or psychological correlates of the steps of a calculation on paper.

We may wonder whether it is helpful to have recourse to these considerations in order to elucidate our dialogue about the game of chess between Adelheid and the Bishop. It seems to me that at least one thing can really be learned from them. The argument that Rodolfo uses in denying the reality of the game of chess is basically an argument from analogy. He claims that inasmuch as the game does not have a beginning in the play the game is not a real one for the reason that a game is a real one only if it has a beginning. And now Valentino gives the impression of joining in the dispute and replies that the game does have a beginning, for otherwise it would not be a real one.

But here Valentino only pretends to accept the premisses of Rodolfo's reasoning. In effect he proceeds in a way similar to that employed in Wittgenstein's remarks about calculating in one's head and uses these words in order to reject the entire style of argument and to indicate a completely different way of looking at the issue.

If you wish to decide whether in a play something is to count as a real game you will have to take into account all kinds of circumstances; and your decision will for instance depend on what you take to be the intentions of the author, and the words or gestures of the actors will also play an important role. The criteria we use in order to find out whether two people who are sitting in a café are really playing chess cannot without further ado be applied to what happens on the stage. Similarly, genuine stage money need not be genuine everyday money. If a prosecuting officer intervened and arrested an actor for the reason that on the stage he had used counterfeit money to pay his bill, we should try to explain to the officer what a play is, what kinds of function the props have within the play, and so forth. After he has grasped that he will release the actor, and perhaps he will say to himself, 'I see, in the play it is possible to use counterfeit money to pay your bill; consequently it is genuine money and there is no reason for me to act'. And if the officer has a good deal of imagination he may continue and reason as follows, 'If it were money which in the play counts as counterfeit, then the Public Prosecutor would have to interfere; but the person to be arrested would not be an actor but Jack the Knife. I myself, however, am not in a position to arrest him because I do not occur in the play.'

The case of our game of chess is fairly similar to that. Of course, a chess champion who is sitting in the audience may get excited and inform the Bishop (or would it be the actor?) that he is not defeated yet: by making a certain move he could escape Adelheid's attack, and so on. In the game which is taking place on the stage, however, the Bishop has been checkmated even though the same arrangement of chessmen would have to be interpreted in a completely different way if it occurred in a tournament. And in that sense in which this arrangement means 'checkmate' in the play, the game does have a beginning. In the play it is a real game after all.

Thus Valentino's reply according to which the game does have a beginning (for otherwise it would not be a real game) is in effect a rejection of Rodolfo's objection. If Rodolfo were right in voicing his misgivings he would also be justified in saying things like 'Adelheid is not real because she has not been born' or 'The Bishop is not real because he has not been consecrated'. But a stage character need not be born on the stage in order to count as a real human being (in contrast to a ghost for instance). And in the play a game can be a real one even if its beginning has not been mentioned in the play. To explain that it has no beginning has no point (it is *'witzlos'*, to use Wittgenstein's expression). And in order to indicate this Wittgenstein uses the puzzling words 'Of course it has; otherwise it would not be a game of chess'.

Raising a question about the beginning of the game would be similar to a child's question regarding the future lot of certain figures from a story. In that case you will either have to tell the child that, as the story is just a fairy tale, you know nothing about it or you will simply make up your own plot and try to continue the story in a more or less plausible fashion. And this is the way Valentino *alias* Wittgenstein proceeds. He does not reply in this vein:

> What's the point of talking about a beginning? In the play there is no beginning, and that's that. In so far as it is possible to talk of reality with respect to a play, this game of chess is a real game. But in order to count as a real game it need not have a beginning in the play and it cannot have a beginning that occurs outside the play.

This reply could be seen as making use of a distinction between what is or holds true in a make-believe world, on the one hand, and what is presented or represented in it, on the other. In accordance with this distinction something may be said to hold true in a make-believe world without being represented (notably that the game of chess had a beginning) while other matters are left indeterminate (like the specific opening). But instead of responding in this manner Wittgenstein behaves like an adult who continues the story he has been telling a child off the cuff and says, 'Of course, those two have been playing chess, haven't they? So the game must have a beginning.'

Now Rodolfo's misapprehension will be clear. Still, the reader will have to be careful, and avoid taking Valentino's words literally, otherwise he may fall into confusion and blame

Wittgenstein for having misled him. And then he will be tempted to agree with the judgment of Liebetraut, who, in the same scene of Goethe's *Götz von Berlichingen*, exclaims, 'If I were a great lord, I should not play that game but forbid it at court as well as in the whole country.'[7]

NOTES

1 Cf. Donald Davidson, 'Communication and Convention', *Inquiries into Truth and Interpretation*, Oxford, Clarendon Press, 1984, pp. 269f.

2 'An die Freunde': 'Sehn wir doch das Große *aller* Zeiten/Auf den Brettern, die die Welt bedeuten'.

3 This qualification is necessary to exclude the possibility (mentioned below) that the actors are as it were privately playing a game (which could then be won by the actor who is representing the Bishop).

4 This passage is referred to by Garth Hallett in his *Companion to Wittgenstein's 'Philosophical Investigations'*, Ithaca, Cornell University Press, 1977, p. 422.

5 At this point of his commentary Hallett refers us back to our §365. Cf. Hallett, op. cit., p. 444.

6 There is no explicit mention of a portrait in §365, but I think it is quite legitimate to suppose that a portrait is precisely what is meant at this point. Cf. some of the remarks on p. 86 of Wittgenstein's *Last Writings on the Philosophy of Psychology*, Oxford, Blackwell, 1982, and on p. 205 of the so-called second part of his *Philosophical Investigations*.

7 'Dies Spiel spiel ich nicht, wenn ich ein großer Herr wär, und verböt's am Hofe und im ganzen Land'.

Chapter 8

The visual room*

Andreas Kemmerling

Exactly two hundred years ago in 1789, the Austrian philosopher
K.L. Reinhold said:

> The idea [*Vorstellung*] is all there is about which all philoso-
> phers agree that it is real. At least if there is anything at all
> about which there is agreement in the philosophical world, it
> is the idea; no idealist, no egoist, no dogmatic skeptic can deny
> the existence of the idea.[1]

About one hundred years ago, Frege had begun to question the
philosophical relevance of the concept 'idea'. Frege never denied
the reality or existence of ideas which Reinhold had claimed to be
immune from philosophical doubt. But he flatly denied that the
concept of idea is of vital importance for a philosophical theory
of human knowledge. For, first, ideas are not what human
knowledge is about. (This holds, of course, only with the
exception of the few things we know about ideas.) And, secondly,
ideas are not the kind of things in which human knowledge
consists. What knowledge consists in must be something that
intrinsically fixes a truth value, and it must be something that
remains the same when different people have it. (This holds at
least in those cases in which we want to say that different people
know – or might know – exactly the same things.) But ideas do
not intrinsically fix a truth value, nor can two people ever have
the same idea. Frege's conclusion is that the concept of idea plays
no important role in a philosophical theory of knowledge; its
proper place is in a psychological account on what goes on in
human beings when they acquire or apply knowledge.

Traditional conceptions of ideas – such as the Cartesian one –
are not very well characterized. The word 'idea' is often used to

cover a variety of things which we nowadays consider as distinct. Perhaps the most telling characterization of what is meant by this word can be found in the 'Third Meditation': they are *tamquam rerum imagines*, as it were pictures of things. That is what the word 'idea' appropriately applies to, according to Descartes. The qualification ('as it were') is fairly indeterminate but necessary, for at least some ideas are said to be not like pictures at all (e.g. our innate idea of God).

When Frege attacks the tendency to attach central importance to the concept of idea, he assumes that ideas have at least the following interconnected characteristics:

(i) Ideas are entities of a psychological kind. They are not brain-states or some other kind of physical thing.
(ii) Ideas are essentially subjective; they are contents of a particular mind or consciousness. If x is an idea of mine, it cannot be an idea of yours. (To say that x is a content of my mind is not to say that x is in me. Strictly speaking, ideas are nowhere. When we say that a certain idea is in a certain person, this is, for Frege, just a metaphorical way of expressing the essential subjectivity of ideas.[2])
(iii) Ideas are *had*. They cannot be sensed or thought; they can neither be 'perceived' nor 'comprehended'. It is external objects which one might see, smell, taste, etc. Thoughts one might grasp (or 'comprehend'). But ideas one has. 'Having' is the word which Frege selects for the purpose of referring to the special relationship which obtains between a person and any of her or his ideas.
(iv) There are no ideas which are not had.

According to the above features of ideas, as characterized by Frege, it is fair to say: ideas are relata, i.e. entities that stand in relations (to persons who have them.) And if a person has an idea, this is – in at least one sense – an essentially subjective state of affairs: no one else could have the very same idea. Taking a linguistic turn, it is fair to say that Frege held that '. . . has (the idea) ——' expresses a relation of eminent intimacy: whatever name of an idea is inserted in the second slot of this dyadic predicate, the resulting monadic predicate will be true of at most one person. Name an idea, and you've picked out its 'haver' or owner.[3]

Before we turn to the difficulties that Wittgenstein finds in this conception of ideas, we should note two advantages it has over many traditional accounts. First, the relation that obtains between a person and an idea is not a perceptual relation of some kind. Secondly, the spatial idioms ('in the mind', etc.) involved in our common discourse about ideas are just a manner of speaking; we should think of them as awkward metaphors for the essential subjectivity involved in having ideas.

For the sake of simplicity, let us concentrate on visual ideas, that is ideas of the kind we have when we see or imagine ordinary objects. Let i be such an idea, e.g. the idea that Harvey had yesterday at the stroke of eight. According to Frege's account, it holds that no one else but Harvey ever can have i. A question arises. Given that a sentence of the kind 'x has (the idea) y' entails that no one else (but x) has y, then how should this entailment be rendered in a logically perspicuous notation? There seem to be two possibilities. One way is to characterize the idea in such a manner that the only possible owner of the idea is determined by this characterization. (Accordingly, if D is an appropriate definite description of the idea i just mentioned above, then it follows on purely logical grounds that the predicate 'has' ^D applies to Harvey uniquely.) The other way is to characterize the relation of *having* in such a manner that its first relatum is determined by this characterization. (Accordingly, ideas could be specified 'anonymously', i.e. leaving it open who has them; we could, given the second way, allow for a description like 'the most exciting idea anyone ever had'. Such a description is ruled out by the other analysis.)

The problem is this. According to Frege's account, a sentence of the kind

(v) x has y

expresses that a certain relation obtains between a certain person and a certain idea. Such a sentence entails that no other person stands in the same relation to the same idea. We have noted at least two candidates for a logically appropriate representation of the truth condition expressed by such a sentence:

(vi) $\mathrm{Has}(x, y_x)$
(vii) $\mathrm{Has}_x(x, y)$.

If we choose (vi) as our analysis of (v), we should add a convention to the effect that the subscript of the second relatum-expression must, on pain of analytical falsity (or lack of well-formedness), agree with the first relatum-expression. If we choose (vii), our convention should guarantee an agreement of the relation-expression's subscript with the first relatum-expression. But which should we choose? Either choice seems completely arbitrary. Perhaps, then, what we really need is another, and better, way of analysing sentences like (v).

THE FIRST PARAGRAPH

Frege did not deal with questions like these. But Wittgenstein did, or so I shall assume in trying to understand §398 of the *Philosophical Investigations*. In this section, Wittgenstein attacks some conception of visual ideas which is so much like the Fregean one that it seems reasonable (or at least acceptable for the purpose of identifying a determinate target of his remarks) to suppose that it actually is the Fregean conception. This is of course not to say that Wittgenstein means to criticize Frege. He criticizes a certain conception of ideas. This conception is metaphysically neutral in the sense that it does not entail any of the grand *isms* – Frege held it, and he was a realist; when Wittgenstein used to hold it (as we may suspect), he was a solipsist; and this conception is consistent with idealistic doctrines as well. This is important to note because Wittgenstein's earlier discussions of this conception of ideas are sometimes in the context of a discussion of solipsism.[4] So it may seem that what Wittgenstein really means to attack is solipsism. But this is not so. The topic in §398 is clearly whether it makes sense to assume that having ideas is something essentially subjective. A negative answer will have repercussions for any doctrine that relies on a Fregean conception of ideas, not just for Wittgensteinian solipsism.

Let us turn to §398. And let us imagine that Wittgenstein is sitting in a room with somebody who holds a theory of visual perception and imagination that is based on the Fregean conception of ideas. The Fregean, as we might call him for convenience, has just put forward the outlines of his theory. He holds that whenever a person sees or visually imagines something, he or she has ideas. The idea that one has when one, for example, looks around in this room, the Fregean claims, cannot be had by anybody else; at most, another person might have a similar idea (but this is a dubious claim anyway because there is no possibility of comparing different people's ideas).[5] But how can one characterize the idea one has? It seems very natural to describe the visual idea of a room by mentioning visible features of the room. But if the Fregean tries out a description like 'It is the visual image of a room in which there are two windows and a heater beneath them', then Wittgenstein might object that exactly the same description is true of something that he presently has as well and that the Fregean therefore has failed to describe his idea in such a way that his claim ('it cannot be had by anybody else') is justified. So far, the description of the idea has not yielded anything so special that nobody else might have the thing described.

It is at this point that §398 starts. The Fregean, less confident, repeats his claim, now laying stress on ideas of imagination (but obviously he has not completely abandoned hope of pushing it through for visual perception also):

> But when I imagine something, or even if I actually *saw* objects, I shall after all *have* something which my neighbour has not.[6]

To this Wittgenstein replies, in his inimitable manner:

> I understand you. You want to look about you and say: 'At any rate, only I have THIS.'

Indeed, the Fregean certainly would like to say this, if he only had a way of pointing to his visual idea – this would save him the trouble of searching for an appropriate way of describing that which only he has. But he knows very well that pointing is out of the question. According to his view, his ideas cannot be seen (or otherwise sensed) by anybody, not even by himself. What the demonstrative 'THIS' is meant to refer to is nothing that can be demonstrated.

Wittgenstein makes a short remark on the uselessness of the Fregean's reply[7] and raises a fairly radical question:

> Is it not equally well possible to say: 'There is here no question of a 'seeing' – and therefore none of a 'having' – nor of a subject, nor therefore of the I either'? Might I not ask: In what sense do you *have* that of which you are talking and of which you say that only you have it? Do you possess it? You do not even *see* it.

Of course, the Fregean is prepared to concede that Wittgenstein is right about the first and the last point: he does not see the idea he has. But Wittgenstein seems to want to discard the words that the Fregean badly needs in order to convey what he is driving at: the word 'I' and the word 'have'. If these words – just like the useless demonstrative 'THIS' – should turn out to be unsuitable for the Fregean's current purpose, then he would be at a complete loss. How could he ever hope to make himself intelligible?

Wittgenstein now concentrates on the strange use the Fregean makes of the word 'have'. The first observation is that this word is in need of elucidation if it is meant to express a relation between persons and things that are not visible even in principle. But we can pass over this point – Wittgenstein himself does – for his next point seems to be much more forceful.

> Would you not have to say of it [i.e. THIS something] that no one has it? For it is clear: if you logically exclude another person's having something, it loses its sense to say that you have it.

How can Wittgenstein say that an utterance of 'I have THIS' is senseless if it is made by the Fregean? To see more clearly what is at issue, we should get rid of the demonstrative. For the Fregean should concede that this was just a useful linguistic makeshift to which he resorted overhastily. A genuine demonstrative is used properly only if its referent can, at least in principle, be sensed. No such restriction applies to names, the Fregean might argue. So let us assume that in the meantime he has introduced a name for the visual idea he wants to talk about, for example by saying 'I hereby introduce *Hoc* as a rigid designator for the visual idea I had when I uttered the word "THIS" '. Certainly, Wittgenstein has plenty of objections against this move on tap, but these are not our immediate concern here. To straighten things out, it seems useful to keep the point about the demonstrative separate from the one that Wittgenstein tries to make about the Fregean's use of the word 'having'.

So let us ask again: How can Wittgenstein say that 'I have Hoc', as used by the Fregean, is senseless? What exactly is his argument in the passage just quoted? A first answer is this: in any case, the word 'have', as used by the Fregean, has lost its ordinary sense. Ordinarily, when we say that a person has something, *y*, we say this only if (at least in principle) somebody else might have *y*. Our common concept of *having* includes the possibility of change of ownership. And though the word 'have', as the Fregean prefers to use it, has lost its ordinary sense, it has not yet acquired a new sense; hence what he says is, strictly speaking, senseless.

If this is Wittgenstein's argument, then it seems similar in philosophical design to his first observation (about the visibility of what is possessed). And the Fregean might easily deny all this. He might insist that he is just applying the common concept of having to things about which we ordinarily (outside philosophical contexts) do not talk. Having, he might say, does not essentially involve the possibility of a change of ownership, even if it does so usually (and with regard to things of ordinary interest). Let us escape from the impending quarrel about words and turn to something less dull.

There is a second way of construing Wittgenstein's argument. The Fregean holds the following:

(viii) It is logically excluded that anybody else but I has Hoc.

(viii) entails

(ix) It is senseless to say of anybody else but me that he has Hoc.

Given the truth of (viii) and (ix), we are left with only two possibilities, namely (x) and (xi):

(x) I have Hoc.
(xi) I do not have Hoc.

But assuming that the introduction of the name 'Hoc' was successful, (xi) is a self-defeating statement. Therefore the Fregean is left with (x) as the only statement about who has Hoc that is not ruled out on linguistic grounds. Therefore (x) is what Wittgenstein calls a 'grammatical sentence' [*grammatischer Satz*]. Such sentences have no sense (or shall we say: what is said in using such sentences makes no sense?). To use a grammatical sentence is pointless when it comes to making statements: no information is given, no possible state of the world is excluded.[8]

A third interpretation of Wittgenstein's statement is as follows. Consider the extensions of the two predicates:

(xii) The Fregean has ——.

(xiii) Wittgenstein has ——.

According to the Fregean's conception, these extensions are necessarily disjunct sets of ideas. If an idea belongs to the extension of (xii), it cannot belong to the extension of (xiii), and *vice versa*. But, this being so, how can we assume – as the Fregean does – that there is a common dyadic predicate,

(xiv) . . . has ——.

from which (xii) and (xiii) stem? Should we not rather say that 'has', if it is a genuine relational expression, takes on a different sense each time it is applied to a different person? Put more assertively, the point here is that the word 'has' lacks a uniform meaning when applied to different persons. And if this is so, then it makes no sense to contrast the Fregean's having Hoc with Wittgenstein's not having it, because two different concepts of having are involved. Hence it is senseless, in a way, for the Fregean to assert that he has something which nobody else has. He means to emphasize a contrast which, by his own lights, does not exist.

   Whatever might be the argument Wittgenstein has in mind, the exegetical problem at this stage consists rather in a surplus of prima facie feasible interpretations than in there being no plausible reading in sight. This will change as we move on. But before we continue, let us give a rough summary of the first paragraph of §398. The Fregean has not found a way of specifying, exactly and intelligibly, what he is talking about when he claims that he has it and is the only one who can have it. His attempt at demonstratively referring to 'it' was doomed to failure, and he has not yet offered anything more promising. Moreover, the very intelligibility of his use of the word 'have' has been challenged.

THE SECOND PARAGRAPH

At the beginning of the second paragraph, Wittgenstein gives the Fregean a second chance, or so it seems. Surprisingly, he turns very accommodating, assuring the Fregean of his understanding.

   But what, after all, is it that you are speaking of? I said already that I know inside what you mean.[9]

But Wittgenstein hastens to add that it is not an object or some kind of entity he knows (when he knows, 'inside', *what* the Fregean means). What he knows is rather this: how one feels and tends to behave and speak if one is under the spell of the Fregean's doctrine and tries to explain it.

> But what that meant is this: that I know how one thinks to conceive this object, to see it, to – as it were – refer to it by means of looking and gesturing. I know how one stares ahead and looks about one in this case – and other things as well.

Wittgenstein knows – or so he seems to want to say – what might be called the psychology of holding the Fregean's views, such as what it is like to feel the urge to say such things as the Fregean does say. Yet he does not accept the Fregean's claim that what he means (and what he means to refer to) is a certain entity of a special kind: namely his very own visual idea of the room. Nothing hinges here on 'the real existence' of a material room over and above his idea; his idea might, for the present purposes, be just as well merely an idea of imagination. (We are not concerned at present with any epistemological questions about how reliable ideas-of-a-room are with regard to there really being a room.) Wittgenstein now grants the Fregean a certain way of referring to what he has in mind:

> I think one can say: you are talking . . . of the 'visual room'.

This looks like a terminological concession, a concession which gives the Fregean new leeway for saying what (which object) he means. What does this leeway consist in? Of course, ideas – and among them visual images – on the Fregean conception are not rooms, and they are nothing that is like a room. The Fregean is well aware of this. Yet he is now given credit for describing his visual idea as if it were like a room; in order to mark the difference (between the idea and the real thing, if there is any), the entity previously meant to be referred to as THIS is now being called the *visual* room. This new terminological device seems to enable the Fregean, at last, to talk about his very own visual idea in just the way in which we commonly talk about a room we see or imagine; in describing it, we mention windows, heaters, and so on. The Fregean seems to be led back from his semantical impasse to the richness of the usual ways of making one's meaning intelligible. His use of the word 'THIS' was quite unforthcoming, even if accompanied by some looking around and other equally unhelpful behaviour. Wittgenstein now seems to grant him a terminological gimmick to make his point about the subjectivity of having ideas. He may talk about the *visual* room, making it thereby clear that he is not talking about rooms (namely '*material*' ones).

The Fregean may now, it seems, happily go along and describe what it is that he has. He might say: 'The visual room has two windows and a heater' and more of this kind. But wait a minute. Would it not be better to say: 'The visual room has two visual windows and a visual heater'? Heaters – real *material* heaters – seem to be the categorically wrong kind of equipment for *visual* rooms. Maybe he would be better off to take the pains of saying: 'The visual room has visually-two visual windows and visually-one visual heater.' Should the word 'has', in his description, be 'visualled' also, or has the visual room really got all of its visual furniture? – The Fregean may have a hard time figuring out exactly what is best to say. He has been offered a new way of expressing what he has in mind. But he must now make up his mind about how to put the new terminological devices to determinate use when it comes to describing his particular idea.

The problem the Fregean has to face resembles the problem of the early Cubists. Imagine Picasso and Braque, in late 1912, when they had just invented this new way of pictorial expression, having tried it out, so far, only on paintings representing fruits and musical instruments. Now imagine one of them popping one night into the other's studio and saying: 'How about a portrait of me in this new way?'. The other one would have faced a problem similar to the one that our Fregean has with respect to Wittgenstein's terminological offer. In a new idiom, various solutions to a seemingly straightforward problem of description (or depiction) may suggest themselves. A few sections later on, Wittgenstein characterizes the Fregean's predicament:

As if you had invented a new way of painting.

(§401)

The Cubists, eventually, came up with portraits of persons. May not the Fregean, eventually, come up with a description of the visual room? That seems to be the question at issue.

For the Fregean, there may be no determinate off-hand answer to the question of how to describe the visual room. But one thing is clear. He himself cannot be in the visual room. He knows Frege's doctrine by heart, and Frege says: 'I have an idea of myself but I am not this idea.'[10] And, in the same wonderful passage, Frege goes on to argue that one cannot be part of an idea that one has either. So, there is no place for a faithful Fregean within his visual room.

This is important to note because Wittgenstein immediately turns to the question of ownership again. Who has (or owns) the visual room? Let us take stock before we deal with this question. The Fregean found it hard to say, in the first round, what exactly it is that he (thinks he) has and what he means by saying that he has it. In the second round, he is granted room-talk; he may now fairly freely talk of windows and heaters (as long as he interposes a 'visual' or 'visually' here and there, in the right places). Still he must take a firm stance on the question in what way and in what sense he has the visual room. Otherwise his claim that he *has* something would be as dubious as his descriptions of what he claims to have. And the first thing, on this topic, to put on record is this: he cannot visually-have it, whatever exactly this might be. For in order to visually-have the visual room, the Fregean would have to be inside it. At least he would have to be an entity that can, in principle, be met in the realm of those 'visual' things. But, as we just observed, there is no place for the Fregean within the visual room (and not even within the visual space). The Fregean is no idea, and he is no idea-like entity either. 'The visual Fregean' does not denote the Fregean. But the word 'I', when used by the Fregean, denotes the Fregean himself and none of his visual counterparts.

So then it seems that if the Fregean has the visual room at all, he must, according to his doctrine, have it from the outside. (It must be he himself who has the visual room.) But how could he have it this way, namely, in the way that ordinary material rooms are possessed? There is no obvious answer. For material rooms can, at least in principle, be owned by different people; and it must be distinctive of a visual room that it can, in principle, have only one owner. In what other way may the Fregean claim to have the visual room from the outside? Maybe in such a way as regular material pictures of rooms (be it pictures of rooms, be it pictures of imagined rooms) are possessed? Again, this does not work, and for the same reason: material pictures can be owned by different people, at least in principle.

What else can the Fregean offer in order to elucidate in what sense and in what way he has the visual room? I do not know. The Fregean definitely has a problem at this point. For it is part of his doctrine that he cannot be in the visual room; hence if he has it, he must, so to speak, have it from outside; and if he has it from the outside, the question arises why anybody else is logically excluded from having it. But has it been shown that he cannot come up with an answer? Might he not, as things stand right now, find a way of describing the visual room which makes it acceptable (or at least makes intelligible what he means by saying) that (a) he has it, (b) nobody else can have it, and (c) there is no reason to deny its existence? The Fregean might be very inventive and clever.[11]

But Wittgenstein is at once very apodictic. As soon as he has granted 'visual room' terminology, he continues:

That which has no owner is the 'visual room'.

This is surprising. Here Wittgenstein pounds out his conclusion even before he tries to provide an argument. What he subsequently offers as an argument for this claim is even more surprising. Here is what he says:

I can as little own it (the visual room) as I can walk about it, or look at it, or point to it.

This does not mean that the Fregean cannot own the visual room *because* he cannot walk about it, look at it, or whatever. Wittgenstein has merely repeated his claim. The reason he offers for it is this:

It does not belong to me insofar as it cannot belong to anybody else.

Wittgenstein has made this point before (in the first paragraph). The point is forceful, however, only as long as the Fregean, with regard to sentences of the type

(v) x has y

prefers an analysis like

(vii) $Has_x(x,y)$

to an analysis like

(vi) $Has(x,y_x)$.

An analysis like (vii) burdens the having-relation with the task of guaranteeing exactly-one-havership; an analysis like (vi) does not. If the Fregean adopts (vii), his claim is that there is a special relation of having which, as it were, glues an idea to only one person. This analysis (let us call it *the sticky relation account*) assigns a peculiar meaning to the word 'have' in sentences of type (v). In the first paragraph, Wittgenstein attacked such an analysis. But the Fregean is not forced to opt for the sticky relation account. He may instead prefer an analysis like (vi) which we might call *the sticky objects account*. In this case, the having-relation that he talks about in sentences of type (v) does not carry the weight of logically guaranteeing that an idea is had by only one person. This is to say: in case the Fregean chooses the sticky-objects account, he may well claim that the word 'have', as it occurs in sentences of type (v), has its ordinary meaning – it does not do any extra semantical work. So the Fregean might reply to Wittgenstein's last remark that it attacks the wrong target. What is at issue in the second round, he might hold, is not the sticky relation account; this was dealt with in the first round. The issue of the second round ought to be: can the sticky objects account be rendered intelligible by means of the new terminology? Is there a way to elucidate the content of 'I have the visual room', as this sentence is used by the Fregean, in accordance with the Fregean conception of ideas, namely as a contingently true proposition (about the obtaining of an ordinary relation between the Fregean and some sticky object) which entails that nobody else stands in that relation to this object?

In brief, as long as Wittgenstein concentrates on what it is to have something, he may either doubt the intelligibility of the Fregean's new way of using the word 'to have' (in this case, he attacks the sticky relation account only), or he may claim that 'to have', in the ordinary sense of this word, does not apply to sticky objects. In the second case, Wittgenstein also attacks the sticky-objects account – but only by making a sweeping linguistic claim for which he has not yet offered any good reason. Wittgenstein goes on:

> Or: it (the visual room) does not belong to me insofar as I want to apply the same form of expression to it as to the very material room in which I sit.

To this the Fregean ought to object. He does not want to apply 'the same form of expression' to the visual room as to the material room. By courtesy of Wittgenstein, he has his 'visual'-proviso. As we have seen, the details of this proviso may still be highly unclear, but it has not yet been shown to be for the birds. As a rebuttal of Wittgenstein's charge, the Fregean may point out that the material room can be described as having two windows but that the same form of description does not apply to the visual room: it has two visual windows instead. So Wittgenstein's objection seems not to be valid.

What else does Wittgenstein offer at this stage of his argument? He adds a rather strange remark:

> The description of the latter [i.e. the material room] need not mention an owner, in fact it need not have an owner. But then the visual room *cannot* have one.

This remark is strange because it looks like a humdrum *non-sequitur*. There seem to be two readings for the remark. The first reading is this: (xv) entails (xvi).

(xv) The description of the material room need not to mention an owner.
(xvi) The visual room cannot have an owner.

The second reading is that (xvi) follows from (xvii).

(xvii) The material room has (or may have) no owner.

Obviously, both readings fail to yield a good argument because the alleged entailment-relations simply do not obtain. I fail to see what the suppressed premiss might be which could impress the Fregean. Wittgenstein adds:

> 'For it (the visual room) has no master within it or without it', one might say.

One might say this. But then one still has not given an argument. The Fregean already knows that he cannot own the visual room from within it. But where is the argument to show that he cannot own it from outside either?

To sum up our findings in the second paragraph of §398, the Fregean may well feel undefeated by Wittgenstein's objections. Even if one concedes that Wittgenstein has raised serious problems for the sticky relation account in the first paragraph, one may still have some hope of saving sticky objects. Certainly, the Fregean has not yet found a convincing way of describing his visual idea in such a manner that makes it plain that only he can have it (in the full normal sense of 'having'). But on the other hand, Wittgenstein has not, in this section, offered a knock-down argument against the sticky objects account.

THE THIRD PARAGRAPH

> Think of a picture of a landscape, an imaginary landscape with a house in it – and someone were to ask 'Whose house is that?' – The answer, by the way, might be: 'It belongs to the farmer who is sitting on the bench in front on it.' But then he cannot, for example, enter his house.

This is the last paragraph of §398. There are three kinds of difficulties I have in trying to understand this little passage. The first concerns the question what Wittgenstein is up to. What role is this paragraph supposed to have in the context of the whole section? Is it meant to support, by way of illustration, a point that has been made already? Or is it meant to add something new which has not yet been pointed out?

My second question is: what exactly are we invited to do? What is it that Wittgenstein suggests to the reader? How, for example, are we supposed to imagine the little scene in order to render the answer ('It belongs to the farmer. . .') appropriate?

A third question is this: what is this paragraph about? Is it about the concept of possession? Is it about the distinction between 'in the picture' and 'in reality'? Is it about identity (e.g. about identity conditions for farmers, for farmers as they are pictured, and for picture-farmers)? Or is it about essence (e.g. about questions like the following: 'Is it part of this farmer's essence that he is sitting in front of the house?')

I shall begin with the second question – not because I have a definite answer to it but rather because there is something quite irritating about this little paragraph which I want to point out right at the outset. Imagine the following. Harvey and I have just entered a room in a museum. It contains paintings which have been assembled for an exhibition announced as *Imaginary Landscapes in the Sixteenth Century*. There are paintings by Flemish artists and by the Danube school, and right now we stand in front of a painting which shows a farmhouse in a beautiful scenic setting. In front of the house there is a farmer sitting on a bench. Harvey asks, 'Whose house is that?'. This little scenario is meant to fit the first sentence of the last paragraph:

> Think of a picture of a landscape, an imaginary landscape with a house in it – and somebody were to ask 'Whose house is that?'

Harvey's question may be a little strange, but serious problems of understanding start with Wittgenstein's next sentence:

> The answer, by the way, might be: 'It belongs to the farmer who is sitting on the bench in front of it.'

Whose answer is that? Here are three cases. First case: it is my answer; I amuse myself with giving a stupid answer to a question which I consider stupid. I do not know anything of relevance about the painter; what I know about the painting is just what I see in front of me. Second case: it is the best answer at hand; as it happens, a specialist on these paintings stands right next to us; he has overheard Harvey's question and is kind enough to give this answer. Third case: it is the right answer.

Which case is meant by Wittgenstein? Not the first one, for he would have expressed himself differently; he would have written 'Now somebody might answer. . .', or something like that. Most probably not the second case as distinct from the third, or the third as opposed to the second; again, Wittgenstein would have been careful enough to say more clearly which one of the two remaining cases is meant if his argument were to draw on one of them specifically.

What makes the specialist's answer (about whose house it is) correct? Let us assume that the farmer in the picture is as imaginary as the rest (once again, it is reasonable to assume this because otherwise Wittgenstein should have said explicitly that it is only the landscape which is imaginary). What makes it correct to say that the imaginary farmer in question owns the imaginary house? Obviously, facts about the painter and the painting. Here is what the specialist tells us: this big key which hangs down from the farmer's belt is, in the school to which the painter of this picture belongs, a conventional means to indicate house-owner-ship; moreover, there are passages in the painter's diary and letters in which he refers to the farmer as the owner of the house. And what the specialist tells us is true.

But why, for heaven's sake, should we now conclude that the farmer cannot enter his house? Is he lame? Nothing we have heard so far seems to justify this conclusion. The only way to justify this claim about the farmer's handicap is to introduce further information about the painting. (The picture clearly illustrates, say, a very popular fairytale about a farmer and his bewitched house which he could not enter.) Wittgenstein mentions nothing of this kind. Obviously he means to claim that

(xviii) Given that it is correct to say that the house in question belongs to the farmer in question, still it follows from what has been said so far about the farmer and the house that he cannot enter it.[12]

Offhand, I see no other way of reading the last two sentences of §398. But this reading is very poor. For, first, what is claimed in (xviii) is highly implausible and, second, it does not fit in the context of this section.

To make vivid what I find immediately irritating about the third paragraph, think again of the little museum-scenario. The specialist has just presented his reasons for saying that the house belongs to the farmer, and now Harvey remarks, about the farmer in question, 'But then he cannot, for example, enter his house'. We should be baffled by such a strange comment. Given the previous conversation with the specialist, it is at least eccentric and unwarranted to draw such a conclusion. Harvey must be joking.

Is Wittgenstein joking? But what could be the joke's point? Well, it would be a wonderful point if it were about the impossibility of having ideas from the outside. Such a point is exactly what is still missing in this section. So we might try to read the third paragraph as follows. The house in question corresponds (in Wittgenstein's parable) to the visual room. Nobody outside the picture can own this house, not even the owner of the picture. A house of this kind cannot be owned. And even if we say that it is owned by somebody inside the picture (for example by the farmer in question), we do not mean that literally; for the farmer in question cannot, literally speaking, even enter this house. When we say that he owns it, we are speaking in scare-quotes. Transferring this point back to the visual room (and, more generally, to all ideas in the Fregean's sense), the result is: it is completely out of the question to speak of an idea as being had (or of the visual room as being owned) from the outside, that is, by a real person; and it is at best a metaphorical way of putting things if we say that it is had from the inside, for nothing which is in the realm of ideas can literally be said to own anything.

But this is not a feasible interpretation for the third paragraph. Wittgenstein very clearly does not deal there with the question whether the house in the picture can be owned from the outside. Furthermore, he appears to have no misgivings about the answer to the question whose house it is. On the contrary, accepting this answer is the point of departure for the subsequent remark about the farmer's not being able to enter *his* house.

So let us try another interpretation. It goes like this:

The picture is a product of the painter's imagination, and that is to say, among other things: there is no flesh-and-blood farmer and no stone-and-brick house which are represented. If, in spite of this, we speak here of a farmer and a house, then what we mean is a *picture-farmer* and a *picture-house*. (The qualifying prefix 'picture' in front of 'farmer' and 'house' corresponds to the qualifying prefix 'visual' in front of 'room' and 'window'.) The picture-farmer is no flesh-and-blood farmer, but he is no material part of the painting either: he is no oil-on-canvas farmer. In calling him a picture-farmer, 'picture' refers to the *pictura*, not to the *tabula colorata* of the painting. Compared to a flesh-and-blood farmer or to the oil-on-canvas farmer, the picture-farmer is fairly intangible. Where is he? What is his mode of existence? What is his *principium individuationis*? His very nature gives rise to many difficult questions. One of these questions is: what properties can be attributed to him? Flesh-and-blood farmers can do lots of things: sow and plough, feed the cattle, breed horses, and so on. Moreover, in weaker senses of 'can', they can do a variety of things: they can age, they can have sisters and they can own a house. Oil-on-canvas farmers are more passively gifted: they can lose their brightness, they can be photographed, transported and restored, and much more of this variety. What is it that a picture-farmer can 'do'? Well, he can for example sit on picture benches, in front of picture-houses (which may, or may not, be owned by him). Now if a picture-farmer sits in front of a picture-house, can he enter it?

No, he cannot. For it is part of his essence to do only those things that he may be recognized, by looking at the material picture, to be doing. What he cannot be seen to do in the picture, he cannot do at all. For he owes his existence, identity and essence to the material picture (and in particular to the oil-on-canvas farmer who is part of it). All his possible doings have to be in accordance with what actually is to be seen in the picture. Can he think of his wife? Yes, for nothing which is to be seen in the picture is in conflict with his doing this. Now, if he sits in front of a picture-house, can he own it?

Yes, he can. For owning is not a doing, therefore his owning the picture house is not in conflict with what is to be seen in the picture. The crucial difference between owning the picture house and entering it is this: this very painting allows for a house-owning farmer (or, if you wish, for a picture house-owning picture-farmer); not one brushstroke would have to be added or changed to make it a picture of an imaginary farmer-who-owns-the-house-in-front-of-which-he-sits. But entering the house is different; this very painting does not allow for a house-entering farmer. It takes a different painting to produce a picture of an imaginary farmer-who-enters-his-house. But a different painting generates a new picture-farmer, therefore the original picture-farmer cannot enter the picture-house even if he owns it.

What might be said in favour of this interpretation? First, it solves the problem of how to reconcile the last two sentences of §398, which seemed to be incoherent. This interpretation acknowledges that Wittgenstein wants to claim that (xviii) is true, and it makes sense of this claim. Second, it seems to fit in nicely with other occasional remarks that suggest that Wittgenstein took a strong line with regard to what is in a picture and what is not.[13]

But this interpretation has its drawbacks. First of all, the metaphysical account behind it (whatever its details may be) is hard to swallow for somebody who sticks to our common ways of looking at, and talking about, pictures. Certainly, given our usual ways of looking at pictures of imaginary situations and talking about them, the farmer can enter his house. Comic strips prove this immediately: nobody (except maybe a philosopher) would dream of talking about Donald, the very imaginary duck, in the way that this interpretation forces us to speak about the imaginary farmer. Second, the metaphysical account behind this interpretation is not very attractive even for a philosopher who does not care too much about how we commonly look at pictures and talk about them. For the construct of the picture-farmer seems half-hearted, philosophically speaking; it seems to be an ad hoc entity which, on the one hand, can own a house (if only with scare-quotes around the house and the owning) but on the other hand *cannot* enter it (not even with scare-quotes around 'enter' and 'it'). But the reconciliation of the last two sentences of the third paragraph has drawn exactly on this hybrid nature of the picture farmer; he may own but he cannot enter, *whichever way one prefers to distribute one's scare quotes.*

For this, to be sure, is a basic exegetical problem of the last paragraph of §398: the same farmer (whatever his essence might be) is said both to own the house (if only in scare-quotes) and not to be able to enter it (if only in scare-quotes, again). No farmer-switch between the two sentences is consistent with Wittgenstein's words. In the last sentence of the paragraph he speaks of the same farmer as in the sentence before; the anaphorical pronoun 'he' can only refer to the farmer who was said to own the house in question. There being no flesh-and-blood farmer, we are left with two possible choices: (a) the oil-on-canvas farmer, and (b) some other entity, for convenience called 'the picture farmer'. With regard to (a) the sad fact is that the oil-on-canvas farmer cannot literally be said to own the house in question. But the even sadder fact is this: if he somehow (in scare-quotes of indeterminate meaning) can be said to 'own' the house, he can as well – equally well or equally badly – be said to be able to 'enter' the house. This deadlock eventually, and inevitably, leads to the picture farmer. This, after all, is nothing but an entity that can coherently be said to be an owner (or an 'owner') without being able to enter (or 'enter') its possession. If Wittgenstein were dependent upon some such entity, we might as well believe in Fregean ideas.

A third, and particularly serious, drawback of the interpretation in question is that our overall exegetical problem is not solved. This interpretation may yield a coherent reading of the third paragraph, taken in isolation, but what can it contribute to understanding the whole section? How does the third paragraph, in the light of this interpretation, relate to the rest of the section? How could Wittgenstein hope to persuade the Fregean to get rid of his conception of ideas by drawing on such a strange construction as the picture farmer?

One guess is this. The picture-farmer is a typical Fregean's construct, very much like the visual room and other ideas. When it comes to individuating ideas, the Fregean naturally draws on their content. He insists that the visual room is not a room, but in describing it, the Fregean resorts to idioms that are appropriate, in the first place and without qualification, only for the description of rooms. It is qualities of material rooms which he attributes, if only in scare-quotes, to the visual room. Yet the Fregean must be able to indicate clearly when he is speaking literally and when he is speaking in scare-quotes (or using his 'visual'-modifier). The same holds for the picture-farmer; in describing him, we naturally bring in predicates that, in the first place and without qualification, apply only to people. Because we find it so easy and natural to talk this way, we have a tendency to reify the picture-farmer, to think of 'him' as something over and above the oil-on-canvas farmer. Nevertheless, there is nothing but the oil-on-canvas farmer and our ways of looking at pictures and talking about them. There is no farmer-like entity which is quasi-depicted. There is no picture-farmer, but just a farmer picture with no pictured farmer. He who believes in the picture-farmer misconstrues his way of looking at pictures and talking about them as being confronted with (and referring to) an intangible object. He who believes in Fregean ideas does exactly the same. He misconstrues, for example, his seeing or imagining a room as being confronted with ('having') an object: the visual room.[14]

All this is fine and in harmony with what Wittgenstein says in the next few sections of the *Philosophical Investigations*. But it is not a satisfactory interpretation of the last paragraph of §398. For this interpretation does not elucidate the puzzling wording of the paragraph, and it offers no answer to our pending question: what exactly is Wittgenstein's argument against the Fregean's sticky-objects account?

Let us get back to the puzzling wording first. According to the interpretation just envisaged, Wittgenstein's point is highly general: visual rooms are philosophical monsters of the same kind as picture-farmers; they are the products of a tendency to reify ways of dealing with things. To make this point, Wittgenstein would not have needed to commit himself to such a strange claim as (xviii), nor to imply that the Fregean is committed to it. In so far as Wittgenstein could easily have made this general point much more clearly without bringing in problems of ownership at all, it is doubtful that this is what he is driving at in this passage.

Now what about the still pending question regarding the Fregean's sticky-objects account of his position? Again, the interpretation under consideration offers no satisfactory answer. A satisfactory answer would be an attempt at showing that Fregean ideas cannot, in principle, be described in such a way that their essential subjectivity (their essentially being had by exactly one person) is intelligible. No such attempt is made in this paragraph, according to the interpretation.

So the third paragraph remains puzzling. And we have not found anything in it that could be taken as the argument that Wittgenstein implicitly claims to have presented: an argument to the effect that the visual room cannot be owned from the outside. In the next section, Wittgenstein makes an even stronger claim: the owner of the visual room is not in it, and there is no outside. Certainly, if there were no outside then the visual room could not be owned from the outside. Translating Wittgenstein's statement back into the Fregean's terminology, we get this: whoever has a particular idea is not part of the idea, and ideas are all there is. The Fregean, not being an idealist of any kind, would deny the second part.

But maybe Wittgenstein's argument in §398 after all – and contrary to what we have assumed so far – is directed exclusively against an idealist version of the Fregean conception of the nature of ideas. This does not seem very plausible, since Wittgenstein quite naturally speaks of the material room in the second paragraph; and this would be a flagrant *petitio* if he wanted to refute a certain form of idealism.

In light of our considerations, Wittgenstein in §398 has failed to present an argument that shows that ideas, as conceived by the Fregean, cannot be had.

NOTES

* When I wrote this paper in 1989, the only publication which dealt with §398 of *PI* was P.M.S. Hacker's *Insight and Illusion*, Oxford, Clarendon Press, 1986. Hacker discussed §398 only in the context of Wittgenstein's reflections on solipsism. I find this approach interesting but not fully adequate, as will soon become clear.

If I were to write such a paper today (i.e. two years later), I would certainly try to defend my somewhat negative conclusions against Eike von Savigny's careful and stimulating interpretation (see his *Wittgensteins 'Philosophische Untersuchungen'*, vol. 2, Frankfurt am Main, Vittorio Klostermann, 1989) and Hacker's new exegesis, *Wittgenstein. Meaning and Minds*, Oxford, 1990. Doing this would require a new paper, whereas all I want to do here is to add a footnote to *this* one – and to express my gratitude to Jay Rosenberg and Katia Saporiti for valuable comments on an earlier version of it.

1 Karl Leonard Reinhold, *Versuch einer neuen Theorie des menschlichen Vorstellungsvermoegens*, Jena, 1789, p. 190.

2 Cf. G. Frege, *Die Grundlagen der Arithmetik*, Breslau, 1884, §61. A similar point is made by Berkeley in the middle of the last of the *Three Dialogues Between Hylas and Philonous*. Put in Fregean terminology, Berkeley points out that to speak of ideas being *in* the mind is just to say that they are *had*. Of course, Berkeley would not have accepted Frege's terminology, because his arguments for immaterialism presuppose that ideas can be seen, heard, and so on. Although Frege and Berkeley are in agreement about the conceptual question whether ideas literally can be said to be anywhere, they disagree on the question whether material objects exist and can be sensed.

3 That is, of course, to say: name an idea-token, and you've picked out its haver. We are here concerned only with ideas as particular mental occurrences.

4 Cf. The *Blue Book* and *NFL*, for example. But see also *PR*, §61 and §71, and the *Brown Book* (*BB* p. 175), where our topic is discussed, although solipsism is not at issue.

While on the subject, let me add that neutral monism is not at issue either in §398, although it seems not unreasonable to assume that the first two paragraphs of this section were inspired by a passage in William James's essay 'Does "Consciousness" Exist?'. In the second part of this essay, James argues for a position which, with regard to experiences, avoids any dualism of what he calls *consciousness* and *content*: 'If the reader will take his own experiences, he will see what I mean. Let him begin with a perceptual experience, the "presentation", so called, of a physical object, his actual field of vision, the room he sits in'. This perceptual experience James calls the *'pure experience of the room'*. The ontological nature of such a 'pure experience' he wants to leave open, in this passage, for

[t]he one self-identical thing has so many relations to the rest of

experience that you can . . . treat it as belonging with opposite contexts. In one of these contexts it is your 'field of vision'; in another it is 'the room in which you sit' . . . . The presentation, the experience, the *that* in short (for until we have decided *what* it is it must be a mere *that*) . . . [a]s a room . . . has occupied that spot and had that environment for thirty years. As your field of consciousness it may never have existed until now. As a room, attention will go on to discover endless new details in it. As your mental state merely, few new ones will emerge under attention's eye. As a room, it will take an earthquake . . . in any case a certain amount of time, to destroy it. As your subjective state, the closing of your eyes, or any instantaneous play of your fancy will suffice. . . . As an outer object, you must pay so much a month to inhabit it. As an inner content, you may occupy it for any length of time rent-free.

(William James, *Essays in Radical Empiricism*, Cambridge, MA: Harvard University Press, 1912, 1976, pp. 7–9)

There are striking parallels between the way James puts his point in this passage and how Wittgenstein's interlocutor in §398 expresses what he means. Yet Wittgenstein does not address neutral monism. At most, he borrows from James a way of making vivid what he is trying to get at.

5 Cf. G. Frege, 'Über Sinn und Bedeutung' (*Kleine Schriften*, p. 146) and 'Der Gedanke' (*Kleine Schriften*, p. 352) – for the English translation, see G. Frege, *Collected Papers on Mathematics, Logic, and Philosophy*, ed. B. McGuinness, trans. M. Black, *et al.*, Oxford, Blackwell, 1984: 'On Sense and Meaning' (pp. 159f) and 'The Thought' (pp. 361f).

6 Occasionally my translation differs from E. Anscombe's.

7 Cf. *BB* pp. 171–4, where Wittgenstein remarks in a related context:

I mean the sentence, 'I see this', as it is sometimes contemplated by us when we are brooding over certain philosophical problems. We are then, say, holding on to a particular visual impression by staring at some object, and we feel it is most natural to say to ourselves 'I see this', though we know of no further use we can make of this sentence.

8 Frege might well have been impressed by this argument. At the end of §49 of his *Grundlagen der Arithmetik* he argues that if you cannot deny an existential statement, the affirmation of it would lose its content.

9 As far as I can see, Wittgenstein has not said this before in *PI*. Maybe this mistaken reference is a relic from an earlier version which contained such a remark.

10 Cf. 'Der Gedanke', *Kleine Schriften*, p. 357 ('The Thought', op. cit., p. 366).

11 The visual room, under the Fregean's analysis, might turn out to be something like the common cold: (a) whoever catches it has (caught) it; (b) nobody else can catch – or subsequently 'have' – the very same

(token of a) cold; and (c) there is no reason to deny the existence of the cold-token which has been caught. This is a funny way of talking about catching a cold, but the Fregean might find more convincing examples.

12 'It follows from what has been said so far . . .' is my long-winded attempt at capturing what Wittgenstein means by the word 'then' in the last sentence of §398.

13. Cf. his reservation about saying that something must be boiling in the pictured pot, even if pictured steam comes out of the pictured pot (*PI*, §297), and about saying that the pictured rock supports the pictured castle (*RFM*, VII, §16).

14 Cf. *PI*, §401.

Chapter 9

Making contact in language: the harmony between thought and reality[1]

Robert L. Arrington

For many years, §445 of the *Philosophical Investigations* struck me as one of Wittgenstein's more enigmatic remarks: 'It is in language that an expectation and its fulfillment make contact.' What could this possibly mean? After rummaging around in some of Wittgenstein's other works, I gradually came to see what (I think) Wittgenstein is saying here. I even came to the conclusion that this remark helps us understand the concept of representation as it was developed in the middle period works in reaction to what was said about it in the *Tractatus*.[2] But it is only recently that I have come to look upon §445 as the key to an important series of remarks in the *Investigations* itself. It is, I now think, an interpretative filter that yields an understanding of some even more enigmatic comments about the queerness of thought and the harmony between thought and reality.

There is a clearly demarcated series of interconnected remarks in the *Investigations* beginning at §428 and ending at §465. The series opens with the interlocutor's puzzled expression 'This queer thing, thought', and it closes with a section whose initial comment is again that of the interlocutor, now speaking as confident metaphysician: 'An expectation is so made that whatever happens has to accord with it, or not.' In responding to this last comment, Wittgenstein seems to accept it, rephrasing it, to be sure, at least quasi-linguistically and adding a typical qualification warning against hasty generalization. The remark about expectation and its fulfillment making contact in language occurs about halfway between §428 and §465, as if it were the peak that we struggle to ascend, and from which we then confidently descend. What I offer here is one tour guide's commentary, and one of many possible tours, up and down this peak.

How queer thought is, how odd that it can deal 'with the very object *itself*' (§428). This fantastic ability we thinkers have, to use thought to grasp things in the world! 'We feel as if by means of it we had caught reality in our net' (§428). How can our minds, here in our heads and bodies, think about, be in contact with, the things *out there* beyond the boundaries of the skin? And the mystery compounds itself when we contemplate the fact that we here and now can think of things that themselves do not exist here and now: things in the past, things that exist no more; and things in the future, things that so far have never existed. Queerest of all, perhaps, is the fact that we can think of what *never* exists: we can have false thoughts.

Someone surveying the disappointing history of philosophical reflection on thought and reality might well conclude that thought *is* a queer thing, defying as it does the best efforts of some of the best minds of our species to understand it.[3] Or such a spectator might think this history ludicrous and suggest that it amounts to little more than the compounding of confusion. That, of course, is Wittgenstein's view. After all, he tells us in §428, 'thought does not strike us as mysterious while we are thinking'. And as he says in the *Philosophical Grammar*, 'It isn't while we're *looking at* it that it seems a strange process' (*PG* p. 154). G.E. Moore might have confessed that he never found thought mysterious until he took some philosophy courses. And Wittgenstein might have agreed, for he tells us that it is only when we reflect upon thought (retrospectively and philosophically) that it strikes us as odd. He would have us consider the possibility that the obscurity of the subject is the result of the shadow cast by the inquirer himself!

After noting in §428 the queer appearance of thought to reflective minds, Wittgenstein immediately passes on in §429 to a remark about the harmony of thought and reality. Although the details of this remark are obscure and can best be understood by returning to them later, the spirit of the remark is clear. It alerts us to one important way that thought may seem to be such a queer thing: the way it once appeared problematic to Wittgenstein. Wittgenstein speaks in §429 of the harmony or *agreement* of thought and reality, and the latter is a notion that concerned him throughout his philosophical career. In the *Tractatus*, he

developed a picture theory of representation which explained the
agreement of thought (and language) with reality in terms of an
agreement in form. The elements of a thought and a proposition
must have the same forms as the objects in the world they
designate, form being understood as the possibility of entering
into certain combinations, with, respectively, other names and
other objects. A proposition can be neither true nor false unless
there is an agreement in form between its elements and the
elements constituting the substance of the world.

As we know, Wittgenstein abandoned this picture theory of
thought and language upon his return to philosophy in the late
1920s. With it went those feelers that were names and those
logical forms that permitted thought to be in agreement with
reality. In the place of pictures having logical form, we are given
autonomous language games, *all* of whose elements are to be
explained linguistically and none of which can be justified by
showing that it agrees with or reflects reality. And now the
question arises: where are we to find the agreement between
thought and reality that allows us to think of reality and catch it
in our net? It seems clear that §§428–65 represent Wittgenstein's
attempt to come to grips in his later thinking with the issue of
the agreement between thought and reality. In these sections he
continues to explore a topic that had long concerned him and
which now, in his post-Tractarian days, could be experienced
with greater urgency.

As we leave the periphery and enter the midlands of §§428–65,
the topic under discussion is language and how it allows us to
say things about the world. The first thing we note is that
language may appear to fail in this task. Sections 430–5 give us a
number of examples of these apparent failures. To begin with,
there are rulers (§430) and signs (§432) that appear dead. The
ruler that is put against an object may seem to tell us nothing; it
just lies there, dumbly, unable to achieve what thought achieves.
The sign *by itself* seems dead, unable, like thought, to point to
something, identify it, characterize it, or produce understanding
(§433). Likewise, there are gestures that try to portray but fail to
do so (§434). The ruler is just an inert physical body, so how does
it tell us anything? And the sign is just a sound or set of ink
marks, the gesture just a physical motion – how can they convey
information, represent things, and portray how they are? The
physical entities are complete in and of themselves and so do not

take us beyond themselves – to the other things of this world.
Sentences, of course, are just collections of signs, so how is it that
they manage to represent (§435)? They themselves are just
complex objects, or facts, complete in themselves. And if we give
a verbal order, how do we get from language to *action* (§§431,
433)? If we try to explain what we want done, even by acting out
the execution, what we produce are mere motions which in
themselves say nothing. Viewed from this perspective, it looks,
Wittgenstein wryly comments, 'as if the order were beginning to
stammer' (§433).

Let us try to be a bit clearer about Wittgenstein's reasons for
thinking that language can appear to be dead. The rulers, signs,
motions, and so on appear to fail because *they are not thoughts*
and *not like thoughts*. Thoughts are always thoughts *of* something else, and hence they point beyond themselves. Thoughts
reach out and grasp reality; they latch on to individuals in the
world (such as, 'the thought of *him*'); and they take the measure
of things (such as, 'I was thinking that he should arrive soon').
But any descriptions of the physical instruments of thought – the
rulers, gestures, signs, and sentences – are, on the contrary, self-
contained; they describe the physical instruments in terms of
their own properties alone. They make no reference to *other
things*. Which is to say these physical instruments of thought do
not point beyond themselves, as thoughts do. How, then, can
they serve as instruments of thought? Don't our words fall dead
from our lips?[4]

Something has gone wrong, for surely our signs are alive and
well – full of import and effect. We can easily be tempted here by
the notion of hidden, behind-the-scenes mental processes that
bestow meaning on our signs, and when this manoeuvre leads us
into a philosophical dead-end (§435), we can be misled even more
egregiously by the hocus-pocus of soul magic (§454). Wittgenstein's own way out of our puzzlement is through the land of
wishes – with a brief pass by that imposing and unavoidable
tablet of stone known as the hardness of the logical must. This
landscape, however, is hardly filled with light but rather is itself
obscure and disconcerting. We must wander for a while before we
get our bearings.

Section 437 tells us: 'A wish seems already to know what will or
would satisfy it; a proposition, a thought, what makes it true –
even when that thing is not there at all!'[5] This is, at first sight, a

very remarkable ability. How can a wish know (how can we who have the wish know) exactly what, as yet non-existent, event would satisfy it? How can we prophesy about the future, and with such confidence as to assert that exactly *this* would satisfy our wish? Indeed, how can we go so far as to say, as we do, that this event *must* occur if our wish is to be satisfied? 'Whence this *determining* of what is not yet there? This despotic demand? ("The hardness of the logical must")' (§437). The reference to the logical must alerts us to the fact that it is *logically required* that a certain event take place if a particular wish is to be satisfied. But this surely is not at first apparent. How can there be a logical connection between a wish and the event fulfilling it? The latter may not even occur. Whether a wish is satisfied is a contingent matter – is it not also a contingent matter that a particular event does satisfy it? A wish, after all, is just a *wish*, a mere psychological occurrence, often whimsical and frequently unrealistic – who knows what would satisfy it? How could such a flimsy thing have such an impact on the future that a very specific later event, a substantial occurrence in the world, must occur if the wish is to be fulfilled? At this point, the allusion to the logical must just serves to thicken the fog settling over the land of wishes.

Section 438 begins the constructive task of elucidating wishes and expectations by telling us that they are 'unsatisfied' and by explaining this in the following way: 'expectation is unsatisfied, because it is the expectation of something'. It is an expectation of something real, something outside the process of expectation. A wish is unsatisfied by virtue of being a wish for something that has not yet occurred, and if this something later occurs, the wish is thereby satisfied or fulfilled. But that a wish is *un*satisfied does not mean that one feels unsatisfied until it is fulfilled. And its being satisfied in this sense does not mean that there occur feelings of satisfaction upon the occurrence of the event fulfilling it. Thus, 'Perhaps I should not have been satisfied if my wish had been satisfied' (§441). Finally, in saying that I wish, for example, for an apple, I am not expressing a belief that an apple will quell a feeling of nonsatisfaction I have. I am stating *what* I wish for, not predicting or conjecturing about what might have a certain effect on me at a future time. If I were doing the latter, the question could arise as to whether I really know what would produce this effect. How can I be so confident that an apple will quell my feeling of nonsatisfaction? Some apples are sour; some palates are jaded. But 'the question whether I know what I wish before my wish is fulfilled cannot arise at all' (§441). This question cannot arise because I can be in no doubt about the matter. If I wish for an apple, it makes no *sense* to say that I doubt whether this is what I really wish for.[6]

In §442 interesting questions are raised about the relationship between an expectation and the event that fulfills or satisfies it. Let us say that I expect a shot, and that in fact the shot occurs and my expectation is fulfilled. What kind of 'agreement' exists between the expectation and the shot? The most radical proposal is that the agreement is one of numerical identity: the actual shot 'somehow' already existed in the expectation. If we fail to get a grip on this notion,[7] we might suggest that some parts or aspects of the event expected are already in the expectation (MS 108, p. 213 – cited by Hallett). But no, it was the whole shot I was expecting! Another possibility is this: the shot occurs and at the same time I feel certain feelings of satisfaction. This will not work either, however, because it is the shot I expect and not the feelings; if the former had not occurred but the latter had, the expectation would not have been fulfilled.

Section 443 is a tough, but critical, passage. We jump from expectation to imagination, not knowing how we get there and not for the moment making much sense of what we find. The question is raised whether the red you imagine is the same, or the same thing, as the red you see in front of you. If not, then how can the red in front of you turn out to be what you imagined? Surely we might want on some occasion to say that it *is* the same. But if so, how are we to comprehend this? How could the red you see in front of you, the actual colour of some real object, already be in your imagination? If it were, would it not be an imagined red instead of a real red? And wouldn't the imagined red be a somewhat paler red, less vivid than the real thing? (*BB* p. 60). But no, if I imagined a paler red than what is in front of me, then I did not imagine just this colour now in front of me. In point of fact, however, I did imagine this very colour. How so? Did I have an image in my mind that is itself the same red colour? No, my image was an image *of* a red colour, not a red image.

Wittgenstein proposes to dissolve the mystery by way of analogy:

But haven't we an analogous case with the propositions 'Here is a red patch' and 'Here there isn't a red patch'? The word 'red' occurs in both: so this word cannot indicate the presence of something red.

(§443)

Here I have always had the feeling that this passage 'just goes by too fast'. There is, however, an echo in it of the heretofore unexplained §429 where we heard of the harmony between thought and reality. Maybe we are making progress. How, then, are we to understand this passage from §443? In the following way, I suggest. We can use the word 'red' to refer to or describe the *absence* of something red; hence merely using the word does not imply that there is something red present. It follows that if my imagining red somehow involved the use of the word 'red', this would not require that there actually be something red in my imagination. At the same time, if my imagining red involved the use of the word 'red', that might help explain why we are tempted to think that imagining red requires that red be in the imagination, for there is a temptation, surely among philosophers, to take the meaning of the word 'red' to *be* the colour red. The word 'red', they suggest, is the *name* of the colour red, and the thing named is the meaning of the name. So if in imagining red I am using the word 'red', I must be designating something red – there in my imagination! Or as Wittgenstein puts it in the *Grammar*, 'Doesn't the misunderstanding consist in taking the meaning of the word "red" as being the sense of a sentence saying that some thing is red?' (*PG* p. 135).[8] Given this misunderstanding, it is easy to see how imagining red can be taken to involve something's being red – it is something red, after all, that I imagine. The analogy, then, between imagining red and asserting 'Here there is not a red patch' holds out the promise of both dispersing the mystery surrounding imagination and explaining why it is there in the first place.

We return in §444 to the discussion of expectation. Just as we might think an imagined red colour is not (cannot be) the same as the red colour one sees in front of one (§443), so we might think that the words 'he is coming' have a different sense in the statement 'I expect he is coming' from the one they have in the statement 'He is coming'. In the latter, after all, one is referring to *his actual coming*, whereas in expressing the expectation one is referring to a coming that may never occur. How could 'he is coming' designate the same event or occurrence in that case? But the proposal that the words have different senses in the two contexts is absurd. If it were true, then it would be impossible for the report (that he is coming) to verify that the expectation (that he is coming) has been fulfilled. But it does verify it (*PG* p. 139; MS pp. 108, 271 – cited by Hallett). Moreover, if asked to explain the meanings of the words 'he' and 'is coming' as they appear in the two sentences, one would use the *same* ostensive definitions. Same explanation of meaning: same meaning – a basic Wittgensteinian 'axiom'.

If the same words have the same meaning in the two different contexts, however, this just generates another problem. If 'He is coming' as an assertion means the same as the object clause in 'I expect he is coming', doesn't this suggest that the fact of his coming, the real event, is somehow already in the expectation – just as an imagined red seems already to be there in the imagination? The event or something very much like it – perhaps its shadow (something having the same *form* but lacking in substance, namely, the *possible* state of affairs of his coming)? Surely the expected event and the fulfilling event have to be significantly similar.[9]

But wherein lies the similarity between my expecting him to come and his actual coming? The behavioural criteria for the two events are quite different. Does my walking up and down the room resemble the door opening and someone (him) walking in? Not in the least. If we compare my expectant behaviour and the event satisfying my expectation, they do not seem to 'agree' at all. *Unless*, Wittgenstein points out, in walking up and down, expecting someone, I *say* 'I expect he'll come in'. If this were to happen, there would be a similarity. But, Wittgenstein asks, 'of what kind?' (§444).

And this leads us to our peak, to *Philosophical Investigations* §445: 'It is in language that an expectation and its fulfillment make contact'. Are we prepared for this high altitude? Do the previous remarks lead up to it as a natural conclusion? I think not. But by consulting some of Wittgenstein's other writings, we can see how easy it is to get from the preceding remarks to §445.

Section 444 provides the ideal jumping-off point. My saying 'I expect he'll come in' (as I pace the floor, look at the clock, and so on) is what Wittgenstein calls the expression of my expectation.

He tells us in *Philosophical Grammar* that 'in so many cases it clarifies the grammatical situation to say: let us put the expression of expectation in place of the expectation, the expression of thought in place of the thought' (*PG* p. 140). Following this advice, let us put the expression 'I expect he'll come in' in place of the expectation that he will come in. What do we thereby accomplish? For one thing, 'if you see the expression of an expectation you see what is being expected' (*PG* p. 123). In the case at hand, we see that what is being expected is that he will come in – that is exactly what I *say* I expect. The expression of an expectation contains an indication of its fulfillment.[10]

Where are we to find out *what* wish or expectation someone has? Wittgenstein's answer is unequivocal: 'Where are we to find out what makes the wish *this* wish, even though it's only a wish? Nowhere but in the expressed wish' (*PG* p. 150). By extrapolation, if I say 'I expect he'll come in', then *this* expectation is the expectation that he will come in. But his coming in is the fulfillment of the expectation. Hence finding out what makes an expectation *this* expectation, a particular and distinct expectation, is finding out what its fulfillment is. Expectations and wishes are individuated by their fulfillments, and we make these individuations by looking at the expressions of the expectations and wishes.

A while back we were asking about the relationship, the agreement, between an expectation and the event that fulfills it. Now we are in a position to understand this. In expressing the expectation – 'I expect that he'll come in' – I am at the same time identifying the state of affairs that would fulfill it – 'He'll come in'. This makes the agreement between the expectation and its fulfillment an internal one. 'Describing an expectation by means of what is expected is giving an internal description', Wittgenstein tells us (*PR* p. 68). And he sums up the matter nicely:

> Isn't it like this: my theory is completely expressed in the fact that the state of affairs satisfying the expectation of *p* is represented by the proposition *p*?
>
> (*PR* p. 66)

An expectation and what satisfies it are internally related, so that if we know what expectation it is, we already know what would fulfill it. The description of the latter follows from the expression of the former.[11]

When we passed the stone tablet called 'the hardness of the logical must', we were taken aback by the idea that an expectation could determine in advance what its fulfillment *must* be. How, we asked, could this be? Now we have the answer. It is not, of course, that an expectation logically determines that its fulfillment will occur. Often the fulfillment does not occur, and whether or not it does is a purely contingent matter. But if an expectation *is* fulfilled, it *must be fulfilled in one way and only in that way*, namely by the occurrence of the state of affairs indicated in its expression. To be fulfilled, the expectation that he will come in must be followed up by his coming in; nothing else will serve to fulfill it. And this determination is no mystery at all, since it follows from the simple fact that in expressing the expectation we do so by means of a clause that could be used to describe the event fulfilling it (if it occurs), the event that *must* occur if it is to be fulfilled. We can't know what expectation *it is* without knowing what must occur if it is to be fulfilled.[12]

Now we can understand §445. The contact in language between an expectation and its fulfillment is not a physical one but a logical one, and it occurs in the grammatical nexus set up between expressing an expectation and describing its fulfillment. It is a logical proposition that my expecting him to arrive at a certain time is fulfilled by his arriving at that time. The grammar of 'expectation' is such that expectations are individuated by their fulfillments and such that the *expression* of an expectation involves a clause that can be converted into a description of its fulfillment. This is the way we talk about expectation, and the way we must talk if we are to follow the grammatical rules giving sense to this notion. The contact between an expectation and its fulfillment is prefigured in grammar.[13]

We are now ready for the quick, down-hill part of our journey. During this descent we shall take note of only one of the many attractions available to us.[14]

Sections 446–51 discuss a number of ways in which we can be bewitched by language in areas adjacent to the land of expectation. Let us consider one of these areas: pain. 'If I say "I have no pain in my arm", does that mean that I have a shadow of the sensation of pain, which as it were indicates the place where the pain might be?' (§448). If I say I am not in pain, nevertheless I must grasp the possibility of my being in pain. This possibility seems like a shadow, the spitting image of pain, insubstantial, perhaps, but real enough, as it were pain waiting to materialize.[15]

In response to this philosophical conundrum, Wittgenstein forthrightly lectures us: 'If anyone says: "For the word 'pain' to have a meaning it is necessary that pain should be recognized as such when it occurs" – one can reply: It is not more necessary than that the absence of pain should be recognized' (§448).[16] In the *Philosophical Remarks*, Wittgenstein likened the concept of a dream to a signal dial having two settings: one, dreams; the other, no dreams (*PR* p. 113). Likewise, the concept of pain can be thought of as a signal dial with two settings: one, pain; the other, no pain. We use the concept of pain *in a proposition* to say that someone is in pain *or* to say that someone is not in pain – we put the signal dial at the one setting or the other. The concept of pain encompasses both of these possibilities – that is, the word 'pain' can be employed meaningfully in both of these ways. In saying that I have no pain in my arm, it is not necessary for me to have an image or shadow of pain (§448), but simply to have mastered the concept of pain and hence to have learned how to set the signal dial at the negative position. This relates back to the discussion in §443 of imagining red and saying 'here there is not a red patch'.[17] All of these cases serve to remind us that mastery of a concept is not a matter of having certain experiences, but of being able to use words in multiple, grammatically interrelated ways.[18] We shall return to this point shortly.

Let us now go directly to §465, which I quote in full:

> 'An expectation is so made that whatever happens has to accord with it, or not.'
>
> Suppose you now ask: then are facts defined one way or the other by an expectation – that is, is it defined for whatever event may occur whether it fulfills the expectation or not? The answer has to be: 'Yes, unless the expression of the expectation is indefinite; for example, contains a disjunction of different possibilities.'

In all likelihood, Wittgenstein's emphasis in this remark is on the 'unless' clause. But I want to concentrate on the initial 'Yes'. Doing so allows us to double back to the topic of the queerness of thought, and then to return at last to the issue of the harmony between thought and reality.

An expectation defines or determines, for whatever event may occur, whether or not it fulfills the expectation. If I expect N to arrive, then, whatever in fact takes place, I know how to describe it: *relative to my expectation*, I shall describe it either as N arriving or as N not arriving. And given the one description or the other of what takes place, I know ('necessarily') whether or not my expectation has been fulfilled. I know these 'necessary truths' simply by having mastered the grammar of 'expectation'. This grammar contains a set of logical connections among the expression of an expectation, descriptions (relative to the expectation) of what subsequently happens, and statements of whether the expectation is or is not satisfied.

On page 70 of the *Philosophical Remarks* Wittgenstein provides us with an analogy that helps us understand expectation:

> Expectation, so to speak, prepares a yardstick for measuring the event when it comes and what's more, in such a way that it will necessarily be possible to measure the one with the other, whether the event coincides with the expected graduation mark or not.

I may use a yardstick to determine whether an object is a yard long. If the object does not coincide with the graduation mark of one yard, I am still able to measure the object with the yardstick. I know that the object, in missing the yard mark, is *not* a yard long. Likewise, an expectation that N will enter the room allows one to 'measure' what happens, whether the event that occurs coincides with the expectation or not. If it does not, one knows that N did not enter the room. Both expectations and the use of yardsticks involve something like the concept of pain which we discussed above. The concept of pain, we observed, is similar to a signal dial with two settings, and a proposition about pain sets the dial at one of the settings. Likewise, expectations are signal dials set at one of two marks. If the event that occurs does not coincide with this mark (not being the event we expected), we know that it coincides with the other.

Now let us picture thoughts as being like expectations. As in the case of expectations, we often express our thoughts in language. These expressions of thought may come in many different forms, for example, 'I am thinking of Albert Schweitzer', 'I was thinking that winter will come early this year', 'I think Yugoslavia is on the Adriatic Sea', and so on. Now we ask: how can thought 'deal with the very object itself'? How can it 'catch reality in its net'? If I am thinking of a certain person, how can my thought be of *him*? If I think winter will come early this year, how can I here and now think of this event that hasn't yet occurred? These problems are by now familiar, and their 'solution' is easy. My thought is of Schweitzer if in expressing it I say that I am thinking of Schweitzer. 'Schweitzer' is what we are required, by the grammar of our language, to call the person I am thinking about. If we encounter the person someone says he was thinking of – the person he refers to by a name or definite description – and we too are willing to apply this name or description to him, then we are grammatically required to grant that so-and-so was thinking of *this very person*. Someone can think of another person just to the extent that he (and we) can use the same name, pronoun, or definite description to identify this person that is used in expressing or identifying the thought.[19]

Let's catch a bit of reality in our net. I say I think winter will come early this year, and, by golly, it does. I was right – what I thought actually occurs. There is no mystery here. Given the way I expressed my thought and the way we describe what climatic changes take place, the latter can be derived from the former. Of course I may have been wrong, from which it would follow that winter did *not* come early. How odd, someone might claim, that my thought can dictate how to describe the event that occurs even if my thought is in error! Do we have an opening for idealism here? Well, no – we have only a grammatical proposition that requires acknowledgment. If I say 'I think winter will come early this year' and my thought is in error, grammar dictates that we can describe the weather by saying 'Winter did not come early this year'. Simply knowing that the thought was not fulfilled allows us to describe the weather in this specific way.

Thoughts, then, no less than expectations, are like the use of yardsticks.[20] The use of a yardstick tells us whether an object *is* or *is not* a yard long. A thought tells us whether a fact *does* or *does not* correspond to it. Given our yardstick, a particular object *must* be either a yard long or not. Given our thoughts, what takes place in the world *must* show them correct or incorrect. Individual thoughts *necessarily* catch reality in their net or fail to – some catch it and some don't. And if a particular thought fails – for example 'I think winter will come early this year' – then *another* thought, were someone to have it, would catch the facts –

namely, 'I think winter will not come early this year'. The queerness of thought disappears once we attend to the grammar of 'thought'.[21]

And now we can return, at last, to the harmony between thought and reality. In §429, Wittgenstein has this to say:

> The agreement, the harmony, of thought and reality consists in this: if I say falsely that something is *red*, then, for all that, it isn't *red*. And when I want to explain the word 'red' to someone, in the sentence 'That is not red,' I do so by pointing to something red.

How are we to understand these propositions? As noted before, we need to see them as expressing a position on a topic that was already of great concern to Wittgenstein in his early philosophy. In the *Tractatus*, the agreement between thought (language) and reality was secured by sameness of logical form. In Wittgenstein's later work, the agreement is not a relationship between a proposition and a state of affairs but rather a relationship within language: 'Like everything metaphysical the harmony between thought and reality is to be found in the grammar of the language' (*PG* p. 162; *Z* §55). To grasp this harmony, we need to consult, not the logical form of reality but the rules of grammar, the rules drawing connections among words and sentences, connections which must be maintained if sense is to be preserved.

It is not immediately clear, however, how §429 identifies a new conception of the harmony between thought and reality. It is possible, in fact, to understand §429 in a way that is consistent with the thesis of the *Tractatus*. Let us assume that 'The vase is red' is an elementary proposition and that the word 'red' is the name of an object. To say that the vase is, after all, not *red* (if I have said falsely that it is red) could be taken as a way of claiming that in the false proposition 'The vase is red' the name 'red' refers to the object red. The proposition is false, yes, but it is nevertheless the object red it makes reference to, the very same object it would have referred to had it turned out to be true. By referring to this same object in both true and false propositions, the name 'red' ensures that there is an identity of form between the world and language, whatever turns out to be the fact of the matter about the vase.

Furthermore, if I want to explain the word 'red' to someone as it occurs in the proposition 'That is not red', I can do so, in an

Augustinian, if not precisely Tractarian, way, by pointing to something red. I explain the meaning, that is, by pointing to the object that is the meaning of 'red', even if this object is not a constituent of a particular atomic fact in the world. In the proposition at hand – 'That is not red' – I am describing a possible fact containing the imperishable object red and denying that this fact exists.

Section 429, then, does not in any obvious way distinguish Wittgenstein's later ideas on the harmony between thought and reality from his early ideas on the subject. If there is a difference, as the remark about 'everything metaphysical' in *Philosophical Grammar* and *Zettel* suggests, then we need to look for a totally different construal of §429. I suggest that §445 will help us here.

If I say, falsely, that the vase is red, it must be the case, assuming sincerity, that I think the vase is red. Just as an expectation and its fulfillment make contact in language, we have seen that a thought and its fulfillment also do so. And what this means is that from the expression of the thought we can derive a description of the state of affairs that would fulfill the thought, that is, make it true. In the case at hand, the vase's being red would make true the thought that the vase is red. Furthermore, we have seen that from the expression of an expectation, we can derive by means of a logical step in grammar a description of the state of affairs that must exist if the expectation is to be unfulfilled. Likewise, we should be able to derive a description of the state of affairs that must exist if a thought is to be false or unfulfilled. And, indeed, from the thought expression 'I think the vase is red' we can derive just this description, namely, 'The vase is not red'. As a matter of grammatical necessity, this latter description, 'The vase is not red', *must* be true of reality if the thought expressed in 'I think the vase is red' is unfulfilled. Under the condition of my thinking falsely that the vase is red, it must be the case, as a matter of grammar, that 'The vase is not red' is *true*; it must be the case that the vase is not *red*. Thus if I think and say falsely that the vase is red, then, for all that, it isn't *red*.

But what does this show us? How have we established a harmony or agreement between thought and reality? How are we to construe 'harmony' and 'agreement' here? What do they signify? And what would it be like if thought and reality did not harmonize or agree?

When Wittgenstein urged in the *Tractatus* that thought and

reality have an agreement in form, this was to be understood in terms of reality and thought having the *same* form. In the later philosophy, do reality and thought have something in common? They do not necessarily have the same linguistic expression – a thought, after all, could be false – but they do have in common a set of grammatically related expressions. We could talk here of their being in the same grammatical space (*PG* pp. 142–3) or say that the same grammar applies to our talk about reality as applies to our talk about thought. Wittgenstein explicitly makes this claim about expectation: 'what expectation has in common with reality is that it refers to another point in the *same* space' (*PR* p. 70). Let us say, then, that thought and reality 'share' a grammatical system.[22] And within this system, we can describe the world relative to our thoughts and express our thoughts relative to the world: thought-expressions and reality-descriptions are coordinate. It is this common grammatical system which allows thought to harmonize, agree, or 'connect' with reality. Wittgenstein tells us in the *Grammar* that 'It is the *calculus* of thought that connects with extra-mental reality' (p. 160) and in so far as he also asserts that 'it is the *system* of language that makes a sentence a thought' (*PG* p. 153), we can conclude that it is the calculus or system of grammar which allows thought to be in agreement or harmony with reality – that is, coordinated with it through a set of interrelated linguistic expressions.[23]

In expressing a thought, we use language that in part could be used to describe the bit of reality that would fulfill it. This common element, however, is not discovered by examining reality, examining thought, and discovering that the same language is appropriate for both. For it is clear that in examining reality we may fail to find the event that fulfills the thought – the latter may be forever unsatisfied (false) since the fulfilling event may never occur. The identity of the two linguistic expressions is not found in an observed relationship between a bit of reality and a piece of thought; rather, it is found in grammar. It is forged by the rules that govern our expressions of thoughts.

Someone might object that if thought and reality are said to have in common a grammatically connected set of linguistic expressions, this simply begs the question about whether there is harmony or agreement between thought (language) and reality. It amounts to assuming that at least some of our descriptions of reality harmonize with it, and this is the very question at issue.

But there is no *petitio* involved in our grammatical observations; there is only confusion in this objection to them. The objection (mis)interprets 'harmonizing' as 'being true of', whereas in fact the harmony of thought and reality consists just as much in our ability to have thoughts (and construct descriptions) that are false of reality as those that are true of it.[24] In sharing a grammar, thought and reality share a set of meaningful linguistic expressions, whether these expressions are true or false when used to describe reality. To the extent that a meaningful form of language can be used to express a thought *and* to describe (truly or falsely) a bit of reality, there is harmony between thought and reality. Thought and reality share possibilities of meaningful articulation. What question could be begged in claiming this? Is anyone prepared to assert that the linguistic expressions we use with respect to thought are not meaningfully applied (correctly or incorrectly) to reality?

In a sense, as Wittgenstein notes in the *Blue Book* (p. 30), it is the fact that thoughts can be false which is at the heart of our puzzlement over thought. False thoughts may seem to require extra-special, real but nonexistent objects, just as, we have seen, unfulfilled expectations may seem to require shadow fulfillments, and the absence of pain may require shadow-pain. But by placing the expression of a thought in a grammatical system, we can see that an unfulfilled thought is coordinated with a *statement* about what comes to exist in reality – a false statement. It is also coordinated with another statement which is true, but this is the *negation* of what was thought. We understand the expression of the (unfulfilled) thought to the extent that we understand these grammatical connections; we do not understand it by having some queer event come before the mind. As Wittgenstein tells us early on in his rethinking of the agreement between thought and reality, 'the sense of a proposition only presupposes the grammatically correct use of certain words' (*PR* p. 67).[25]

Can we even conceive of a disharmony or lack of agreement between thought and reality? What if there were no grammatical connection between the expression of a thought and the description of the fact that would make it true? Can we imagine this? It might appear so: we might simply express thoughts in one way and describe reality in another. Then we could not know what would fulfill a thought simply by examining its expression. We would have to go in search of some third thing which assured that the thought, expressed one way, was fulfilled by a certain fact, described another way. And it might happen that we failed in this task and were forced to conclude, at best, that we cannot know whether or not thoughts and reality harmonize, or, at worst, that they do not.

But this thought experiment cannot really get underway. When we speak of *thoughts* whose expressions do not involve language that would describe the reality fulfilling them, we only seem to be speaking sensibly. In fact we fail to do so, because a thought just *is* something expressed by means of language that is descriptive of its fulfillment.[26] This is what we mean by a thought, what in our grammar the word 'thought' means. We have tried to imagine severing this connection between the expression of thoughts and the descriptions of their fulfillments and *still* being able to talk about thoughts, indeed able to construct a scepticism with regard to their harmony with reality. But once the connection is severed, it is no longer *thoughts* we are talking about. Hence, we must conclude, it is impossible to conceive of thought and reality not being in agreement or harmony. Their harmony is guaranteed by the rules of grammar, by the rules governing sensible speech. Needless to say, this harmony is not a matter of *metaphysical affinity*; it simply is built into the way we talk.

NOTES

1 I wish to thank P.M.S. Hacker and C.G. Luckhardt for reading an early draft of this paper and making very helpful comments on it. References to Hallett are to Garth Hallett, *A Companion to Wittgenstein's 'Philosophical Investigations'*, Ithaca, Cornell University Press, 1977.

2 See my 'Representation in Wittgenstein's *Tractatus* and Middle Writings', *Synthese*, 1983, vol. 56, pp. 181–98.

3 An Irreverent Synopsis of the History of Philosophical Reflection on Thought and Reality.

Consider first the example of Democritus. Democritus believed that, in thinking, the outer atoms or surface of an object – its idol, effluence, or image – comes before the mind. That is one way to catch or grasp reality – by Zeus – to have the thing itself, or a significant part of it, inside the mind. Other ancient Greeks, in no obvious way less discerning, apparently pictured the soul, the organ of thought, as leaving the body and wandering among the things of the world, knowing them as a tourist by travelling, *sans* Baedeker, to visit them. Consider next the solution of Aristotle: in thought, the mind and its object, although made of different matter, take on the very same form. Well, after all, we *have* known some people whose minds were as crooked as the schemes they hatched, and some students whose minds clearly resembled the blank sheets of paper they contemplated. Passing on to the modern scene, we find the hugely popular theory that, in thinking, we have parading before the mind, in various modes of association, images that partially resemble the objects in the world they represent – partially, the theory insists, leading us to surmise that images represent their objects much in the way our contemporary politicians represent their constituents. It remained a bit of a mystery just how these ideas or images take on some of the features of the objects they represent – is Democritus due for a recall? – and perhaps even more of a mystery how they come to have some colourful properties that in no way whatsoever resemble those of their impoverished constituents – hanging out in a bad neighbourhood, one might expect. These mysteries were never solved, for philosophy soon took a critical turn, and shortly thereafter discovered idealism. Kant showed us how the mind can grasp at least some of the features of objects – their more pervasive and 'necessary' ones – by pointing out how these features are contributed by the mind itself. Unfortunately, the objects themselves, throwing off their mental garb, escape from the clutches of the mind and go off naked into a secret and forbidden place – like coy lovers, ardently desired and pursued, but unknown and unpossessed, mere teases. Thought is foiled once again. But only, apparently, as a result of timidity, uncertainty, and immaturity. As thought came to adulthood in Hegel, it confidently 'solved' the problem of itself and the world by establishing that, after all is said and done, it *is* the world. The problem of how thought can grasp objects in the world is really only the problem of how the mind can know itself, and that does not seem much of a mystery: it knows itself by being itself. But now we have a different problem: how can the mind be *ignorant* of the things of the world; if thought and its object are one and the same, how can thought fail to deal with the very object itself and catch it in its net? At this point, it may seem opportune to embrace existentialism and to stare, with some degree of unpleasant nausea, at our own nothingness. At least the problem would disappear.

4 It might appear that the solution to this problem is simply to add thoughts to our signs, gestures, and sentences – are not these accompanying thoughts what give meaning to their instruments? Perhaps it is the thought itself that breathes life into the sign and the sentence. But how does thought, divorced from these physical manifestations, accomplish the task of representation? Disembodied thought, after all, *is* a very mysterious thing. So the fact that signs without thoughts fail to signify just makes it more mysterious that the thoughts themselves *are* able to signify. It renders thought 'an

incomprehensible process' (*PG* p. 155). 'The mental act seems to perform in a mysterious way what could not be performed by any act of manipulating symbols' (*BB* p. 42).

5 The analogy drawn here between a wish and a proposition is an intriguing one. We were initially perplexed about signs and sentences, about how they represent and convey understanding, and this is surely a concern about what philosophers call propositions. And how does Wittgenstein propose to deal with these perplexities? By talking about *wishes*, and, as we shall see, *expectations* and *hopes*! We are to get at what looks to be a *big* problem, a major and fundamental philosophical one, by attacking what seems to be a problem of little concern to philosophy. This is, I think, an illustration of Wittgenstein's claim that the alleged super-concepts traditionally studied by philosophers are in the end just ordinary citizens of the conceptual realm – the concept of a proposition is just as humble as the concept of a wish.

6 This suggests that it makes no sense to speak of my knowing what I wish for. Wittgenstein implies, however, that it not a complete howler to say that I know what I wish for before I actually get it, for he writes, 'Suppose it were asked "Do I know what I long for before I get it?" If I have learned to talk, then I do know' (§441). So in a sense, or possibly in certain circumstances, 'I know what I wish for' is meaningful – perhaps its use is simply to say that doubt cannot arise in the case (see Hallett, p. 476).

We are not to assume, however, that it always makes sense to speak this way about our wishes. In §441 Wittgenstein grants that there is a sense of 'wish' in which it is not always the case that we know what we wish for (' "I don't know myself what I wish for" '). Here as elsewhere, we should not assume that a word has only one use. This second use of 'wish', however, is one that will no longer occupy Wittgenstein's attention in the current discussion.

7 After all, 'The objects he is thinking about are certainly not in his head – any more than in his thoughts' (*PG* p. 143).

8 In his Cambridge lectures of 1930–2, Wittgenstein notes that 'when we say the word "toothache" it does not stand for anyone having *toothache*, unless it occurs in a proposition' (*L30* p. 32); he also warns: 'We confuse a name or word or meaning of a word ("red") with the *proposition* in which the word occurs ("this is red") ' (ibid. p. 35).

9 'The strange thing is expressed in the fact that if this is the event I expected, it isn't distinct from the one I expected' (*PG* p. 134).

10 And how else might we find out what is expected? 'And in what other way, in what other sense would it be possible to see it?' (*PG* p. 132 and *PI* §452) If someone observes my other, nonlinguistic, expectant behaviour – my pacing the floor, looking at a clock, going to the door, even looking at a picture of him – he doesn't necessarily get an identification of what I am expecting. All of these forms of behaviour could be interpreted in a vast variety of ways: they might show, for instance, that I hope he won't come, or that I am frightened that he may come, or that I wish someone else would come, and so on. It

does not, for example, follow logically from my looking at a picture of him that I am expecting him. What if one tried to get behind the behaviour that expresses my expectation and examine the expectation itself, say by miraculously looking in my head? What would one observe? Perhaps an image in my mind of his coming through the door. Or would that be what goes on, not in my expectation of him, but rather in my fear that he may come? Images, we have all learned from Wittgenstein, are subject to multiple interpretations. Perhaps I observe some mental process in my head which is the expectation itself, that which gives meaning to the image (the intention that informs it) or stands alone without any image, directly being the expectation itself. But how could a *process* point beyond itself and be an expectation of *him*? Any process, by virtue of being a process, seems self-contained and complete in itself, this being the case whether it is a physical process or a mental one (*PG* pp. 144, 148). The grammar of 'process', Wittgenstein tells us, prevents us from thinking of any kind of process as being an expectation and consequently containing an identification of *some other thing* that would fulfill it. Even God would be unable to discover what I expect by looking into my mind and surveying its processes.

Still another possibility is that one discovers what I expect by observing what happens to me, specifically, say, by observing what happens when my expectation ceases. Wittgenstein annihilates this suggestion with the following sarcastic remark: 'If I wanted to eat an apple, and someone punched me in the stomach, taking away my appetite, then it was the punch that I originally wanted' (*PR* p. 64). This, of course, is a *reductio ad absurdum* and an example of Wittgenstein's wild wit.

Another *reductio*: 'I have a wish for an apple, and so I will call "an apple" whatever takes away the wish' (*PG* p. 134). We don't define the object of a wish or want in terms of whatever relieves or assuages it. If I wanted an apple, but discover that all of them have been poisoned, my desire vanishes, but that hardly means I desired uneaten, poisoned apples.

11 And thus we are able to explain the similarity between the expectation and the fulfilling event in terms of the internal relation between the expression of the one and the description of the other. As Wittgenstein remarked in his lectures of 1930–2, 'the similarity of expectation to fulfillment is shown by the fact that both are expressed in the same words in language, and not by any further proposition' (*L30* p. 33).

12 This explains why the question cannot arise as to whether the person who has an expectation knows what would fulfill it. There can be no doubt on his part about the matter, for to the extent that he has a certain expectation he has already expressed, or is capable of expressing, what would fulfill it.

We also can understand now the connection Wittgenstein alluded to in §441 between a psychological matter like expectation and language ('Suppose it were asked "Do I know what I long for before I

get it?" If I have learned to talk, then I do know' (*PI* §441)). If I know
how to talk, and I say 'I long for the summer break', then, in bleakest
winter, I already know that it is the summer break I long for. *I say so.*
It is in language that the connection is made allowing one to know
in advance what one longs for, expects, hopes for, plans, and so on.

13 Inevitably, I fear, the question will arise as to whether I or others
know what will fulfill my expectation if I do not express my
expectation in language. We have learned enough from Wittgenstein
about psychological affairs to realize that when a person expects
something, any of a number of psychological states and events may
occur, but none of them are essential. And surely I may expect N to
arrive soon without ever saying out loud or to myself that I expect
him to arrive soon. How am I aware, in such a case, of what
expectation I have? How can I 'know' that his arrival is what I
expect? How can others know this? If expectation and its fulfillment
make contact in language, what if, on a certain occasion, there is no
language within which this contact can be made?

We have also learned enough from Wittgenstein to know how to
handle this problem. Of course I may not actually say to myself that
N will arrive shortly if I expect him to do so, but I might have said it
if someone asked me what I was up to, or what I expected; and I
might have said it if I asked myself, 'Now, let's see, just whom am I
expecting?' In so far as I have mastered the language of expectation,
the expression was there for my use, were the proper occasion to arise
on which it was called for. And one criterion for my expecting N
(silently) is that I would express my expectation in this fashion were
one of these occasions to arise.

But what if a person has not mastered language? Could he then
expect N to arrive soon? Could he expect anything? All sorts of
feelings and images might occur in such a person (or animal), but
what right have we to link these up with expectation? The dog has
an image of his master walking through the door – is he thereby
expecting him? Why not say that he is hoping that he will come? Or
doubting that he will come? Why say anything at all? In this case we
simply do not have available the kind of criteria that allow us to say
confidently that someone expects something to happen, criteria
which importantly include the actual or hypothetical expression of
expectation in language. There may be behavioural traits from
which we infer that a dog expects his master, for example, he waits at
the door before the master's arrival. But it does not follow logically
from the existence of this behaviour that the dog expects his master,
nor can we specify the conditions under which this behaviour would
be criterial for the dog expecting his master. But from the (sincere)
assertion 'I expect N to come' it follows logically that N's coming
will fulfill my expectation.

14 The following is a synopsis of some of the attractions we are unable
to visit and discuss in the body of the paper:

We return in §452 to the topic of expectation, and we appropriate some of the results of our earlier explorations. Someone might think that if we could see the mental process of expectation itself, we would directly see what was being expected. And Wittgenstein's response is that this indeed is true, but only because in directly grasping the expectation via its expression, we do discover what the object of the expectation is. Section 453 takes us a step further. It raises a question about all this talk of *perceiving* an expectation. Do I perceive someone else's expectation? It is a dubious notion indeed, although I may well observe that he expresses his expectation in a certain sentence. Even more dubious is the idea of a person perceiving his own expectation. A person says what he expects, but it would be 'an idiotic distortion of the expression' to assert that he perceives his expectation. It follows from this, of course, that a person does not come to know, or discover, what he expects by perceiving his expectation. He expresses his expectation in words, and the sentence he uses conveys what he expects.

Sections 454–7 follow these remarks on expectation, and they have as their topic the subject of meaning. Here Wittgenstein has some things to say that, while familiar enough, bear on the earlier topic of living and dead signs. Signs considered merely as physical things are dead, Wittgenstein grants. They signify (an arrow points) 'only in the application that a living being makes of it' (§454). But this application of signs is not 'a hocus-pocus which can be performed only by the soul' (§454). Rather, it is the activity of the whole (embodied, living) person. It is an act like going up to someone. Because we ourselves are engaged in acts of going up to someone, of using signs, we frequently will not observe our own activity (§456). Then we may encounter only the dead sign, the physical word or arrow or gesture, and unsatisfied with that as the signifier, we first look inward for something totally nonphysical which will breath life and signification into the physical sign. We simply miss our own living activity.

Early in our trip through §§428–65 we encountered the gulf between an order and its execution. But our study of the logical or grammatical connection between an expectation and its object allows us to see that the gulf is only an apparent one, an illusion. In knowing what order has been given, we know what action will execute it. 'You are ordered to appear for military service at your local armoury' will be executed only by your appearing for military service at your local armoury. If it appears that the person giving the order knows what will fulfill it even before this action occurs, demystification of this appearance requires no more than pointing out that 'if an order runs "Do such and such" then executing the order is called "doing such and such" ' (§458). It is a grammatical fact that we encounter here, a logical connection between the way we express the order and the way we describe its execution. There is no queer sense in which someone giving the order already knows its fulfillment, no mysterious manner in which an order anticipates its execution (§461). The order may or may not be executed; just by giving an order, we do not know the future. Simply in giving an order, we know nothing about what will happen later on, although we may well be aware of the grammatical proposition to the effect that if act *a* occurs, and we have ordered *a*, then our order is fulfilled.

There is no queer way in which an execution is already present in an order, long before the execution actually occurs (if it ever does). We do not have to produce the execution itself and hold it up for view before the mind in order to understand the order. If someone does not understand our order, we explain the words in it, and we can do this in a variety of ways. Our definition may involve our actually doing the action commanded (I may tell a novice at chess to move his rook, and then actually move it for him), but it may involve giving a example of the action, or just giving another proposition equivalent to the order (§459). This is how the explanation of meaning *actually* occurs – it does not require that we enter Platonic heavens (to mingle with eternal actions), Meinongian jungles (to encounter actions that never occur), or Lockean mirror shows (to observe images of actions). And one further thing is certain: to understand the order – to know what would fulfill it – we don't have to wait for someone to act and then observe whether this action produces feelings of satisfaction, either in the agent or the commander: the commander did not order the person to do what would give one or the other of them certain feelings (§460).

Why do we become so confused, and tempted by philosophical 'discoveries', when we attempt to understand matters like expectation? Wittgenstein's suggestion, of course, is that we are bewitched by language, by the forms of expression we use and by analogies among these forms of expression. For example, one can't hang a person who isn't there (§462), and this might mislead us into thinking that one cannot look for, expect, or hope for something that isn't there. But to follow that way of thinking would engender the absurd result that if I look for someone he must 'be there' even if he doesn't exist at all. We have been led to this conclusion by being misled by our grammar. The kernel of truth behind a metaphysics of real, but nonexistent, objects of searches is the grammatical proposition that if we are looking for *p*, we can't say we have found what we are looking for unless we are willing to call it *p*. This doesn't tell us anything about the world, but only about how we talk. Likewise, before we enter the realm of round squares and the trisection of an angle, let us remember that we would not *call* the effort to round the square (to trisect an angle) successful unless we found that the person engaging in the effort actually rounded the square (trisected the angle). And that we would *never* describe what someone did in these terms indicates why the search is not just unsuccessful, but futile and nonsensical.

Wittgenstein identifies very clearly in the *Philosophical Grammar* a couple of other ways in which language can mislead us in this area of discussion. First of all, we are inclined to think of the fulfillment of an expectation as an object.

> We say that the expression of expectation 'describes' the expected fact and think of an object or complex which makes its appearance as fulfillment of the expectation. – But it is not the expected thing that is the fulfillment, but rather: its coming about.
> The mistake is deeply rooted in our language: we say 'I expect him' and 'I expect his arrival'.
>
> (*PG* p. 137)

The tendency, then, to think of the fulfillment as an object results from misleading features of the surface grammar of the way we talk about expectation. And once we have construed the fulfillment as an object, it is difficult, because of analogies among the ways we speak of many objects, not to see this 'object of an expectation' as somehow existing. After all, the hunter says both 'I expect a stag' and 'I killed a stag', and it is clear that one cannot kill a stag that does not exist. Therefore, we may conclude, one cannot expect a stag that does not exist – even if in point of fact there is no stag in the forest. 'Then the stag I expect must have a kind of existence or reality different from that of the stag I kill, but an existence and reality for all that', our philosophical instincts drive us to say. Here, Wittgenstein points out, we have a tempting path leading directly into the dark confines of Plato's *Theaetetus* (*PG* p. 137). The temptations set here by language can lead philosophers to say some strange things about expectations, orders, and so on. When we order someone to undertake an action, it may appear as if the order makes us acquainted with *this very action*, thereby already bringing it into existence – in a certain sense. 'But here we are simply misled by the form of expression of our language, when it says "the knowledge of *what* you have to do" or "the knowledge of the action".' These linguistic traps, which are always planted in our way, can produce an almost hysterical sense of perplexity and generate theories that undoubtedly rise to the challenge.

But nonsense may not appear to be nonsense; arising out of our language itself, it may appear to be the very best of sense, indeed to be a higher form of wisdom. The future that is already here as the object of an expectation, the order that is executed before it is actually followed, the round square that comes into being as we ask about it, and the belief that is true in order that it can be false – these philosophical exotica are grounded in our language. But they are illusions for all that, for they make their appearance only when we divert our attention from the actual use of language and when we confuse grammatical facts about the way we are to talk with realities accessible only to philosophers. Our study of expectations and commands has allowed us to pass from disguised nonsense to patent nonsense (§464). And that, of course, was Wittgenstein's intent all the while.

15 Some other forms of bewitchment: we are told in §446 that we can use language to say that a red patch is there and also that it is not there. And the voice of bewitchment speaks: but surely there is a difference

between one that is and one that isn't; perhaps language just abstracts from the difference, so that what we mean by the words 'a red patch' is something that can both exist and fail to exist, an entity that can participate in existence or fail to do so, a Platonic form, as it were.

And a step further, in §447, we hear the voice of bewitchment again: if I negate a proposition, then I am negating what the proposition describes; what it describes must exist in some sense if I am to negate it. It is as if 'the negation of a proposition had to make it true in a certain sense, in order to negate it'. Now we are positioned to encounter the philosophical wizard who tells us that it is impossible to have a false belief, since for the negation of our belief to be true, our belief itself must be true, in, of course, 'a special sense'.

Bewitchment is to be found in still other, perhaps more likely, places, for example, in dreams. The statement 'I dreamt last night' would be false if I did not do so, but it would still be meaningful. And I must understand that meaning if I am to deny that I dreamed. Does my denial carry with it, then, a 'hint of a dream' (§448), a dream of a dream, not even achieving the reality of illusion but real for all that?

16 If one responds by asserting that to understand not being in pain I would at least have to know what it would be like if I were in pain (I would have to be in touch with, aware of, pain) then the lecture continues: 'We fail to get away from the idea that using a sentence involves imagining something for every word.' This is familiar territory in Wittgenstein's world. We think of words as having meanings, and as being names of the things they mean. And we may take these meanings to be Tractarian objects or to be images in the mind. In either case, we are seeking something real (in one realm or another) that corresponds to our words and sentences. Hence we look (philosophically) for the pain that does not occur, the dream we do not have, the event we expected which did not materialize, the state of affairs we falsely described.

Sections 449-51 respond to one philosophical theory developed to explain the sense or meaning of our words and sentences in terms of some real but rarified entity. This is the imagistic theory, which embodies the assertion that understanding the meaning of a word (the sense of a sentence) involves having in the mind a real but mental entity, an image. In response, §449 reminds us that in operating with words we may indeed translate them into pictures (images are supposed to be like pictures), but no one picture is required – sometimes it is one, sometimes another. No super-image, the very shadow of a thing or state of affairs, is necessary. In §450 we are told that in order to know what someone looks like it is not necessary to be able to imagine that person at all; being able to mimic his expression is just as good. And the telling blow to the imagistic theory comes in §451: what if we are given the order 'Imagine a red circle here'? According to the imagistic theory, to understand this order, I would have to imagine the act that is to be performed. Am I, then, to imagine that I imagine a red circle here? What could that possibly be like?

17 In *Philosophical Grammar*, Wittgenstein speaks of the ambiguity of expressions like 'the colour red as the common element of two states of affairs', and he tells us that 'this may mean that in each something *is* red, has the colour red; or else that both propositions are about the colour red' (p. 135). He goes on to say: 'What is common in the latter case is the harmony between reality and thought to which indeed a form of our language corresponds' (ibid.). This form of language is a set of grammatical possibilities – the ways in which we use 'red' meaningfully: among others, to say that there is a red patch here and that there is not a red patch here.

18 'The sign does its job only in a grammatical system' (*PG* p. 133).

19 There are, to be sure, misidentifications of the person we are thinking about. If I say 'I was thinking of Babe Ruth the other day', it may come out in discussion that I was really thinking of Ty Cobb, not Babe Ruth. This would become apparent if I agreed to a description of the person I was thinking about ('The player who prior to 1950 had the most hits in his career') and then came to see that it was Cobb, not Ruth, who is identified by this description. In spite of my misidentification, however, the person I am thinking about is determined by the linguistic 'label' that I would be willing to use, perhaps upon reflection, in expressing my thought or describing a past thought. It is possible that I could misidentify the object of my thought both by applying the wrong name *and* the wrong description(s) to it, but what I *am* thinking about is identified in the end by a name or description or pronoun I would agree to apply to the person or object.

20 Wittgenstein tells us in the *Philosophical Grammar* that 'thoughts are in the same space as the things that admit of doubt; they are laid against them in the same way as a ruler is laid against what is to be measured' (pp. 142–3). And in likening propositions to yardsticks in the *Philosophical Remarks*, he claims that just as we put all the graduation marks on a yardstick up against the object to be measured, so we put a system of propositions up against reality when we 'measure' it with a proposition (p. 110).

21 Grammar is the great solvent of queerness in adjacent areas as well. Wittgenstein asks in §435: 'How do sentences represent? Don't you know? After all, nothing is hidden'. These questions are not really straightforward questions about a process of representation (see J. F. M. Hunter, *Understanding Wittgenstein*, Edinburgh, Edinburgh University Press, 1985, pp. 155–60). The answer to them is not: 'Yes, of course we know; sentences obviously do it this way.' That sentences represent is a grammatical proposition – that is just what some sentences do, what we mean by the word 'sentence'. Some sentences tell us what to do, others express our feelings, others represent facts, and still others do other, many other, things. But that a particular sentence represents is not a mystery – it is simply one of the things that, as a matter of grammar, sentences are defined to do.

22 In his Cambridge lectures of 1930-32, Wittgenstein had this to say: 'What is common between thought and reality must already be expressed in the expression of the thought. You cannot express it in a further proposition' (*L30* p. 37). And what is this common element that is expressed? As we will observe in a moment, it cannot be the 'description' – the clause that could be converted into a description – used to express the thought, for the thought may be false, in which case the 'description' expressing the thought does not apply to reality. It is the grammar of this 'description', or the grammatical system to which it belongs, that is common to the thought and reality; it is this grammar which is expressed in the expression of the thought.

23 This notion of a grammatical system also allows us to explain how signs have life, this being the problem we encountered on first entering the midlands of §§428-65: 'the system of language seems to provide me with a medium in which the proposition is no longer dead' (*PG* p. 149).

24 'What makes it possible for us to judge rightly about the world also makes it possible for us to judge wrongly' (*L30* p. 37).

25 This presupposition may appear as a 'shadow': 'It looks as if a sentence with e.g. the word "ball" in it already contained the shadow of other uses of this word. That is to say, the *possibility* of forming those other sentences. – To whom does it look like that? And under what circumstances?' (*Z* §138). The concluding questions in this passage warn us that these other possible uses of a word do not have to float before our minds when we use the word in one of its grammatically permitted ways.

26 'Could we imagine any language at all in which expecting *p* was described without using "p"?'

'Isn't that *just as* impossible as a language in which~p would be expressed without using "p" ?' (*PR* p. 69).

Chapter 10

'Das Wollen ist auch nur eine Erfahrung'

Stewart Candlish

Wittgenstein's discussion of the will in *Philosophical Investigations* has not been ignored by subsequent philosophers. But it has received very little in the way of systematic exegesis,[1] even though it is refined almost to the point of unintelligibility. Instead, it has usually been quarried: individual remarks have been ripped from their context (the most common example of this is the question posed in §621) and discussed or developed in isolation. If my own reading of the secondary literature is anything to go by, hardly anyone seems to have felt the bafflement which I had always felt when confronted with the discussion's opening sentence in §611: ' "Willing too is merely an experience", one would like to say.' Why on earth should this be something that one would like to say? What is going on here? Are we just witnessing Wittgenstein's struggle with some private obsession? Or, perhaps more interestingly, is the idea that willing is merely an experience something which had been put forward independently, so that it seemed to Wittgenstein worth writing about? Or, as the impersonal 'one' suggests, is there some reason which, regardless of other philosophical commitments, anyone might share for thinking in his apparently quite unappealing way? It was through asking myself such questions as these that I came to examine the much rougher and more discursive texts that lie behind the polished surface of the discussion in *Philosophical Investigations*, texts which are far more revealing and which cast a great deal of light on the purpose and outcome of that discussion. I do not claim to have made any startling discoveries or to have a dramatic new interpretation with which to confound other students of Wittgenstein. More modestly, I offer readings of superficially puzzling passages which render them less puzzling and which show Wittgenstein's discussion of the will to exemplify certain themes which are *leitmotifs* of the *Philosophical Investigations*.

THE CONTEXT OF THE DISCUSSION

Despite Wittgenstein's decimal numbering system's illustrating non-sequential connections among its various propositions, it is tempting to read the *Tractatus* page by page, like a conventional book. Yet of course unless we read it non-sequentially, we shall be unlikely to understand it – for a start, the references of the pronouns will often escape us. But what is far more tempting is to read *Philosophical Investigations* sequentially, for here we have not even a decimalization scheme to remind us that it is constructed in much the same way as the *Tractatus*. So it is much more difficult to read than the *Tractatus*, for we have in effect to construct our own numbering as we proceed, and we must do this solely on the basis of internal connections among its sections – connections which may be very far from obvious until one has a numbering system which shows them up. Of course, even a Tractarian system may be insufficient to catch the various interconnections amongst the sections of the text. My point is that we need *at least* such a system, even if it is not made explicit; if we read the book sequentially, we risk getting into trouble.

Again, the references of the pronouns can be problematic: there is, for example, a particularly troublesome 'here' in the first sentence of §618. And to illustrate further, if we read sequentially, the discussion of the will seems to come from nowhere at §611, immediately following an apparently unconnected discussion of the description of the aroma of coffee. Losing its context, we may miss its sense. To get the context, I suggest, we must first look back to §571:

> Misleading parallel: psychology treats of processes in the psychical sphere, as does physics in the physical.

After §571, Wittgenstein discusses in its light *expectation, belief, hope,* and *intention*. Following these discussions, we get §598:

> When we do philosophy, we should like to hypostatise feelings where there are none. They serve to explain our thoughts to us.

(This passage is clearly subordinate to §571; in a Tractarian system, it would get just one extra digit.) Then, after some illustration of what is said in §598, the discussion of the will begins: we should expect its point to be that in the case of the will, too, 'we should like to hypostatise feelings where there are none'. With this context, it should now be no surprise that the discussion begins with one of Wittgenstein's interlocutors suggesting that 'Willing too is merely an experience', a suggestion to which, apparently *in propria persona*, he responds sharply. But whom does this interlocutor represent?

OTHER RELEVANT TEXTS

The *Tractatus* is of course a constant reference point in trying to identify the targets of *Philosophical Investigations*. But there are other possibilities too. First, Bertrand Russell's views are often lurking in the background of Wittgenstein's later writings. Second, Wittgenstein himself mentions (in passing) St Augustine. Third, in *Zettel* he makes a remark (§597) which indicates that lying behind his later treatment of the will is his reading of William James's *The Principles of Psychology*. For Wittgenstein mentions there (and again in *Zettel* §33) a characteristic Jamesian theme in the matter of the will, namely the idea that in voluntary action there is a feeling of innervation. (The idea was Wundt's; James was opposed to it.) This point indicates that we may also find *Zettel* itself useful here.

The source of *Zettel* §597 is §845 of volume I of *Remarks on the Philosophy of Psychology*. This shows that it was written in the period 1945–8, and that may suggest that it was composed too late to be taken into account when trying to understand remarks in Part I of *Philosophical Investigations*. But there are some reasons for not being as cautious in our interpretative efforts as this. One is that the later remarks in *Philosophical Investigations* Part I appear to have been composed not just pre-war but extending into the period just mentioned. Secondly, *Zettel* §580, although a more explicit rendering of the second half of *Philosophical Investigations* §613, is unintelligible without the first half, which means they must be read together and presumably that Wittgenstein would eventually have arranged that they should be; indeed, von Wright has even conjectured[2] that Wittgenstein intended the material in *Zettel* to be incorporated into *Philosophical*

Investigations itself. Be that as it may, and despite the somewhat dubious status, as part of Wittgenstein's oeuvre, of *Zettel* in the only form in which we have that work, it is nevertheless clear that, whereas Wittgenstein's remarks on this subject in *Philosophical Investigations* are mostly questions or are negative, in *Zettel* we find the sketch of a positive view of the will, without which the earlier discussion is seriously incomplete. (It is worth noting, though, that this incompleteness is, in a sense, to be expected. The emphasis on the philosophical primitiveness of human practice which is at the heart of *Philosophical Investigations* explains both why Wittgenstein includes a discussion of the will - although it no longer features as a *problem* for him as it did in the *Tractatus*, he can hardly leave so central a topic neglected - and why that discussion should largely consist of rejections of attempts to make familiar bodily human action itself something derivative.)

'WILLING TOO IS MERELY AN EXPERIENCE'

I asked just now whom Wittgenstein's interlocutor represented when he said:

> 'Willing too is merely an experience', one would like to say (the 'will' too only 'idea'). It comes when it comes, and I cannot bring it about.

One obvious answer is the author of the *Tractatus*, who included just such a doctrine in that book (6.373-4; 6.423). But as I have already indicated in arguing that we should also consider *Zettel* here, other possible sources are James and Russell. (St Augustine can be ruled out.) Russell explicitly asserted that his 'main thesis [is] that all psychic phenomena are built up out of sensations and images alone',[3] which seems to make him a natural target of much of *Philosophical Investigations* as well as someone who thinks that willing is just an experience; and later in the same chapter he says of the will that he sees no reason to doubt the correctness of James's view. I have already mentioned that *Zettel* gives us good reason for thinking that James is prominent in the background in general during Wittgenstein's discussion of the will. There is much circumstantial evidence for this, found mainly in ideas common to both men's discussions. But there is conclusive proof of this prominence in the manuscript known as *Eine Philosophische Betrachtung*,[4] Wittgenstein's 1936 attempted reworking in German of the *Brown Book*. There, in a discussion of the will which is a clear forerunner of that in *Philosophical Investigations*, but which is absent from the *Brown Book* itself, Wittgenstein makes explicit mention of James's chapter on the will in *The Principles of Psychology*.[5] So any content common to the views of Wittgenstein's interlocutor in §611 and those of James is unlikely to be a coincidence. And here are two passages from James which reveal just such a common content:

> *whether or no there be anything else in the mind at the moment when we consciously will a certain act, a mental conception made up of memory-images of these sensations, defining which special act it is, must be there.*
>
> Now *is there anything else in the mind when we will to do an act?* We must proceed . . . from the simpler to the more complicated cases. My first thesis accordingly is, that *there need be nothing else, and that in perfectly simple voluntary acts there is nothing else, in the mind but the kinaesthetic idea, thus defined, of what the act is to be.*
>
> (pp. 492-3)

> With the prevalence, once there as a fact, of the motive idea the *psychology* of volition properly stops. The movements which ensue are exclusively physiological phenomena, following according to physiological laws upon the neural events to which the idea corresponds. The *willing* terminates with the prevalence of the idea; and whether the act then follows or not is a matter quite immaterial, so far as the willing itself goes. I will to write, and the act follows. I will to sneeze, and it does not. . . . In a word, volition is a psychic or moral fact pure and simple, and is absolutely completed when the stable state of the idea is there. The supervention of motion is a supernumerary phenomenon depending on executive ganglia whose function lies outside the mind.
>
> (p. 560)

These quotations demonstrate beyond all shadow of doubt that James, as well as Russell and the author of the *Tractatus*, held the view expressed in at least the opening sentence of §611 (I shall leave open for a moment the question of whether James was committed to that expressed in the second sentence); and together with the other evidence marshalled earlier, they show that James was a principal target of Wittgenstein's later discussion of the will, since that sentence introduces the doctrine which forms the discussion's central theme.

We now have three foci of the attack on the doctrine of §611. But this still does not explain why Wittgenstein says in §611, 'one would like to say'; for this phrase indicates some source of the view other than the mere influence of books by him and by James. Wittgenstein, in using the impersonal '*man*', is identifying a perennial temptation, as he says, 'when we do philosophy', and the particular holders of the view that willing is an experience feature here merely as an exemplification of that general tendency. So we should at least try to consider why the idea that willing is merely an experience is supposed to be tempting. Is it just because of that general tendency towards hypostatizing feelings which Wittgenstein mentions, or is there something about the will itself which makes the idea especially alluring?

Part, at least, of the answer comes from our authority on our own willing. One of the themes of *Philosophical Investigations* could be summarized in this way: contrary to Russell's main thesis, difference in mental state is not always reflected in difference in mental content, if content is defined narrowly so as to exclude essential reference to the outside world. (I have in mind, for example, Descartes's *Principles of Philosophy*, I, ix.) To illustrate this, we could cite the discussion of *seeing as* (*PI* II, xi), and the famous remark that 'If God had looked into our minds he would not have been able to see there whom we were speaking of' (p. 217); the idea is prefigured in the *Tractatus* in the discussion of the Necker cube (5.5423) and in its Kierkegaardian suggestion that the ethical will cannot alter events in the world but can, nevertheless, alter the world as a whole. But the significance of the idea was not developed or appreciated in the *Tractatus*, and it would only be natural for someone who had not yet seen this significance to assume that the exercise of the will is phenomenally distinguishable in experience. For how else could we explain our seeming authority on this matter? One seems to know for sure that and what one is willing, and how could one know this unless the willing and its content could be read off from one's experience at the time? This is the way in which

Wittgenstein was thinking at one stage during the composition of *Notebooks 1914–16*:

> The will seems always to have to relate to an idea. We cannot imagine, e.g., having carried out an act of will without having detected that we have carried it out.

> (*NB* p. 86)

Moreover, the will typically does not err in finding its object, and Wundt thought that this ability too must be underpinned by an experience, according to James (*Principles of Philosophy*, p. 493). Wundt offered the feeling of innervation as this underpinning. And James – rejecting the supposed feeling of innervation, but still looking for an underpinning – assumes that the answer must lie in some other phenomenon, and finds the sole remaining one to be the kinaesthetic idea:

> *All our ideas of movement,* including those of the effort which it requires, as well as those of its direction, its extent, its strength, and its velocity, *are images of peripheral sensations, either 'remote', or resident in the moving parts, or in other parts which sympathetically act with them in consequence of the 'diffusive wave.'*

> (pp. 493–4)

> Let the reader try to direct his will towards a particular movement, and then notice what *constituted* the direction of the will. Was it anything over and above the notion of the different feelings to which the movement when effected would give rise? If we abstract from these feelings, will any sign, principle, or means of orientation be left by which the will may innervate the right muscles with the right intensity, and not go astray into the wrong ones? Strip off these images of result, and so far from leaving us with a complete assortment of directions into which our will may launch itself, you leave our consciousness in an absolute and total vacuum.

> (p. 500)

James, we might say, is from Wittgenstein's point of view half-right: he has rejected a spurious phenomenon, but has not made the final step of rejecting all phenomena. (We shall see that this summary of the position needs modification.)

That was part of the answer to the question of the sources of the temptation to think of the will in terms of experience. But Wittgenstein himself, on page 236 of *Eine Philosophische Betrachtung*, identifies for us another source. After mentioning the experiment where one crosses one's hands, intertwines one's fingers and then is unable to move a finger specified merely visually until it is touched as well, he says:

> This experiment, just like that in which the task is to draw a square with its diagonals in the mirror, shows, so one would like to say, that willing too is only an experience (the 'will' only 'idea'). 'It comes when it comes; I cannot bring it about.' – Or: 'One can't will whenever one wants. It just happens.'
>
> (My translation: the closeness of this passage to *PI* §611 is obvious)

But why should these experiences lead one to the view that willing is only an experience? The connection is not obvious. One hypothesis is that it works through there being something in each experiment which I cannot bring about, despite my being someone of normal faculties, so that the second sentence of §611 is treated as grounds for the first. What is this something? All there seems to be is the action itself, but an *action* is hardly 'merely an experience', and anyway, the discussion arising from this passage, in *Philosophical Investigations* §§613–19, appears to be concerned with the idea that willing is an event prior to the action itself. The solution to this puzzle can be found in *Notebooks 1914–1916*. It is clear there that Wittgenstein was intrigued by the mirror-writing experiment from an early stage (*NB* p. 87), and he says of it

> one notices that one is only able to manage it if one prescinds completely from the visual datum and relies only on muscular feeling. So here after all there are two quite different acts of the will in question. The one relates to the visual part of the world, the other to the muscular-feeling part.

(This idea of the duality of the will in this case persists in attenuated form in his later discussion of it in the *Brown Book* (*BB* p 154).) Now this does lead to the idea that one cannot produce the requisite experience of willing prior to the action. For all we can get is the visual anticipation of the projected action, and that leads, as we know, to the wrong action – the wrong finger being moved, or the pencil being moved in the wrong direction. It is only when we obtain the kinaesthetic idea of the required motion that we can bring off the action, and this is not something we can obtain for ourselves directly, but something which 'comes when it comes', for example by someone touching the required finger in the intertwining experiment, or moving the hand for us in the required direction in the mirror-writing experiment, or by our accidentally making the right movement in either experiment.

Now despite its having apparently occurred to Wittgenstein independently, this is a characteristically Jamesian idea, for, as we saw earlier, James talks of willing as a prior occurrence of memory-images of kinaesthetic sensations. One might even say that, for James, willing an act is just thinking about it kinaesthetically, and indeed this seems a fair summary of his ideomotor theory of action, according to which such thinking is automatically translated into action unless inhibited by contrary thoughts: 'consciousness is *in its very nature impulsive*', he says (p. 526), and the bare idea of a movement's sensible effects can be that movement's sufficient mental cue, failing to be so only when there is some '*conflicting notion in the mind*' (ibid.).

I have already mentioned how close the passage I translated from *Eine Philosophische Betrachtung* is to *Philosophical Investigations* §611:

> 'Willing too is merely an experience', one would like to say (the 'will' too only 'idea'). It comes when it comes, and I cannot bring it about.

What is the logical relation between the first and second sentences here? One possibility, as we have seen, is that the second is offered as grounds for the first. If that were so, there should be independent reason for supposing the second to be true. What reason is there? If we think again of the author of the *Tractatus*, we can see that this idea was forced on Wittgenstein by other doctrines of that book. As Winch points out, the sole connection of the ego to the world is via the proposition, and it is impossible for the ego to constrain directly the course of events in a world in which the only necessity is logical necessity and everything that happens is contingent. But this is only an answer to the question, 'Why might Wittgenstein have held this view?'; it does not show us why *anyone* could be tempted by it. We might show this by considering that willing is traditionally the ego's original executive relation to the world, the origin of all our bringing-about. As such, it cannot itself be brought about by some different and more original agency; and if an episode of willing is brought about by a further episode of willing, we face the question of what brought about the further episode. If we are to avoid an infinite regress, then there must be some episode of willing not itself brought about; and if there is one such, we have to explain the nature of the difference between the unbrought-about and the brought-about kinds. But *ex hypothesi* there is no such difference. (The relation to Ryle's most effective argument against the doctrine of volitions is apparent.)

We have seen that the second sentence of §611 could be taken as giving the grounds for the first. But could the first be taken as giving grounds for the second? There is some slight textual evidence that Wittgenstein intended §611 to be read this way. This evidence appears in §97 of *Philosophical Grammar* (written in 1932-4), where Wittgenstein compares willing with meaning and intending and this time expresses the opposite view to the one expressed at the opening of *Philosophical Investigations* §611, so that to get the desired reading we have to apply transposition and cast the result into the subjunctive mood:

> This is like when we say: 'The will can't be a phenomenon, for whatever phenomenon you take is something that *simply happens*, something we undergo, not something we *do*. The will isn't *something* I see happen, it's more like my being involved in my actions, my *being* my actions.'

I think the truth is, however, that Wittgenstein saw the first two sentences of §611 as expressing the same view in two different ways, for on page 235 of *Eine Philosophische Betrachtung* he says:

> 'The will is an experience' –, in contrast with what? – I could instead also have said: 'The will *happens* to me'.

And perhaps all that can in the end be said about why Wittgenstein thought this view tempting was contained in my remarks about the two experiments which inclined Wittgenstein himself towards it. But there is one other potential source of temptation which might be worth mentioning. This is introspection. James automatically turned to introspection when seeking insight into the nature of some psychological phenomenon; this tendency is exhibited in the first quotation from James in this paper, and in the following striking passage from his chapter on the will:

> It was in fact through meditating on the phenomenon in my own person that I first became convinced of the truth of the doctrine which these pages present.
>
> (p. 525)

When asked about the nature of the voluntary act, and how it differs from the involuntary movement, a natural reaction is for us to scrutinize ourselves inwardly while we set about doing something, thinking about what we are doing. In such circumstances, where we forget that most voluntary actions are not performed so reflectively, we are likely to land on some sort of mental event as the willing event, and particularly upon some thought of what the act is to be, just as James landed on 'the kinaesthetic idea of what the act is to be'. Once we have done this, an equally natural inference would be that we cannot bring about this experience, for it does not lie within our power to bring about any experience directly (though indirect bringing-about is a different matter), and the exercise of the will is supposed to influence events directly (cf. *PI* §613). The apparently obvious implication (explicit in the *Tractatus*) is that, being unable to bring about my willing, I am powerless.

This consequence of the view that willing is merely an experience is combatted in §§612–14 of *Philosophical Investigations*, in a discussion which overlaps with a not obviously motivated attack on the idea that willing is a sort of wishing, an attack which runs from §614 to §616. The puzzling thing is to see how the idea that willing is wishing is connected with the Jamesian view that willing is an experience. But in fact James's theory is precisely a theory in which willing and wishing are conflated, and even where he apparently distinguishes them, the impression of his having done so does not survive close scrutiny. For example, speaking of the effort of will required to get out of a warm bed on a cold morning, he says:

> It was our acute consciousness of both the warmth and the cold during the period of struggle, which paralyzed our activity then and kept our idea of rising in the condition of *wish* and not of *will*. The moment these inhibitory ideas ceased, the original idea exerted its effect.
>
> (p. 525)

If we read this carefully, we find that the distinction between the ideas belonging to *wish* and those belonging to *will* is a distinction entirely external to the ideas themselves, dependent purely upon whether or not the mind contains contrary inclinations. Notice that this position is, in fact, a logical consequence of James's ideo-motor theory described a moment ago. The conflation of willing and wishing was something towards which Wittgenstein was tempted in the *Notebooks* (though he firmly rejected it in one of the passages suppressed from the text of the *Tractatus*), and which appears explicitly in the *Tractatus* at 6.374; unpalatable when spelled out, it is nevertheless a fair summary of the consequence of supposing willing to be an experience, for on the ideo-motor theory of which that supposition is an expression, no distinction other than a merely external one can be drawn between willing and wishing, and thus on that theory it can be no more closely related to action than is wishing; that is why such an unpromising idea figures prominently in *Philosophical Investigations*.

'THE WILL IS NOT AN EXPERIENCE'

The historical and metaphysical roots of the idea that willing is merely an experience proved to be tangled, but those of the opposite idea are easier to deal with. In the passage from *Philosophical Grammar* which I quoted in the last section, we see a reaction against the idea that willing is an experience. And in that reaction are the roots of the idea of the ineffability of the will, of the impossibility of there being any experiences characteristic of willing. Wittgenstein will resist this view too, as he resists the view of §611; and this double resistance is typical, as we can see when we reflect on how he refuses either to identify thinking with some mental phenomenon like imaging or to conclude that it must therefore be some ineffable mental act which lies beyond the reach of all phenomena. The setting of *Philosophical Grammar* §97 itself displays this similarity between his treatment of the will and his treatment of thinking, via its discussion of intentionality.

Again, *Eine Philosophische Betrachtung* is helpful here. In *Philosophical Investigations* the oscillation between the views that willing is phenomenal and that it is non-phenomenal is half-smothered, perhaps because Wittgenstein is now more interested in what the views have in common – that is, the idea of willing as our executive relation to our physical acts; and when the latter view does appear explicitly, at §620, no particular attention is paid to the contrast between it and its opposite. Whereas on p. 235 of the earlier work we find Wittgenstein bringing it out quite explicitly:

> Here there is a curious conflict of two ideas: one would like to say, 'the will is not an experience' and – 'but the will is only experience'. What in general do these two sentences mean, and why does one want to say both?

Just as I explored the background to the view that willing is merely an experience, now it is time to do the same for the opposing view. Here again the idea can be found in the *Tractatus*. This is not to say the *Tractatus* is blatantly inconsistent; rather, it contains a doctrine of the bifurcation of the will, distinguishing in 6.423 between 'the will as a phenomenon . . . of interest only to psychology' and the will as 'the subject of ethical attributes', about which 'it is impossible to speak'. Wittgenstein's early reading of Schopenhauer is well known, and this odd view of the ethical will has its historical roots in Schopenhauer's critique of Kant (*The World as Will and Representation*, vol. II, p. 196):

> 'As perception can furnish only *phenomena*, not things-in-themselves, we too have absolutely no knowledge of things-in-themselves.' I admit this of everything, but not of the knowledge everyone has of his own *willing*. This is neither a perception (for all perception is spatial), nor is it empty; on the contrary, it is more real than any other knowledge . . . . In fact, our *willing* is the only opportunity we have of understanding simultaneously from within any event that outwardly manifests itself; consequently, it is the one thing known to us *immediately* and not given to us merely in the representation, as all else is.

But again, Wittgenstein does not merely single out his past self for criticism; again, he says that *one* would like to say 'the will is not an experience', and so again we have to look for some pressure towards this idea which anyone could feel. The pressure is given expression in *Philosophical Grammar* §97, in a form far more articulate than anything we find in *Philosophical Investigations*, after he has just been talking about how intention cannot be a phenomenon, because no mere phenomenon could contain the thing intended as an intention does:

> This is like when we say: 'The will can't be a phenomenon, for whatever phenomenon you take is something that *simply happens,* something we undergo, not something we *do.* The will isn't *something* I see happen, it's more like my being involved in my actions, my *being* my actions.' Look at your arm and move it and you will experience this very vividly: 'You aren't observing it moving itself, you aren't having an experience – not just an experience, anyway – you're *doing* something.'

The point might be put this way: if, looking for the real action, the unmoved mover, we try to fix on some phenomenon, this phenomenon will always appear to us as itself something produced, not as producer. (The problem appears graphically, and catastrophically, in Jennifer Hornsby's theory of the will.)[6]

BOTH VIEWS REJECTED

Wittgenstein criticizes both the inclination to identify willing with some item of experience and the contrary inclination to render willing ineffable. Against the view that willing is an experience which I cannot bring about, he employs a variety of tactics. He first (§612) relieves the pressure to think like this, by reminding us that we should never be inclined to say of an ordinary action that 'it comes when it comes'; he then (§613) disentangles a perfectly ordinary sense of 'bring about' in which it is quite possible for me to bring about my willing, thereby making it clear that no such ordinary sense was in question in the original metaphysical remark such as we found in the *Tractatus.* But the extraordinary sense, identified next, is no sense at all, – 'it makes no sense to speak of willing willing'; if it did, then 'willing' would be the name of an act, but it is not – one cannot, for example, obey the command to will, as nothing is specified thereby. An implied point here is that 'bringing about' is the wrong way to think about our actions; and it is worth noticing that the German *'herbeiführen'*, which I have so far followed Miss Anscombe in translating as 'bring about', can also be translated as 'cause'. It would be impossible to translate the whole of §613 in this way, for we could not then make sense of *'ein unmittelbares, nichtkausales, Herbeiführen'*, but since this last notion is itself rejected as arising from a misleading analogy, one which supposes the causal nexus to be a sort of intervening mechanism, we can perhaps read Wittgenstein as anticipating Donald Davidson's insight that we do not in the normal case cause our own actions, whether this causation be direct or indirect.[7]

In any case, according to Wittgenstein, I employ no means[8] to bring my actions about; and he seems to me to be deriving this conclusion in §§614–16 via the claims that any willing which was an experience prior to action would have to be a kind of wishing, and that ordinary action excludes wishing. But whatever the precise order of his thought here, its conclusion is clear: if we are to speak of willing as involved in my acts at all, then it is so involved not as their source, but as the actions themselves (§615), another idea with its roots in the views of Schopenhauer (*The World as Will and Representation*, vol. I, p. 100).

At §617 he mentions the example which, as we saw previously, he himself had found particularly inclined him to the view that willing is an experience prior to action, over whose occurrence one had no real power, namely, the intertwining experiment. He expresses this inclination here by saying, 'One would like to describe this experience as follows: we are unable to *will* to move the finger.' But then he immediately contrasts that experiment with the case where the finger is merely prevented from moving by being held, and the reminder of this contrast modifies our view of the experiment, so that the inclination now is to describe it not in terms of an inability to will but in terms of an inability to find any point of application for the will. (This is the point which marks the beginning of the shift, completed in §620, from consideration of the will as a phenomenon in experience to considering it as something which lies behind all possible experience, something ineffable.) He tries to combat this new inclination by suggesting that what we suppose to restore to us a point of application in fact can do no such thing. The implicit conclusion is that this whole conception of the will as something prior to the bodily act is mistaken.

At §618 we continue with the idea of the ineffability of willing.

I think the word 'here' in its first line cannot possibly be interpreted as referring to the immediately preceding paragraph. Rather, it seems to me that it must refer to §613's 'willing as an immediate, non-causal bringing-about', not working through a mechanism which can offer resistance, a phrase which strikes me as an elaboration of the underlying idea which I suggested was common to both the view that willing is phenomenal and the view that it is ineffable. He explores this in §618 through the suggestion that it makes sense to say that my body does not obey my will, but not that my will does not, and refers us here to Augustine. In the relevant passage in the *Confessions* (book 8, ch. 8), Augustine says something which seems to me very close to this: having isolated a class of acts (mental, as opposed to bodily, acts) in which to will them is identical with performing them, Augustine finds himself unable to perform one of them. We need not trouble ourselves here with Augustine's resolution of this difficulty; the immediate point is that this strikes him as at least superficially a contradiction. Wittgenstein seems to agree, remarking that one cannot say 'My will does not obey me'; the point blossoms into metaphysical luxuriance at §620, with the observation:

> *Doing* itself seems not to have any volume of experience. It seems like an extensionless point, the point of a needle. This point seems to be the real agent. And the phenomenal happenings only to be consequences of this acting. 'I *do* . . .' seems to have a definite sense, separate from all experience.

But the fact has been obscured that with his very next sentence Wittgenstein brings us immediately back from this rarefied atmosphere. The crucial word 'But', which should open §621, has been omitted from Miss Anscombe's translation, so that the point, which is to remind us that there *are* phenomena involved in action, has been lost. Once it is restored we can easily see the connection between the last sentence of §620 above and the first of §621:

> But let us not forget this: when 'I raise my arm', my arm goes up.

The restoration of 'but' also helps us to come to terms with the famous question of §621, which comes next:

> And the problem arises: what is left over if I subtract the fact
> that my arm goes up from the fact that I raise my arm?

This question is often excised from its context, and assumed to
have an obvious sense which survives the surgery; by some
writers, 'fact' is, remarkably, interpreted as 'event', as though
Wittgenstein thought that the metaphorical subtraction might
even be done literally and the right event identified. But now we
can see that since §621 is a response to §620, its question should
not be assumed to be capable of standing alone wearing its sense
upon its face. The context makes it clear that what is being asked
is, given that 'I *do* . . .' *seems* to have a sense separate from all
experience but that action does involve experiential phenomena,
are these phenomena merely consequences of that doing? What
do we find if we attempt to subtract the seemingly non-active
consequential phenomena from the total action? It will help in
thinking about this question if we add some historical context
too, for there is an obvious connection with the earlier and rather
easier discussion at *Philosophical Grammar* §97:

> Very well; but there's no doubt that you *also* have experiences
> when you voluntarily move your arm; because you *see* (and
> feel) it moving whether or not you take up the attitude of an
> *observer*. So just for once try to distinguish between *all the
> experiences* of acting plus the doing (which is not an exper-
> ience) and *all* those experiences without the element of doing.
> Think over whether you still need this element, or whether it
> is beginning to appear redundant.

It seems to me that Wittgenstein was inclined to think that it *was*
redundant, for here only the metaphysical answer of §620 is
under consideration. And in *Philosophical Investigations* it
seems that he may be prepared to contemplate the answer
'Nothing is left over in experience' to §621's question, without
his regarding this as a proof that there is something left over
which is *not* in experience, an 'extensionless point' which is the
real doing.

Nevertheless, he considers two things which might be held to
be possible candidates for the role of a phenomenal doing. The
first is one which has anyway been quite popular in recent action
theory, namely, *trying*. Apparently thinking of trying as something involving experienced effort, he rejects this candidate very

quickly (§§622–3) on the grounds that it is not true that I try to do something which there is no difficulty in doing.[9]

What he spends more time over (§§624–6) is the unpromising-looking suggestion, appearing at the end of §621 in double brackets,[10] that what is left over might be the kinaesthetic sensations of action. (The words 'for example' – German *'etwa'* – in the opening sentence of §624 may mislead us into thinking that §624 refers to §623; but what is exemplified is nothing to do with the discussion of trying in §§622–3; rather, it must be the experiential interpretation of §621's idea of what is left over once we subtract the seemingly non-active consequential phenomena from the total action.) This suggestion draws on the fact that a voluntary physical action simply *feels* different from an involuntary movement.

Wittgenstein's procedure in this short section is worthy of remark. In §624 we are invited to consider two experiments. One is an imagined laboratory experiment in which the subject is induced by means of the application of an electric current to judge that he is moving his arm when in fact the arm is still; the other is one which Wittgenstein asks us actually to do for ourselves – we are to move an arm to and fro with our eyes shut, and then to try to tell ourselves that the arm is still and that we are only having peculiar feelings in it. The latter experiment appears to have two ancestors: one is the opposite invitation by William James (p. 527):

> Try to feel as if you were crooking your finger, whilst keeping it straight.

The other is a significantly different experiment described in *Philosophical Grammar* §97:

> But shut your eyes, and move your arm so that you have, among other things, a certain experience: now ask yourself whether you still can imagine that you were having the same experience but without willing it.

We might call these three experiments which one can do for oneself 'domestic', in order to distinguish them from the laboratory experiment. The three appear to have in common that the described outcomes are meant to be impossible, and this impossibility is itself supposed to prove something. James wanted to show that the imagining of bodily movement leads inexorably to the occurrence of that movement; in *Philosophical Grammar*, Wittgenstein appears to be wanting to use the experiment to oppose the doctrine of the ineffability of the will.

But in *Philosophical Investigations* he is attacking a certain conception of the relationship between bodily sensation and willing; hence the difference between this domestic experiment and its ancestor in *Philosophical Grammar*. To see what this conception is, it is important to notice that there is no implication at all that the *laboratory* experiment with its outcome is inconceivable. (Though a moment's thought shows that there is some reason to suppose that it is: what on earth would the subject say when asked *why* he was moving his arm up and down?) On the contrary: what he sets his face against here is the *construction* which we may be inclined to put upon the apparent conceivability of that experiment, the construction that the procedure produces in the subject some special kinaesthetic feeling, which is the willing itself, and on the basis of which he can judge that he is willing an arm movement when the arm remains still. It is in reaction to this construction that the domestic experiment is proposed. The invitation to conduct the domestic experiment is an invitation to isolate that supposed special feeling in one's experience, by moving the arm (and thus, if there is such a thing as willing at all, and if this willing is indeed a special sort of kinaesthetic sensation, of necessity willing the arm movement), but imagining that the arm does not comply and that everything is just feeling as though it has done so. One finds by this experiment that it is impossible to bring oneself to believe that the arm remains still, as it did (*ex hypothesi*) in the imaginary laboratory experiment, and this failure shows that there is no such feeling as was suggested. Hence what we encounter in the way of actual kinaesthetic sensations cannot be the required event of willing, something which could be left over from the subtraction of the fact that my arm has gone up.

What then is left over if I subtract the fact that my arm goes up from the fact that I raise my arm? In the case where my arm does go up: nothing of the kind that a proponent of the idea of willing would be looking for. Whatever we find, it is not an event. This observation throws us forward to the hint of §628, which is taken up in the final section of this paper.

Instead of thinking of the occurrence of feelings as something on which we base our judgments as to whether we have acted or not, Wittgenstein tries to convince us, in §625, that the judgment is the criterion of the feeling.[11] Given that the only sort of judgment we are capable of making here is a judgment which explicitly refers to the position and movement of the limb in identifying the supposed feeling which is supposed to inform us of that position and movement, I think that what this comes to is that, if we are to speak of such feelings at all (given that much of our authority to pronounce about ourselves is not based on feeling in even the broadest natural sense of that term), these bodily and kinaesthetic feelings come to us already laden with, or at least accompanied by, spatial and dynamic information; that an extreme empiricist view according to which we construct this information for ourselves on the basis of noticing various correlations among these feelings (the sort of view still infecting his thought even in the *Blue Book*, *BB* p.52) is something which is just flatly contrary to the phenomenological facts of the matter; that these facts, with their spatial and dynamic information, are revealed by the impossibility of success in the domestic experiment of §624; that our bodily and kinsthetic feelings are importantly different in their informational status from, say, our visual sensations; and that this point is yet a further stone in the edifice of the case against the idea of a private language. (Notice that Wittgenstein does not say that such judgments can't be wrong, that is that the spatial and dynamic information on which they are based is infallible; all the experiment shows is that we cannot pretend to ourselves that the information does not exist.)

The treatment of the will in *Philosophical Investigations* closes with a positive hint at §§627–8: that 'voluntary movement is marked by the absence of surprise'. But this is little more than a hint; there are obvious exceptions to the rule; and what is said is so sketchy that he can hardly have thought it satisfactory. For a start, more needs to be said about the *kind* and *basis* of this absence of surprise. *Zettel*, on the other hand, indicates something of what might be said about the will once one has absorbed the negative lessons of *Philosophical Investigations*.

ZETTEL: A MIDDLE WAY

My injunction to read *Philosophical Investigations* non-linearly applies *a fortiori* to *Zettel*. For here we have lost any chance there may have been of discovering, prior to interpretation, what Wittgenstein's intended ordering of the fragments was, let alone what it would have been had he been satisfied with it. In one way this relieves us of a burden, for we are not obliged to give a coherent reading of any particular set of pages; instead, we are quite entitled to do something which most commentators on Wittgenstein have done habitually without entitlement (and in a far more extreme fashion than I propose here), that is to quarry the text for individual passages which suit our purposes and then put them together. I suggest that the following passages should be treated in this way: §§577, 587, 588, 593,[12] 594, 596 and 599.[13]

It seems to me impossible to put a uniquely correct ordering on this collection of remarks (though it is certainly possible to get a better ordering than Geach's). Despite that fact, certain themes are clearly discernible in them:

(i) Voluntary movement is characterized by its susceptibility to orders, involuntary by its insusceptibility (§593).

(ii) The previous point is in some way connected with the possibility of deciding whether or not to do something, which also characterizes the voluntary (§588).

(iii) Voluntariness is reflected in the very character of the movements and their relations to other surrounding events and circumstances (§578). Thus someone asked to do something doesn't necessarily do it automatically (§§587, 594). This connects with the first point in this list: it is not just the susceptibility to orders which counts, but the manner of this susceptibility – orders should not normally be *automatically* obeyed (§593).

(iv) We cannot speak of the voluntariness of movements in abstraction from their normal surroundings (§577).

(v) We can learn about the concept of voluntariness by considering the behaviour of children (§§593, 594, 587).

(vi) One characterization of the difference between voluntary and involuntary is that one draws different conclusions from them (§599).

(vii) It is unusual to have movements which are now voluntary, now involuntary; a special surrounding is required (§577).

(viii) Surroundings include intention, learning, trying, acting, foreseeing, thoughts, feelings, orders, reactions, knowledge of the action by the agent, lack of surprise (§§577, 584, 588, 593, 594, 596, *PI* §§627–8).

We have here a discernible positive pattern of thought on the subject of the will. The first thing to notice is that the idea of 'willing' as our executive relation to our bodily acts, which I suggested was common to both the idea that willing is phenomenal and the idea that it is ineffable, has disappeared altogether. The only way in which willing is now conceived is as nothing other than our ordinary actions themselves. The distinction between the voluntary and the involuntary does not lie in the presence or absence of an extra element of willing; and *a fortiori* willing is not the source of our voluntary actions:

> One produces a sneeze or a fit of coughing in oneself, but not a voluntary movement. And the will does not produce sneezing, nor yet walking.
>
> (Z §579)

The new pattern of thought is that the distinction between voluntary and involuntary lies in the circumstances, and the type, of the movements concerned. While any particular movement of the mouth might in isolation be involuntary, *eating* is not (Z §578). This is a very radical idea in this context. It is not very difficult to accept the same point applied to other matters in the philosophy of psychology, such as the idea that we might have different colour-concepts so that what is in some sense the very same experience might be of a different colour in a society which drew its colour-boundaries in places different from ours. But to apply this to the will looks like going too far. For the impression that particular actions are *essentially* voluntary is very deep-rooted in our thinking.[14] It can seem just inconceivable that our voluntary movements do not have some special origin which gives them their voluntary character. Although Wittgenstein's ideas on, say, thinking have been taken up and successfully exploited,[15] I do not know of anyone who has exploited these parallel ideas of his on the will.[16]

NOTES

1 There is one outstanding article in the area, by Peter Winch ('Wittgenstein's Treatment of the Will', *Ratio*, 1968, vol. 10, pp. 38–53), but this focuses mainly on the *Tractatus*, and what I say here is

supplementary to, rather than rivalling, what he says. Garth Hallett has some useful comments in his *A Companion to Wittgenstein's 'Philosophical Investigations'*, Ithaca, Cornell University Press, 1977. There is one other article, by Don Gustafson, 'Wittgenstein and a Causal View of Intentional Action', in *Philosophical Investigations*, 1984, vol. 7, pp. 225–43, which treats this passage rather more extensively than Winch does. My views are rather different from Gustafson's. An article by H.E. Mason, 'On the Treatment of the Notion of the Will in Wittgenstein's Later Writings', *Philosophical Investigations*, 1988, vol. 11, reached me only after this paper had been completed in its first full draft, but has in any case very little overlap with what I have said.

2 'The Origin and Composition of the *Philosophical Investigations*', in J.V. Canfield, ed., *The Philosophy of Wittgenstein, Vol. 4: The Later Philosophy – Views and Reviews*, New York, Garland, 1986, p. 168.

3 *The Analysis of Mind*, London, Allen & Unwin, 1921, p. 279.

4 Wittgenstein, *Schriften*, vol. 5, Suhrkamp, Frankfurt am Main, 1970, p. 234.

5 All references here to *The Principles of Psychology* are to volume 2 of the 1890 edition (Henry Holt & Co.). Italics in all quotations in this paper are always author's originals. (This point needs emphasis in James's case, as the reader will observe.)

6 Jennifer Hornsby, *Actions*, London, Routledge & Kegan Paul, 1980, p. 106.

7 For a proof of this claim, see my *'Absque Labore Nihil'*, *Australasian Journal of Philosophy*, 1986, vol. 64, section 4.

8 As I prefer to translate *'Mittel'* in §614, rather than Miss Anscombe's 'instrument', which seems to me less general in its application than the German word.

9 This move has commonly been rejected since Grice's influential paper 'The Causal Theory of Perception' (*Aristotelian Society*, 1961 supp. vol. 35), but I shall not try to sort out this difficult matter here. The interested reader can find a discussion of the claim that Wittgenstein replaced an account of meaning in terms of truth conditions with one in terms of assertibility conditions in Peter Winch's writings on Wittgenstein's views on truth, such as his paper 'Facts and Superfacts', reprinted in his *Trying To Make Sense*, Oxford, Blackwell, 1988. A related matter is this: that an imaginary example of sudden paralysis, where the imagined subtraction is of a very different kind, is not considered by Wittgenstein. I think this unfortunate, especially as much recent discussion of the will has turned upon the question of its significance.

10 The editors say of sections appearing between double brackets that they are 'Wittgenstein's references to remarks either in this work or in other writings of his which we hope will appear later'. I have been unable to find any passage in the published writings which would be the reference of this remark. (*PI*, II vii seems to me not to qualify.) Hallett implies that the remark refers to James; and indeed it might –

but if it does, it attributes to James a view which he never held, for he is quite clear that willing is not the kinaesthetic sensations themselves, but the ideas or thoughts of these sensations. There is textual evidence that Wittgenstein did not distinguish these two views, and I do not know whether he thought the distinction unimportant or his reading of James (or his recollection thereof) was faulty.

11 Here is a genuine connection with *PI* II, viii.

12 There is a mistake in the translation or printing of §593 which persists, along with others, even in the 'corrected' second English edition of *Zettel*. One of Wittgenstein's questions should read, not 'What are the *tokens* of involuntary action?' but 'What are the *tokens* of voluntary action?' Only if we notice this can we make sense of the translation to the subsequent question, 'Then what are the tokens of involuntary movement?'

13 Also of interest is §590, where 'our main problem' is connected with the epistemological problem of willing. The 'main problem' is surely that of *meaning*: what makes a mental image an image of X, for example? The connection is, what makes a movement a *willed* one? (This has its correlative epistemological problem, 'How do we tell when a movement is willed?') In both cases there is a temptation to give an answer in terms of a special causal background: this comes out in the form of a special act of mind, one that is ineffable, non-phenomenal in character, since any phenomenon seems dead until intentionality is breathed into it in the form of either meaning or willing. But in both cases Wittgenstein is inclined to answer the question as in §§587 and 588: 'Character and surroundings.'

14 The latest and most powerful expression of this idea is Brian O'Shaughnessy's book *The Will*, Cambridge, Cambridge University Press, 1980. What I go on to say next should not be taken to imply that O'Shaughnessy does not exploit other ideas of Wittgenstein's on the will: on the contrary.

15 See, for example, the first chapter of Hilary Putnam's *Reason, Truth and History*, Cambridge, Cambridge University Press, 1981.

16 Earlier versions of this paper were discussed in Munich, Bielefeld, Berlin, and Canberra, and this version is greatly improved as a result.

Chapter 11

Wittgenstein on believing in *Philosophical Investigations* part II, chapter 10

John F.M. Hunter

The short chapter on believing in Part II of the *Philosophical Investigations* generates more puzzlement per page, I think, than any other stretch of Wittgenstein's prose. The job of making sense of the chapter as a whole is like that of forming a picture out of pieces, any of which can be shaped or coloured, not in just any way at all, but in more than one way. In such a case a number of quite different pictures would be possible, depending on how we decided to shape or colour the pieces; and also if we wanted the picture to come out in a certain way we might have to cut or stretch or colour pieces in ways they seemed to resist.

If there is any coherent whole into which all the pieces, when sagely adjusted, fit, I have not found it. What I find rather is a major theme, a couple of minor themes, and a number of things that are also interesting, whatever the proper place for them might turn out to be. It is as if chapter 10 reproduced the contents of a file in which Wittgenstein collected thoughts on believing, perhaps not himself yet knowing what he would do with all of the miscellaneous deposits. In setting forth what I have made of this material, I will begin by presenting what seem to me the major themes, showing as I go along where some of the smaller parts fit, and what shape I have given them to make such fitting possible.

The central theme of the chapter, I suggest, is that believing is no kind of phenomenon that we might have noticed and given a name to, and that we are not reporting anything about ourselves when we say we believe such and such. If I am right about what Wittgenstein is contending here, the most important consequence will be that the innocent-sounding question what (which phenomenon) believing is, the question to which mentalistic, behaviouristic, and materialistic theories alike are offered as answers, will not arise, and will not call for an answer. A great deal of philosophical effort will thereby be shown to have been expended in vain.

I am assuming that Wittgenstein would give negative answers to the questions, whether we came to use the expression 'I believe . . .' through becoming aware of a phenomenon (of belief), and whether we observed ourselves and others and so discovered belief (*PI* p. 190(b)). To answer these questions negatively would be to make a very radical claim about the use of 'believe', at least in the first person present indicative: that, contrary to the strongest grammatical appearances, it does not report anything about the person who so uses it.

One could say: the speech act that is performed here is one, not of reporting, but rather of affirming. What happens is not that people notice that something they call believing is going on in them and proceed to inform others of this. If we say we believe that P, we are not answering the question 'Is believing that P going on in you?', but rather the question 'Who here declares P to be true?' (or '. . . *says* P is true?', *PI* p. 192(h)).

Let us call the main claim here the non-reporting theme. One of the ways it connects with the remarks at *PI* p. 190, paragraphs (c)–(e) about Moore's paradox is this: if believing were an experienceable phenomenon, it would be unparadoxical to say 'It is raining, but I don't believe it'. It might be quite unmistakably raining, while the phenomenon of believing was simply not occurring. If we asked why this never occurred, the answer might be that human beings are so cunningly designed or so well brought up that when they could see that it was raining, the phenomenon of believing it is raining just never failed to occur. But even so the description of this state of affairs would be altogether intelligible and not in the least paradoxical. (What is supposed to be paradoxical here is that on the one hand it seems clearly wrong to say 'P is true, but I do not believe it', while on the other it very often happens that a person does not believe something, although it is true. If P can be true, although I do not believe it, why can I not *say* 'It is true, but I do not believe it'?)

If 'I believe . . .' is not used to report something about me, then how *is* it used? Wittgenstein's answer is at *PI* pp. 190(c), 190(e), and 191(j): 'I believe it is going to rain' has a meaning like, that is to say a use like, 'It is going to rain'. That is to say, in both cases we are saying it is going to rain, and, so far at least, are talking about the weather, not about ourselves.

Since Wittgenstein only says there is a *resemblance* between 'I believe P' and 'P', it is possible that the way in which they differ is that 'I believe P', unlike 'P', is *partly* about myself. If I am right in saying that Wittgenstein subscribes to the 'no reporting' thesis, how does he get around this difficulty? What, in his opinion, is the difference between saying 'P' and saying 'I believe P'?

Here we must remember that we are so far just talking about the first person present indicative, and a different treatment will have to be worked out for other cases. If (as I suggest) the difference between 'P' and 'I believe P' were that the latter, as well as asserting P, acknowledges that the question whether P is true is one about which people may reasonably disagree, that would be another representation about P, not one about the person speaking. I can find no clear indication that Wittgenstein would agree that this is where the difference lies, but there is not much doubt that we *are* acknowledging the debatability of a proposition we say we believe, and it is also clear that in saying we believe it, we are for our part anyway saying it is true. We are neither expressing any actual doubt about its truth nor saying it is probably true. If we believe it is probably true, that is what we should say, and if we have some actual doubts about it, we may describe ourselves as inclined to believe it, but not as believing it. Saying we believe it is saying it is true and is inconsistent with saying we are in actual doubt about its truth.

There is still a problem about the past tense, the third person, and the hypothetical mood. The attribution to a third party or to oneself in the past, of a belief that it rained or would rain, unlike the first person present indicative, does not say anything about whether it did or will rain; and there may seem nothing left for the word 'believe' to be doing in these cases than reporting or hypothesizing something about the person described as believing. There will be this much reason for supposing that, whether or not 'I believe . . .' says something about me, 'he believes . . .', when it refers to me, does say something about me, and so does 'I believed . . .'.

Whereas it would perhaps be quite characteristic of Wittgenstein to say that 'believe' is just peculiar in sometimes recording a phenomenon, sometimes not, I think he in fact takes the radical position that in no case does 'believe' ascribe anything to the person to whom, grammatically anyway, it is attributed.

We could of course say that 'He believes it is raining' says something about him, namely that he believes it is raining, but whatever this might mean it cannot express Wittgenstein's opinion, since at the very outset of these pages he denied that the word 'believe' came into use through our noticing something and giving it that name.

Paragraphs 192(f) and 192(g), although very difficult to make clear sense of, can be taken in such a way as to explain what we *are* doing with 'believe' in persons and cases other than the first person present indicative, and may represent a major breakthrough:

> Even in the *hypothesis* the pattern is not what you think.
>
> When you say 'Suppose I believe . . .' you are presupposing the whole grammar of the word 'to believe', the ordinary use, of which you are master. – You are not supposing some state of affairs which, so to speak, a picture presents unambiguously to you, so that you can tack onto this hypothetical use some assertive use other than the ordinary one. – You would not know at all what you were supposing here (i.e. what for example would follow from such a supposition), if you were not already familiar with the use of 'believe'.
>
> (*PI* p. 192f)

When Wittgenstein says 'You are not supposing some state of affairs which, so to speak, a picture presents unambiguously to you', is he thinking that we *are* supposing some state of affairs, just not *that* kind – or does he mean that we are not supposing *any* state of affairs, including one which, so to speak, a picture presents to us unambiguously? If he were just denying that it was a particular kind of state of affairs, it would be remiss of him to give no hint of what state of affairs he thought that, instead of it, we *are* supposing. And it would be unclear why he would say that, rather than supposing a particular state of affairs, we are presupposing the grammar of the word 'believe'. Given a blanket denial that we are supposing a state of affairs, he could offer instead something of a quite different kind, like presupposing the grammar; but the natural replacement for a particular state of affairs is, in the first instance anyway, another state of affairs, or perhaps one of a family of them.

So I am inclined to think Wittgenstein was suggesting (a) that saying someone believes something is never attributing a state of affairs, and (b) that instead 'believe' is used here for grammatical reasons. The hard question is how to see grammatical considerations as an alternative to the supposition that we are attributing a particular state of affairs when we say that someone believes something. We may be presupposing the grammar of the word 'cat' if we say 'He fed the cat', but that is not to say that we are not reporting his feeding a cat; yet Wittgenstein seems to hold that when we say a person believes such and such, we are presupposing the grammar of the word 'believe' (whatever that means) *rather than* attributing something called believing.

What is it to presuppose the grammar of a word, and how can the recognition that we are doing this get us out of the present tangle?

We could get started on this question by noting that we say 'She believes . . .' rather than 'She knows . . .', not because there are differences between the phenomenon of believing and that of knowing, and we think the former, not the latter, prevails in her, but because if we said she knew, we would be committing *ourselves* to the truth of the proposition we said she knew – when perhaps we either disbelieve it or have no opinion about its truth. 'She *believes* . . .' does not commit us in that way.

That is some of the grammar of 'believe' and 'know'. We choose between these words in part because of what *we* want to say, not about the person to whom we are attributing belief or knowledge, but about the proposition we say is believed or known. There are no states of persons that require that these words should be used in the way described, but the fact that they *are* used in that way makes the word 'believe' fit nicely in some contexts: it does not commit the attributer of belief to the truth of the proposition said to be believed, but neither does it assign the doubts the attributer may have to the person said to believe.

A second kind of case in which it is grammatical rather than psychological or other considerations that make the use of the word 'believe' apt in certain contexts lies in the fact that the past tense of 'It is going to rain, so I had better close the windows' is not 'It was going to rain, so I had better . . .', but rather 'I believed it was going to rain, so I reckoned I had better . . .'. If there is scarcely room for doubt about whether it will rain soon, there may be no need to say 'I *believe* it will rain', and in such cases at least the word 'believe' is dispensable in the present tense; but when we move to the past tense, 'believe' is called for, not because something called believing prevails in this case and not in the other, but because in explaining reasons for acting, we often want a word that is indifferent to whether or not the expected rain (for example) materialized – and grammatically 'believe' satisfies that requirement.

Although normally when a person says 'It is going to rain, so I had better . . .', she will believe rain to be imminent, she has not, in just saying it will rain, omitted to mention the fact that she believes it. We might say she omitted to mention the belief if we thought it was in view of the phenomenon of believing, rather than of the oncoming rain, that she closed the windows, but that is false. She might indeed say 'I closed them because I believed it would rain soon', but she could not alternatively say '. . . because I noticed myself believing . . .' – as if to go on: 'and I have found repeatedly that when believing it will rain happens, it soon rains'. We could compare the case with finding aching joints to be a reliable indicator of forthcoming rain. One would say 'I am closing the windows because my joints are aching', not in the belief that the joints ached more when the windows were open, but rather through having found very often that when joints ache, it soon rains.

When we say 'I am closing the windows because I believe it will rain soon', it is not the belief but the fact that it will rain soon that is the reason for closing the windows. We can see this better if we write the above sentence '. . . because (I believe) it will rain soon' – or '. . . because it will rain soon, I believe'.

Here we touch on one of the intriguing minor problems in the interpretation of chapter 10: what is the mistrusting of one's belief that is mentioned in pp. 190(h) and 190(i), and why can we not do it? Does Wittgenstein believe that try as we may, we will be unable to distrust any belief we have?

The answer is already in hand: there is no phenomenon called 'belief', and hence nothing that one might *either* trust or mistrust. It is not that we *have* to trust it, but that neither trusting nor mistrusting makes sense. One can say 'I believe it is raining, although I know it is conceivable that this may not be true', but not 'I believe it is raining, but I doubt if it actually is'. The reason for this is that saying one believes something is in part saying it is true, and to say 'P is true, but I doubt if it is' is in the same breath to assert and decline to assert P.

If believing were something one could introspect, or see on an X-ray plate, or study with the help of a mirror or a video camera, it might make a kind of sense to mistrust one's belief: some people might find 'beliefs', that is, on the present supposition, either inner states, shadows on X-ray plates or patterns of behaviour, to be reliable indicators of such things as whether it will rain, in somewhat the way aching bones will often foretell damp weather. Such people would have reason to trust their 'beliefs', while others who found no significant correlation between the facts about themselves that were called their beliefs and what turned out to be true, would of course do well to be distrustful. What they would distrust, however, is not what *we* would call beliefs. We could see this most clearly if we called the brain states, behaviour patterns, mental pictures or whatever else some people trusted and others not, their *bee leafs* – and asked 'Is bee leafing the same as believing?' If Mary said she bee leafed it would rain, meaning that she was experiencing a lively mental representation of rain, she need not yet have any opinion about whether it would in fact rain. She might, on the basis of having found in the past that her bee leafs nearly always turned out to depict accurately something that had happened or would happen, trust this one and conclude that it would rain. Here she would have had a bee leaf about rain before she came to believe that it would rain, and bee leafing would not be the same as believing. Only when she concluded, whether from the occurrence of the mental picture or from meteorological indications, that it would rain, would she in the usual sense now believe it was going to rain.

Generalizing from this, if we suppose that believing is some phenomenon – *whatever* phenomenon we suppose it to be, whether something psychological, behavioural, or physiological – that supposition will have the consequence that saying 'I believe P' will not be a way of saying that P is true but only a way of saying that a certain state of a person prevails. In imaginable worlds people might be able to 'trust their bee leafs' and from them conclude such things as that it will rain this afternoon, but although in *our* language coming to such conclusions would be coming to have the belief that it would rain, it would not (in *their* language) be coming to have the corresponding bee leaf.

The bee leafers can have such bee leafs as that it will rain before they come to regard it as true that rain is imminent, and so their bee leafing something cannot be regarding it as true, and hence cannot be believing.

It is never very clear what Wittgenstein means by 'grammar', but there is an indication in *PI* p. 192(g) that to know the grammar of a word is in part at least to know what would follow from an attributive use of it:

> [If you suppose you believe such and such] you would not know what you were supposing (i.e. what, for example, would follow from such a supposition), if you were not already familiar with the use of 'believe'.

I think that what is suggested here is that, rather than the attribution of belief alleging that a state of affairs of a particular kind prevails, from which in turn we can make various sorts of inference, the assertion that someone believes something itself tells us what we can (and I think also what we cannot) conclude. We cannot conclude that what that person is said to believe is true, but we can conclude that she is in no actual doubt about it, even if she may recognize that in holding it to be true she is going beyond what the evidence available to her would fully warrant. Since in saying 'I believe it is raining' she is saying it is raining, and since it makes no sense to say 'It is raining and I have some doubts whether it is', if she has any actual doubts about the rain then she can neither say she believes it is raining nor can she be described by others as so believing.

It is not from some phenomenon we call believing that such prohibitions, permissions, and requirements derive; rather they are, as it were, packaged together under the heading 'belief'. And the belief package does not consist of a phenomenon called 'belief' together with various consequent permissions and so on; it just consists of the permissions, prohibitions, and requirements. Parts of the package govern the relations between believing and knowing, some of which are: we can go directly from A's saying B knows P to the conclusion that A holds P to be true. And P need not actually be true for it to be *grammatically* in order for A to describe B as knowing it. From a grammatical point of view, everything is in order here as long as A believes P. Whereas A seems to be saying something about B, she is also, if not saying, at least showing something about herself. And if, although P is in fact true, A does not believe it, this fact about her makes it wrong for her to say B knows P but leaves it permissible to say she believes it, regardless of how certain she may be of its truth.

That completes what I have to say about the larger themes in chapter 10. I would like now to make some suggestions about the interpretation of a number of passages, some of them extremely perplexing, and not all of which I know where to place in the larger picture.

1) At *PI* p. 190(j) Wittgenstein, in encouraging us to see it as a most remarkable fact that 'believe', 'wish', and 'will' display all the inflexions possessed by 'cut', 'chew', and 'run', seems to imply that they do display all those inflexions, whereas it is clear that we do not say 'I will believe it tomorrow, if I get a chance'. 'Believe' lacks that inflexion, and it would be most surprising if Wittgenstein had not noticed this. It is therefore likely that he is just encouraging us to expect that verbs like 'believe' will lack some inflexions – as might have been clear from the start if the English had read, not '. . . see it as a remarkable fact *that* "believe" etc. display all the usual inflexions', but '. . . a most remarkable fact *if* they do'. He is not saying that these words do display all the usual inflexions (and it is amazing that they do) but rather recommending that we approach them expecting that they will not function in the usual way, and be amazed (or at least surprised) if they do.

We might connect this with the similar business at *PI* p. 191(g), where it is extremely puzzling how the fact that one can predict one's own future action by an expression of intention shows that it should not surprise us that there should be a verb lacking one inflexion. What may confuse anglophones here is that we think of predicting as working out (as in weather forecasting) what is going to happen – and have difficulty understanding how our sometime ability to do this shows that it is not surprising that a verb should lack an inflexion. The way out of this perplexity is quite simple, I think: Wittgenstein wanted to say that 'to intend', *when it is used to say beforehand* (predict) *what we will do* (as distinct from when it is used in such sentences as 'I intended it as a joke'), is another verb that lacks an inflexion – showing missing inflexions not to be so very rare. (I suppose the missing inflexion here would be exemplified by the fact that we do not say for example 'I can't intend it just now, but I will tomorrow before breakfast, if I remember'.)

2) How would 'I believe . . . and it isn't so' be a contradiction in the language-game in *PI* p. 191(b), if it is not one otherwise? Perhaps the point is that whereas we tend to think we are talking primarily about ourselves when we say 'I believe it is raining', and only indirectly about the fact believed (cf. *PI* p. 190(g)), in the language-game here imagined, the assertion that it is raining would stand out as being what we were primarily bent on saying, and the words 'I believe' would patently just be tacked on. If we are primarily saying it is raining, it is then obvious that going on to say it isn't turns the utterance into a contradiction. As I suggested in a similar context earlier, the point might come out most clearly if we wrote 'It is raining, I believe, and it is not'.

3) It is not obvious what is meant in *PI* p. 191(d) by 'casting light on my state' as contrasted with hinting at it. I am inclined to suppose that by 'casting light' Wittgenstein here means something like 'speaking explicitly about my state', the suggestion being that we fancy we are saying something about our state as much when we say we believe something as when we say we eat something. We take both 'to believe' and 'to eat' to record familiar phenomena, and in that sense to cast light on our state, whereas by contrast 'I believe that something wonderful will happen' might be described as hinting at the excitement I feel without *saying* I am excited. People will guess that I am excited if I say I think something wonderful will happen, but they do not have to guess what is happening if told that I am eating. (This point perhaps connects with Wittgenstein's use of the words 'of belief' in *PI* p. 190(a): the excitement or anxiety that may be hinted at by an attribution of belief is not itself the believing. Moreover it is not that the two are different phenomena, but that excitement is a phenomenon while believing is not.)

4) If, as Wittgenstein says in *PI* p. 191(i), we do not infer our conviction from our words or from the actions that arise from our conviction, and do not feel it within ourselves either, the question how we *do* know we are convinced will be left crying for an answer, but we will be hard pressed to think of one, other than those excluded by the question itself; and no clue seems to be

provided by anything Wittgenstein says hereabouts. The following argument might resolve this problem.

If I say 'I am convinced the weather will clear by early evening', I may be asked what makes me so sure, but not how I know I am convinced. The former question calls for meteorological evidence – about the quality of the light, recent windshifts, typical weather patterns in this part of the country. By contrast the evidence that I am convinced would consist of facts about me, not about the weather. What I have been saying and doing is the kind of information another person might cite – why can I not proceed in the same way? I suggest it is not because I have to employ *another* method, perhaps introspection, but because for me the question does not arise. If it is important to me to know whether the rain will stop and the winds subside, I may usefully review the meteorological evidence so far available, or go in search of more, but there will be no point in my wondering whether I am convinced. It is not as if in well-trained people, being convinced were an identifiable state that set in sometimes and could be cited as valuable further evidence of the truth of what one was inclined to think true. To say one is convinced is not to record the onset of something called conviction, but to *pronounce* the evidence or the reasoning adequate. (Hume was not averse to the question how we know we are convinced. He thought that belief (conviction) *felt* different. According to him we know we are convinced by the vivacity of the idea we have, and the aim of arguing is to bring about the having of vivacious ideas.)

5) At *PI* p. 191(k) Wittgenstein seems to subscribe to something there is much reason to think he does not believe. He says

> This is how I think of it: believing is a state of mind. It has duration, and that independently of the duration of its expression in a sentence, for example. So it is a kind of disposition of the believing person. This is shown me in the case of someone else by his behaviour; and by his words.

Yet in all probability this is *not* how Wittgenstein thought of it. That is indicated quite strongly, not only by *PI* p. 190(g), where he appears to deny that 'I believe' describes his state of mind, but also by the way he continues at *PI* p. 191(k):

> What about my own case: how do I myself recognize my own disposition? Here it will have been necessary to take notice of

> myself as others do, to listen to myself talking, to be able to draw conclusions from what I say!

I assume he expects us all to see at once how absurd this is; and if there is any doubt about that, it is removed, partly by the exclamation point with which the quotation concludes, partly by the next paragraph but one:

> That different development of the verb would have been possible, if only I could say 'I seem to believe'.

Here I take Wittgenstein to be saying that if believing were a state of mind, it would make sense to say 'I seem to believe'. That we believe this or that would be something about us that we could *conclude* from the evidence of our feelings, our behaviour, and so on. The fact that we make no sense of such constructions as 'I seem to believe' is evidence that believing is not a state of mind. Hence when he says 'This is how I think of it', he must mean that he is naturally inclined to think of it that way, even though it is a mistake to do so.

(We do say 'I seem to believe it is bad luck to have a black cat cross one's path', but not 'I seem to believe she is living in Winnipeg now'.)

It is admittedly uncertain what is meant by a state of mind here. We *might* suppose that the reason he says he cannot say 'I seem to believe' is that he reckons a belief to be something he can be immediately conscious of, and so he will *know* whether he believes and not have to figure it out from sundry indications. But even if believing were a particular conscious state, we could say we seem to believe whenever it was uncertain whether the present conscious state was one specifically of believing, and not something very like believing, and easily mistaken for it.

6) By the 'development' of a word, for example in *PI* p. 192(b), I think Wittgenstein means the sentence forms into which significantly the word will and will not fit. Thus a proposition can be 'hard to believe', but it is not very clear whether it can be 'a cinch to believe', and it will not become easier to believe through becoming a skilled believer. One cannot set about believing something, believe it twice over for good measure, or get it believed expeditiously and go on to other things. Such facts as these about a word show what kind of a word it is, and are important because so many of our philosophical difficulties stem

from failing to appreciate what sort of a word we are dealing with. The grammatical considerations just mentioned go a way towards showing that believing is not an action, in spite of the fact that, just as actions can be hard to perform, propositions can be hard to believe.

If we could say 'I seem to believe P', 'I am convinced I believe it', or 'I doubt very much if I do', that line of development of the word would lead in the direction of the conclusion that believing is a state of a person, having various defining characteristics about which mistakes are easily made. Then we could also say 'It came and went so quickly that I could not be sure it was a belief, but certainly it was very like one.'

7) What may count in *PI* p. 192(i) as concepts touching and coinciding over a stretch can, I think, be safely illustrated by the above point about being hard to believe, or again by the apparent datability of believing in sentences like 'When he told me what he had been doing, I believed him', which is like 'When he told me what he had been doing, I laughed'. Here there are apparent concurrences between believing and other things, suggesting (in the former case) that believing is an action and (in the latter) that it is a datable occurrence. The stretch in which words run parallel is what generates the illusion that they are the same kind of word, while the divergences that emerge as we probe further show this to be false. But I am not able to suggest what tendency in our thinking might illustrate Wittgenstein's remark in the same paragraph that 'you need not think that all lines are *circles*'.

8) At what point in our thinking do we veer close to regarding a hesitant assertion as an assertion of hesitancy (*PI* p. 192(1)), or what mistakes might we be better able to avoid if we became quite clear about this difference? I suppose that 'Well, I *believe* that's true' would rank as a hesitant assertion, while 'I just don't know whether that is true or not' would be an assertion of hesitancy. In the first case I am, with whatever qualms, asserting the truth of something, and I am not *saying* I have qualms. Hence so far I have not said anything about myself. In the second case I say something about myself and nothing about the proposition about which I am hesitant. It is perhaps by running the two together that we blind ourselves to the fact that even when a believer is hesitant, he is not recording that fact about

himself when he says he believes, and not recording anything else about himself either.

Index